D1032432

The Confederate States of America

What Might Have Been

ALSO BY ROGER L. RANSOM

The Academic Scribblers:
American Economists in Collision
COAUTHOR WITH WILLIAM BREIT

One Kind of Freedom:
The Economic Consequences of Emancipation
COAUTHOR WITH RICHARD SUTCH

Coping with Capitalism:
The Economic Transformation of the United States, 1776–1980

Explorations in the New Economic History:
Essays in Honor of Douglass C. North
COEDITOR WITH RICHARD SUTCH AND GARY M. WALTON

Conflict and Compromise:
The Political Economy of Slavery, Emancipation,
and the American Civil War

For information about permission to reproduce selections from this book, write to
Permissions, W. W. Norton & Company, Inc., 500 Fifth Avenue, New York, NY 10110

Manufacturing by R. R. Donnelley, Harrisonburg
Book design by Lovedog Studio
Production manager: Amanda Morrison

Library of Congress Cataloging-in-Publication Data

Ransom, Roger L., 1938–
The Confederate States of America : what might have been / Roger L. Ransom.— 1st ed.
p. cm.
Includes bibliographical references and index.
ISBN 0-393-05967-7 (hardcover)
1. Confederate States of America—History. 2. United States—History—
Civil War, 1861–1865. I. Title.
E489.R36 2005
973.7'13—dc22
2005000947

W. W. Norton & Company, Inc., 500 Fifth Avenue, New York, N.Y. 10110
www.wwnorton.com

W. W. Norton & Company Ltd., Castle House, 75/76 Wells Street, London W1T 3QT

1 2 3 4 5 6 7 8 9 0

THE CONFEDERATE STATES OF AMERICA

What Might Have Been

For Richard & Susan

ROGER L. RANSOM

Richard, There is more of you in this book than meets the eye. Thank you for all that we have shared over the past 38 years.

As Ever,

Roger

W. W. NORTON & COMPANY
NEW YORK   LONDON

To my brother David,
who has offered me moral
and technical support for as
long as I can remember

eventually appeared in *Civil War History*. That manuscript was my first attempt to put my ideas about a counterfactual war down on paper, and the favorable reaction it received encouraged me to continue my efforts to construct the imaginary world described in this book. Among the many people who offered helpful feedback on that manuscript, and the various drafts and presentations that followed, were: Richard Bensel, Stanley Engerman, Eric Foner, Michael Holt, John Hubbell, James Huston, Frank Lewis, Rebecca Manes, James McPherson, John Majewski, Peter Temin, and Gavin Wright.

The people at W. W. Norton, particularly Steve Forman, who went through the entire manuscript with a fine-tooth comb and offered countless helpful suggestions, have been generous with their help. Sarah England provided the editorial and production assistance that is essential in turning a manuscript into a finished book.

Finally, my wife, Connie, was, as always, my greatest fan and one of my best critics. Connie read the penultimate draft of the book in its entirety and offered invaluable advice from someone who is *not* wrapped up in Civil War history. Her enthusiasm for pursuing this task at times proved to be more than I could handle. On several occasions I had to remind her that she could read much faster than I could write.

Thanks to her efforts and those of so many others, the final draft is much improved.

—Roger L. Ransom
Riverside, California
June 2004

Contents

LIST OF MAPS, FIGURES, AND TABLES

Maps

Figures

Tables

PREFACE

THIS IS A BOOK about what might have been. It contemplates a world that never existed. A world where Pickett's charge, if it occurred at all, was a stunning success, not a disastrous failure. A world where the Confederate States of America emerged from the American Civil War as a full-fledged nation. A world that is unlike the one we live in today. It is a world that has intrigued me since I was a boy of fifteen.

In the summer of 1953 I checked a novel entitled *Bring the Jubilee Again* out of the local library.[1] It is a story written by Ward Moore that relates the adventures of a young man named Hodge Backmaker, who grew up in a United States that had lost the Civil War. "How well I remember my mother and father talking bitterly of how the war ruined everything," writes Hodge, "they were speaking of . . . the War of Southern Independence which still, nearly 40 years later, blighted what was left of the United States." The "Peace of Richmond," Hodge observes, "was a just and even generous disposition of a defeated foe."[2] Nevertheless, the victors forced the losers to pay heavy indemnities and made territorial demands that left the United States destitute. The Confederacy, by contrast, proceeded to conquer Mexico and eventually ruled over an empire that stretched from Alaska to the southern tip of South America.

As the story unfolds, Hodge, who is studying to be a historian at a small Pennsylvania college, gets involved in a bizarre experiment to transport people back in time. Hodge volunteers to be the first major test of the machine. The machine works, and he is transported through time to the afternoon of July 2, 1863, on a road just outside the town of Gettysburg. In the course of wandering around, Hodge encounters some Confederate soldiers on their way to take up a position on Little Round Top, one of two hills at the southern end of the Confederate line of battle. Hodge has agreed as part of the experiment that under no circumstances is he to become involved in any actions while he is in the past. But the Rebel soldiers accost him and insist he is a Union spy. From there things go badly for the Confederates. Their commander is killed in an argument over what to do with Hodge, and the men elect not to occupy the position on Little Round Top. Years later Hodge recalls his experience on the following afternoon when he witnessed the final day of the Battle of Gettysburg: "All my life I'd heard of Pickett's charge on the third day. Of how the disorganized Federals were given the final blow in their vitals. Well, I saw Pickett's charge on the third day and it was not the same charge in the historic place. It was a futile attempt to storm superior positions (positions, by established fact, in Lee's hands since July first) ending in slaughter and defeat. All because the North held the round tops."[3] With that, Hodge Backmaker is trapped in a world where the South has lost the Battle of Gettysburg.

In the years since I first read *Bring the Jubilee Again* I have felt the urge to create my own version of what might have happened if the South had won the American Civil War many times. When I got to graduate school in the 1960s, I learned that my childhood fascination with what might have beens not only had a very fashionable name—counterfactual analysis—but was also actually one of the cornerstones of the "new economic history" taught by Douglass North at the University of Washington. Somewhere in my subconscious I knew that I had found my calling. I remained a closet counterfactual historian while teaching in the economics departments at the University of Virginia and the University of California at Riverside for the next twenty years. When I moved from the economics department to the department of history at Riverside in 1985, I promised myself that someday I would write a book examining a counterfactual world in which the South won the Civil War.

Several years ago I volunteered to teach an introductory course on the twentieth-century world. Explaining the global history of the twentieth century to undergraduates gave me a new perspective on what matters in history. As I pored over the materials preparing to teach that course for the first time, I was struck by how little attention the American Civil War has received as a historical turning point in the textbooks on world history. The more I thought about it, the more I became convinced that in Lincoln's words, the war was a struggle for the "whole family of man." My objective in constructing a counterfactual world in which the South won the war, therefore, is not only an attempt to satisfy the curiosity that we all have about what might have been but is intended also to demonstrate that the American Civil War was both an important turning point in American history and a decisive event for the course of world history.

One of the problems facing those who would write a history of what might have been is that there are no historical records to document a counterfactual world. I have therefore had to draw upon both my own imagination and the speculations of many other scholars. In this age when cries of plagiarism echo through the halls of academe, I have taken care to document my debts to other people's work. The one exception to this rule is my own work—much of it in collaboration with Richard Sutch—which forms the intellectual foundation for many of the arguments in the book. Let me acknowledge at the outset, therefore, that ideas that Richard and I have developed over the course of three and a half decades of research on the economic history of the United States permeate the text of chapters 1 through 4.[4] Our collaboration is founded on a friendship that dates back to the year we spent at Berkeley in 1967–68. My intellectual debt to Richard is too enormous to calculate.

Among the many legacies of my work with Richard Sutch was the creation of the maps of county-level data in chapter 1 of this book. More than a decade ago Richard and I hired Dovey Dee, an art student who happened to have a talent for working with GIS files, to create county-level base maps for the decennial censuses taken in 1840 through 1880. Using the Atlas Graphics program, we have been able to build computerized maps from the published data of the 1860 census published by the U.S. Census Bureau. The physical and political maps of chapters 2 through 5 are of more recent vintage; they were constructed using computerized maps available from Digital Wisdom, Incorporated, in Tappahannock, Virginia. I appreciate the assistance of the technical staff at Digital Wisdom in providing me with a set of customized Mountain High Maps. I am also greatly indebted to Dave Scharfenberg, who provided me with a customized computer that could handle the enormous files that the maps demanded.

For the past decade my friends, students, colleagues, and I have amused ourselves with speculations about a world where Southern dreams came true in 1865. My debt to those who offered even the most casual comments on those thoughts is considerable. If nothing else, their interest and suggestions fed the enthusiasm that kept the project going. Among those who deserve special credit is a cadre of faculty colleagues and graduate students here at UCR who offered comments over a long period. The most persistent of these include: Michael Bonner, Kimberly Earhart, Tom Cogswell, Peter McCord, and John Neff. My longtime friend and editor at Cambridge University Press Frank Smith deserves a vote of thanks for the encouragement and editorial suggestions he offered during the painfully slow period of gestation while this project was maturing.

In the summer of 1998 I circulated a manuscript for an article dealing with the consequences of a Southern victory in the Civil War that

WHAT IF?:
THE HISTORIAN'S
FAVORITE
SECRET QUESTION

Yesterday won't be over until tomorrow and tomorrow began ten thousand years ago. For every Southern boy fourteen years old, not once but whenever he wants it, there is the instant when it's still not yet two o'clock on that July afternoon in 1863, the brigades are in position behind the rail fence, the guns are laid and ready in the woods, and the furled flags are already loosened to break out and Pickett himself with his long oiled ringlets and his hat in one hand and his sword in the other looking up the hill waiting for Longstreet to give the word and it's all in the balance, it hasn't happened yet, it hasn't even begun yet, it not only hasn't begun yet but there is still time for it not to begin . . . yet it's going to begin, we all know that, we have come too far with too much at stake that moment doesn't need even a fourteen year old boy to think This time. Maybe This time with all this much to lose and all this much to gain: Pennsylvania Maryland, the world, the golden dome of Washington itself to crown with desperate and unbeliev-

*able victory the desperate gamble, the cast made two years
ago. . . .*

[T]omorrow night is nothing but one long sleepless wrestle with yesterday's omissions and regrets.

—William Faulkner, *Intruder in the Dust*

LIKE SO MANY OF his Southern brethren, William Faulkner distilled the outcome of the American Civil War down to those few moments at Gettysburg when the Confederate troops under George Pickett were about to launch the final assault of the battle. Pickett's charge was indeed a "desperate gamble." Lee knew it; Longstreet knew it; Pickett knew it; Pickett's men knew it. But they realized that the Army of Northern Virginia had come too far to turn back at that point. So, against all odds, Lee and his lieutenants rolled the dice in the hope they might somehow gain an "unbelievable victory." Lady Luck, who had smiled so often in the past, failed them that day. Pickett's men were thrown back in disarray, and Lee's grand invasion of the North ended with an ignominious retreat back across the Potomac. The battle was lost, and with that loss went the South's last hope of winning the war. Generations of Southerners were left to wrestle with the "omissions and regrets" of that fateful day in July and wonder what might have been if the flags had remained furled and Pickett's charge never been made. Could the Army of Northern Virginia have avoided the disaster that befell it on the third day of Gettysburg? Could it have avoided defeat and perhaps even have finally gained the larger prize it sought when it had gambled on war two years earlier?

These questions have been posed by historians many times, yet few of them have bothered to pursue the issue in any depth. Given the general aversion of historians to counterfactual history, this is hardly surprising. "If they have considered counterfactuals at all," observes Geoffrey Hawthorn, "[historians] have done so only nervously, in asides."[1] In the pages that follow, I propose to move counterfactual history out of the realm of shadowy asides and place it at the center of my historical analysis. I shall examine a series of counterfactual questions dealing with the consequences of something that did not happen: a Southern victory in the American Civil War. My principal aim in this fanciful exercise goes beyond idle speculation; I hope to demonstrate that the Civil War was not only a watershed in American history but also a crucial turning point in the history of the Western world. The North's military triumph ensured that the United States would remain unified and eventually grow to be one of the dominant economic and political powers in the world. But suppose not only that the South had won the war but that there was a *Confederate States of America* alongside the *United States of America* at the end of the nineteenth century. Only by carefully considering the long-term consequences of having two rival nations competing for political and economic dominance can we fully appreciate the significance of a war that threatened to dismember the largest nation in the Americas.

There is a further reward to this exercise. In the process of explaining the importance of the war to world history, we shall also shed light upon the ongoing debates within the United States regarding the causes of the Civil War. That conflict was a bitter dispute between two sections of the country that had "conflicting visions" regarding the future of the United States in the middle of the nineteenth century. On one side was a Southern vision of an agrarian slave society that would continue to expand throughout the Western Hemisphere. On the other side was a Northern view of the world shaped by the emerging ideology of individualism and a free market society. By the middle of the century a growing number of Americans were convinced that these two visions could no longer be reconciled within a single political entity. The result was the largest military conflict in the Western Hemisphere, a war that took almost as many lives as all the military actions of the United States through the end of the twentieth century. A counterfactual analysis of that war and its consequences will illustrate why this irresistible conflict could not have been avoided and emphasize how close the Southern Rebels came to creating a very different world.

Before we take up these issues, it will be useful to explore what we mean by counterfactual history. Historians tend to be of two minds on the worth of taking a counterfactual approach to examining the past. On the one hand are those, such as the eminent British historian E. H. Carr, who insist that "history is a record of what people did, not what they failed to do." To this set of scholars, counterfactual analysis is little more than playing "a parlour game with the might-have-beens of history."[2] Arguing over possible alternatives available at some particular time is, according to Carr, a pointless exercise, inasmuch as those options have been "closed by the *fait accompli*.[3] Carr's view of the value of counterfactual history may represent a majority position within the historical profession, but there are notable dissenters. Hugh Trevor-Roper, for example, objects to this summary dismissal of historical alternatives simply because they were never realized. "History," he insists, "is not merely what happened: it is what happened in the context of what might have happened."[4] The "might-have-beens" of history are not simply idle conjectures; they are an essential part of the historical narrative.

While counterfactual history may not have been eagerly embraced by historians, even a casual glance at historical literature reveals that virtually every historian flirts with counterfactual possibilities at one time or another. Robert Cowley, one of the leading practitioners of counterfactual military history, observes: "It has been said, that 'what if' (or the counterfactual, to use the vogue word in academic circles) is the historian's favorite secret question. What ifs . . . can reveal, in startling detail the essential stakes of a confrontation, as well as its potentially abiding consequences."[5] While the reason for asking what if questions is obvious enough, so is the challenge confronting those who would pursue counterfactual analysis. For any historical event there is not one but an infinite set of counterfactual events that could have happened. No one seriously argues that historians should track down *all* these potential outcomes. But how do we constrain the number of counterfactual options in order to make the analysis not only more manageable but insightful to the exploration of a specific historical issue? This, it seems to me, is the question at the root of the debates over the usefulness of counterfactual history.

It is important to emphasize at the outset that a counterfactual may not be a useful tool for analyzing or describing some historical situations. Phenomena or narratives that stretch across many years and many places may not offer the historian a manageable set of possible events to examine. It is difficult, for example, to identify a single invention or idea that by itself substantially altered the course of the Industrial Revolution. Nor is it obvious that a single voyage of discovery was so important that its omission would have forestalled the exploration of the New World. This is not to say that inventions or voyages of discovery are unimportant. The problem is that there are so many possible outcomes that it is difficult, if not impossible, to come up with a single set of counterfactual events with which to construct a picture of what might have happened that would be useful for historical analysis. Counterfactual analysis *can* be of considerable assistance, however, in elucidating situations in which a few events in a reasonably short time have had a decisive impact on the course of history. Wars are among the very best examples of this kind of situation. The critical impact of warfare is acknowledged by historians of virtually every methodological persuasion, most of whom chronicle the "eras" of history by the outcome of major wars. This practice is more than a matter of chronological convenience; it reflects a belief that the outcomes of wars play a major role in shaping the course of history.

The fact that they are significant historical events is only one reason that wars are popular subjects for counterfactual speculations. Warfare also invites the consideration of alternative outcomes because it presents the historian with a relatively short window of analysis and a limited number of counterfactual outcomes that must be considered.

When all is said and done, most battles are decided on the battlefield. This means there are only three outcomes that can result from a military campaign or battle: One or the other of the two sides may be victorious by driving its foe off the field of battle, or the battle may end in a situation in which both sides back off for the time being, the fighting to be resumed in a subsequent campaign of battles. This means that the military historian can focus his or her attention on the answer to a single counterfactual question: What if the other side won? What makes this hypothetical question so intriguing is the element of unpredictability that is inherent in military conflict. "War," writes the German military historian Carl von Clausewitz, "is the realm of chance. No other human activity gives it greater scope: no other has such incessant and varied dealings with this intruder."[6] For Clausewitz, whose treatise *On War* remains one of the most insightful studies of the causes and nature of military conflict, "there is an interplay of possibilities, probabilities, good luck and bad that weaves its way throughout the length and breadth of the tapestry. In the whole range of human activities, war most closely resembles a game of cards."[7] Though *On War* was first published in 1832, subsequent history has not diminished the force of these insights into war and chance. Time and again victory or defeat has been the result of good luck as much as of the skill of generals or the courage of the troops that fought in the battle.

While the outcome of battles is unpredictable, in most cases this unpredictability comes down to a few significant events that determine the eventual outcome of the battle. The military historian constructing a counterfactual scenario needs only to identify the turning point in the battle and then imagine what might have happened in the fighting had this turning point gone the other way. William Faulkner's account of a pivotal moment at the Battle of Gettysburg is a case in point. Had Lee not launched the desperate charge on the third day, or had Pickett's charge by some stroke of luck broken the Union line and resulted in a Confederate victory, the Gettysburg campaign might have ended quite differently from the version schoolchildren have etched in their memories. That in turn might have changed the course of the war. Indeed, as we shall see in chapter 2, there were several turning points at Gettysburg that could have changed the course of that battle, and the same could be said for many other battles in the American Civil War. Over the years writers have argued that there were turning points that could have changed the outcome of almost any famous battle, from ancient times to the present. What makes these counterfactual speculations of interest to historians is the realization that a set of relatively innocuous departures from what actually happened on the battlefield could have accumulated into significant shifts in the course of history for a nation—or indeed for the entire world.

DESPITE ITS usefulness for the exposition of their subject, most military historians seldom offer more than a few sweeping remarks that suggest how a different outcome to a battle might have changed the outcome of a war. These forays into what-might-have-been situations usually consist of brief essays that deal with particular events and battles.[8] An exception to this rule is a group of historians who have applied themselves to what they call alternative outcomes of military history. In numerous articles and books these writers search for serious answers to the question of how battles and wars might have turned out differently. In the care they take to present detailed narratives of their counterfactual military scenarios, these scholars stand apart from a host of earlier what if writers. The practitioners of this "new" alternate history treat their subject as if they were dealing with real, not imaginary, events in the past. Writing about a counterfactual Battle of Gettysburg, historian Peter Tsouras insists that "alternate history has to be entirely within the bounds of the genuinely possible, and therefore accurate in all technical details."[9] Another writer claims that this genre of history "is not fiction, but simulated fact. We don't just ask 'what if things had been different?,' we actually put the question to the

test, make it happen, stand back and watch the results."[10] These writers become so engrossed in their alternative worlds that they no longer
feel a need to deal with the real world. "There is no attempt to com-
pare the 'alternative' with the 'real,' " writes David Downing in his
World War II account of the German invasion of Russia in 1942; "the
alternative is written as if it really happened, in the manner of a bare-
faced lie 80,000 words long."[11] The *"raison d'être* for writing histories
of this sort, lies in the fresh light it throws on the underlying processes
of real history by its shifting of the more familiar events taking place
on the surface."[12]

The studies by alternative military history scholars emphasize
Clausewitz's point that the outcomes of battles and wars are inherently
unpredictable. However, offering plausible alternative scenarios for
military conflicts is only the first step in examining the impact of wars
on history. As we noted earlier, wars offer one of the few instances in
which discrete historical events can significantly alter the course of
history in a very short time. The alternative histories discussed above
present counterfactual outcomes that provide important insights into
what Cowley called the "essential stakes" and "abiding consequences"
of alternative military outcomes, and in this regard, the attention to
detail and the careful scholarship of alternative military history lift
their analysis far above the level of a parlor game. But how do we venture beyond the confines of counterfactual battlefields to explore the
social or economic consequences of an important military outcome?
Indeed, one must ask if there will be any major consequences at all. In
an essay exploring the possibility that the Spanish Armada might have
defeated the English fleet in 1588, Geoffrey Parker raises the possibility that what he calls "second order counterfactuals" could offset the
effects of a military victory and produce a situation in which "the previous pattern may reassert itself."[13] Parker employs this concept to
point out that in the case of the Spanish invasion of England, there is
good reason to expect that Philip II might not have been able to
exploit the opportunity that a Spanish victory at sea might have

offered for the conquest of England. Even if they had failed to defeat the Armada, the English might still have defeated the Spanish attempt to invade their island.

Professor Parker's idea of a second order counterfactual emphasizes the need always to view our counterfactual analysis in the context of larger historical forces that must shape any counterfactual scenario. What I shall call the historical mold allows us to extend our counter-factual story beyond the immediate consequences of an event. The possibility of a victory by the Axis Powers in the Second World War offers an excellent example of what we mean. David Downing presents a military scenario whereby the German *Blitzkrieg* has captured Moscow and most of European Russia by the end of 1942. German forces also drive the British from the Mediterranean islands of Crete and Malta and advance past Egypt into Palestine. But in the end these advances by the Nazis prove to be hollow victories. "*Blitzkrieg,*" writes Downing, "was never more than a stopgap answer to the military problems of continental war. It could only work over a limited period of time; it could only be sustained, as was now obvious, over a limited area of space."[14] Wade Dudley reaches a similar conclusion when he claims: "It is difficult to imagine any simple circumstances that would have allowed Japan to win any form of victory in World War II."[15]

Both these historians are placing their alternative history scenarios of Axis military victories in 1941–43 into a historical mold that suggests the victors will ultimately not be able to transform military success into long-term economic or political domination. What is significant to note from these examples is that although the outcomes of military battles may be unpredictable, the historical factors that determine long-run success or failure in major conflicts may not be so susceptible to chance. As Downing notes with regard to the long-run prospects of Nazi Germany, "economic realities cannot be indefinitely denied. Such a society lives on its expansionism, on consuming the lands, the work and the lives of others. It lives on its own momentum, until the momentum dies, and then it begins to consume itself. Such a society has nowhere else to go."[16] This historical mold therefore must take a broader perspective that goes beyond the sphere of military affairs and delves into economic and social trends. What began as an exploration of military turning points will evolve into a broader analysis of subsequent turning points.

WRITERS OF alternative military history have developed a methodology that asks counterfactual questions with an imaginative approach, but they remain focused on a very narrow set of issues dealing with the outcome of battles or wars. Where can we find historical molds into which our counterfactual scenarios might be placed? One area is the work of cliometricians, scholars trained in economics who use statistical inference and economic theory to address problems in economic history.[17] What I have termed a historical mold economists would call an economic or a historical model. At the core of cliometrics are the models that are employed to interpret evidence to support various historical interpretations. Our interest in cliometric research is in the way in which these models can be used to develop the wider implications of something as dramatic as a Southern victory in the Civil War.

Cliometricians have not been particularly interested in the details of war itself. They are, however, very interested in the impact that wars have on the economic development of the combatants. In the early 1960s a group of scholars turned their attention to a major question in American history: Did the Civil War accelerate economic growth and open the way for industrial growth after 1865? At the time most historians endorsed the view of Charles and Mary Beard, two well-known historians who argued in 1927 that the Civil War was nothing less than a "Second American Revolution."[18] For the Beards, the crisis facing the United States in 1860 was a clash of two very different societies, and resolving that conflict was an essential step in the evolution of the United States. In the early 1960s a number of scholars challenged the Beardian interpretation of the war by showing that economic growth actually *slowed* during the decade of the war.[19] This interpretation carried with it a powerful counterfactual implication: *Had the war not taken place*, the rate of growth in the American economy of the 1860s would have been significantly higher than the rate of growth that we actually observe for that decade. By the end of the 1970s the accepted wisdom on the question of economic growth and the Civil War was that the war had probably *not* accelerated growth.[20] Counterfactual methodology had been responsible for a major reinterpretation of American history.

This was not the only area in which research undertaken by cliometricians had a profound effect on the historiography of the antebellum United States. Another major debate among historians was whether or not slavery was profitable to planters in the antebellum South. The accepted wisdom of historians before 1960 was that slavery was *not* profitable. A major problem with this interpretation was that it undermined the equally widespread view that slavery was the cause of the Civil War. If slavery were not profitable, why would the South fight a war to preserve it? In 1958 Alfred Conrad and John Meyer published an article that convincingly demonstrated that slavery *was* profitable to Southern planters.[21] Their conclusion had profound implications on the historians' debates over the causes of the Civil War. "It seems doubtful," Conrad and Meyer said, "that the South was forced by bad statesmanship into an unnecessary war to protect a system which must soon have disappeared because it was economically unsound. This is a romantic hypothesis that will not stand against the facts."[22] Once again, counterfactual methodology had provided insights that led to reassessments in historical interpretations. Quantitative research had shown that the historians' implicit counterfactual—that without the Civil War slavery would have died out of its own accord—was not supported by the data on the rates of return on slaves.[23]

Cliometricians bring a strong sense of order to the counterfactual debates, but all too often they then become locked into an analytical straitjacket that limits the scope of their analysis. In a sense, they become too preoccupied with "predicting" the past with ever-greater precision rather than with developing a historical analysis of what might have happened. The most ambitious attempts to construct sweeping narratives of a world in which the South won the Civil War have been undertaken not by historians or cliometricians but by novelists who develop fictional plots that are set in counterfactual worlds where the South wins the Civil War. These novels, a genre of literature that I term alternative historical fiction, intersperse real characters and major events with fictional characters and events that form the basis for the plot. An example of alternative historical fiction that develops a detailed narrative of a world with an independent Confederacy is the series of novels of Harry Turtledove. Turtledove develops a fascinating and eminently plausible scenario whereby a Confederate victory eventually leads to the involvement of both the United States and the Confederacy in a worldwide war early in the twentieth century.[24] While writers of alternative historical fiction offer insights into the world that would have existed had the Confederacy won, they necessarily subordinate their historical analyses to the interactions of the fictional characters in the novels that form their plots. Like the historians who avoid exploring counterfactual questions in any depth, the novelists writing alternative historical fiction avoid dealing with the myriad of historical details that arise from their choices of counterfactual worlds. They simply present the counterfactual events as backgrounds to the plots rather than the focus of historical inquiry.[25]

WE HAVE looked at the different approaches that historians apply to counterfactual history: Military historians reconstruct alternative outcomes of battles in excruciating detail and economic historians employ statistical data and economic models to "test" counterfactual questions framed within theoretical models. As historian Niall Ferguson notes, neither group has been able to generate a great deal of enthusiasm among other historians. The explanation for this lack of enthusiasm, he notes, is that the work of the first group is "essentially the product of imagination" but lacks "an empirical basis," while the second is "designed to test hypotheses by (supposedly) empirical means, which eschew imagination in favor of computation."[26]

Ferguson's dichotomy is perceptive, but it begs the larger question of whether or not the two approaches could be combined into a complex story that goes beyond the immediate effects of a single counterfactual event and explores the possibilities that might evolve from a series of counterfactual changes. We noted earlier that interest in counterfactual analysis pertains to events that are turning points in history. It is clear that historians are able to use their historical analyses to identify these turning points. Moreover, having chosen the turning points, they have sufficient imagination to come up with various possible alternative outcomes that would have changed history. The problem is that even if you are able to unravel the alternative possibilities from one turning point, you will soon encounter a new juncture at which history could again take a different course. What is extremely difficult to construct is a meaningful narrative of counterfactual history beyond the first imaginary turning points. How do we keep the counterfactual story from exploding into a myriad of different tales, all going in different directions?

One answer is the use of what I have called the historical mold to shape the initial burst of possibilities to fit the world around them. That is what economic historians do best; they provide theoretical paths along which our counterfactual story must travel. A second constraint is the issue of plausibility. Historians and economists alike would agree to exclude those possibilities that go beyond the limits of what is plausible. But what is "plausible"? Niall Ferguson carries this criterion to its most extreme limit when he argues that we should consider "as plausible or probable *only those alternatives which we can show on the basis of contemporary evidence that contemporaries actually considered.*"[27] While his point about tying the counterfactual to contemporary evidence is well taken, his requirement that contemporaries be able to consider subsequent events is highly restrictive. Can we expect that contemporaries who are considering the possibility of going to war in 1860 will accurately foresee the enormous changes that might result from the war? Probably not. Indeed, it is clear that they did *not* anticipate those changes. Ferguson's criteria would therefore restrict our story to only the most immediate effects of the war. There are many alternatives that contemporaries could not foresee but that our historical perspective tells us were indeed not only possible but perhaps even likely. We must be careful not to throw out the baby with the bath water in discarding alternatives as "infeasible" in terms of the options apparent to people at the time.

While it may be too limiting to curtail the broad scope of our analysis, the emphasis on limiting the range of possible counterfactuals to those that could be imagined by contemporaries does bring out an important use of counterfactual analysis in history. Up to now we have been discussing issues of what might have been. That is, we are considering the possible outcomes of some turning point in history after the fact. But what historians looking at the problem years later treat as "counterfactual" possibilities that did *not* happen, contemporaries at the time viewed as possibilities of the future that *might* happen. They were considering alternatives of what might be. As David Potter notes in his counterfactual analysis of the crisis of 1850, "this reading of possible options involved beliefs as well as facts, and historians, of course, do not agree on them as if they were factual."[28] His point is crucial to an understanding of how counterfactuals can shed light on the coming of an event such as the Civil War. Like most wars, the Civil War did not "just happen." Political and military leaders chose courses of action that produced a conflict. The what-might-be alternatives formulated by contemporaries subsequently became the historians' what-might-have-been counterfactuals. Examining how these what-might-be options were formulated can provide valuable insights into the decisions on which what-might-have-been counterfactuals will provide the best insights into the historical turning point under investigation.

WHERE DOES this leave us in our search for a counterfactual "methodology"? In his book *Plausible Worlds* the philosopher Geoffrey Hawthorn suggests that since there are no definitive criteria for determining the parameters of the "best" alternative world, perhaps we should simply "take our commonsensical experience of the human world seriously."[29] This seems to be sound advice. Yet even if common sense prevails, there may still be a tug-of-war between the views of historians who insist that counterfactual analysis must always be plausible and cliometricians who claim that the emphasis on plausibility is overstated and that what matters is having an analytical model to provide insights into the problem at hand. Part of the difficulty here is that both groups have strong preferences for the style in which counterfactual history should be written. Historians want the counterfactual scenario to unfold as a historical narrative, picking up the story at the point where things have changed and relating the plausible consequences. What follows, in their minds, must be a direct extension of the immediate past. Cliometricians take the existing historical situation as the basis for their model and explore several counterfactual possibilities by tweaking various elements of the model to produce a different set of outcomes. How "real" the adjusted outcome is depends on the properties of the model. One of the key issues here is the cliometricians' unquestioning acceptance of the rule of ceteris paribus, the dictum that "other" things *do not change.*

All of which brings us back to Ferguson's dichotomy. Historians rely on imagination but fear that it may get out of hand; cliometricians rely on crunching their numbers and must correspondingly limit their analyses to the fixed parameters of their theoretic models. Common sense can help both groups make reasonable decisions, but it will not provide either with an obvious way to escape the fetters placed on the scope of their analysis. We are still confronted with the question of how one can construct a narrative counterfactual story that will be plausible enough for the historians and offer useful analytical insights to the social scientists. There is, it appears, no way to completely escape the problems of scope and continuity in counterfactual history. Short stories are OK but not too illuminating; longer narratives, even when they promise illuminating insights down the road, tend to get lost in the branches of the counterfactual narrative.

What of the possibility of addressing a "big" question by combining a number of shorter stories? The idea of linking together a series of smaller counterfactual questions in order to provide insights into a larger historical question seems a good one. What is needed is a clearer identification of the larger counterfactual question driving the analysis. We began this chapter by posing just such a question: What If the South Won the Civil War? To explore the implications of a Southern victory, it is necessary to look at a number of turning points, both real and imagined. Some of the turning points will use counterfactual insights to explore the coming of war and the ways in which the South might win the war; others will consider counterfactual situations that would arise if the South won. These counterfactual situations will be derived from the outcomes of the earlier turning points, but they will also be constrained by a secondary counterfactual scenario that places the two North American states in a larger historical environment of the mid-nineteenth-century world. At the end of each chapter our analysis can be "reset" for the next set of turning points. Thus we will begin with an analysis of choices in the 1850s that is firmly grounded in the historical reality facing Americans at that time and eventually move on to some highly speculative projections of what a world with two rival states in North America might look like in 1900. Our narrative will combine the analysis of what we know about the world in the late nineteenth century with a sufficient dose of historical imagination to project the impact of a Southern victory in the American Civil War.

We have discussed the basic ingredients of counterfactual analysis at some length, and a few general guidelines have emerged. Any counterfactual analysis must rest on a solid foundation that is based on *historical reality*. When that historical reality is changed, it is important that counterfactual possibilities be *plausible*, though we cautioned that care must be taken to see that the attention to plausibility does not become stifling. We suggested that *imagination* and *common sense* are useful ingredients to allow the counterfactual narrative to range far enough afield to offer interesting insights to the historical situation. Finally, we argued that analytical models can provide an important guide to the formulation of a *historical mold* that allows us to examine the larger ramifications of our counterfactual situation in the context of historical change. Useful though these guidelines might be, there are no hard-and-fast rules for constructing counterfactual historical scenarios. Like the chef who carefully combines the ingredients to prepare his signature dish, each historian uses his own "recipe" for shaping fact and counterfact into his finished counterfactual narrative.

Following is the best approximation I can offer of the recipe that I used in my examination of an American Civil War that was won by the South:

ROGER'S RECIPE FOR COUNTERFACTUAL HISTORY PUDDING

Take:

2 parts historical plausibility
1 part common sense
1 part imagination

Mix ingredients until they are blended into a smooth, even texture. If the texture seems uneven or coarse, try a little more common sense. If the pudding seems gray and boring, add imagination.

Carefully pour ingredients into a mold shaped in the form of a well-defined historical setting.

Allow to set until pudding has firmly gelled. Be careful not to remove pudding from historical setting.

Serve with a large dose of skepticism, and remember that there is no proof in this pudding.

Bon appétit!

Chapter One

CONFLICTING VISIONS: WAS THE CIVIL WAR INEVITABLE?

Shall I tell you what this collision means? Those who think that it is accidental, unnecessary, the work of interested or fanatical agitators, and therefore ephemeral, mistake the case altogether. It is an irrepressible conflict between oppos-ing and enduring forces, and it means that the United States must sooner or later, become entirely a slaveholding nation or entirely a free-labor nation.

—William Seward (October 1858)

FEW SPEECHES IN CONGRESS have proved more prophetic than Senator William Seward's declaration to an audience in Rochester, New York, in the fall of 1858 that the bitter disputes between the free and slave states of the American Union reflected nothing less than "an irre-pressible conflict." Just over two years after his speech South Carolina passed an ordinance of secession that led to the eventual creation of the Confederate States of America. When Confederate artillery bombarded

Fort Sumter in the spring of 1861, the war of words turned into a war of bullets and blood. The irrepressible conflict was no longer repressed.

What made Seward, and many of his fellow Americans in 1861, think that they were headed for an "irrepressible" conflict? The answer to this question involves two what-might-be questions. Even if we allow for the excess of emotion in the rhetoric that filled the air in the crisis of 1861, it is clear that people in the Northern and Southern states of the Union had very different views of the world and that each group was prepared to fight to see that its view prevailed. The crisis of 1861 was one of those turning points in history where there are only two possible outcomes: Either the Union would be preserved, or it would be broken apart. Our approach to the question of whether or not the war was irrepressible will be to examine the alternative paths that events might take as contemporaries saw them. In this chapter we focus on the origins of what I term the "conflicting visions" that people held for the future of their society and how those visions shaped expectations of the alternatives facing them in 1861.

Ours is hardly the first attempt to explain the causes of the Civil War in terms of conflicting views in the North and South. Seward's speech was delivered amid the passions roused by a crisis that had evolved out of years of acrimonious rhetoric in which each side damned the other. Sixty years later, when those passions and the wounds from the war had subsided somewhat, historians Charles and Mary Beard revived Seward's apocalyptic description of the war in their seminal two-volume study *The Rise of American Civilization*. "The roots of the controversy," wrote the Beards, would not be found in the rhetoric that offered "varying degrees of righteousness and wisdom, or what romantic historians call 'the magnetism of great personalities,' "[1] The core of this conflict centered on the problems posed by an expanding industrial, commercial, and agricultural capitalism of the Northern states clashing with the expansion of a slave plantation agriculture that dominated the South. "Had the economic systems of the North and the South remained static or changed slowly," speculated the

Beards, the political compromises of the first half of the nineteenth century might have kept the sectional antagonisms "within the bounds of diplomacy."[2]

That of course is not what happened. Yet it is worth noting that the counterfactual scenario implied by the Beards' comment was in fact quite close to the view of the future that many Americans had shared as they struggled to form their new nation in the last two decades of the eighteenth century. As we look back today on the extraordinary changes that took place in the United States during the first half of the nineteenth century, it is easy to forget that in 1783, the year that the former colonies signed a treaty with Great Britain to form the United States of America, neither the economic nor the political prospects looked all that favorable for the new nation. The Articles of Confederation soon demonstrated not only the pitfalls of a weak central government but also the depth of the rivalries that existed between the various states. Tobacco, the major staple crop that had supported the Southern colonies, was floundering in a stagnant European market, and the foreign markets for other colonial goods were in similar disarray. Nor did it appear likely that the rest of the economy would quickly recover from the doldrums following the peace with Britain. The United States was a small and fragmented market where both capital and labor were in scarce supply. With a weak economy threatening to get worse, the prospects of forming a federal government strong enough and stable enough to deal with these problems seemed remote at best.[3]

By 1787 the situation had deteriorated to the point where various groups called for a constitutional convention to consider significant changes in the structure of the government. After much deliberation, the delegates to the convention drew up a proposal to adopt a constitution that would remedy the most egregious flaws in the Articles of Confederation. Although the rights of individuals and the protection of property were proclaimed as the philosophical basis for the new government, a more immediate objective of the delegates was to forge a strong enough political union among all thirteen former British colonies to survive the political and economic threats at home and abroad. To maintain the fragile solidarity among the various interest groups represented at the convention, they were willing to compromise on a number of key points. Nowhere was this more evident than in the concessions made to the slaveholding class of the Southern states.

In 1790 roughly one out of every three persons in the Southern states was a slave. Thus, even though the *total* population of the slave states roughly matched that of the North, the *free* population of the South was considerably smaller than that of the North. To offset this significant demographic disadvantage, Southerners insisted on a bicameral national legislature in which the number of representatives in the House of Representatives would be determined according to population, while in the Senate each state would have two representatives. In the public debates over the ratification of the Constitution, the argument for the rules of apportionment in the Senate and the House were framed in terms of protecting the interests of "small" states from the domination of the "large" states. But the real issue here was the protection of slavery. In his notes from the convention, James Madison wrote that "it seemed now to be pretty well understood that the real difference of interests lay, not between the large and the small, but between the N. and the Southn. States."[4] Six of the original thirteen states (Delaware, Georgia, Maryland, North Carolina, South Carolina, and Virginia) were slave states. With the admission of Kentucky in 1792 as a slave state, a balance was established between slave and free states that would be carefully maintained for the next six decades. All this was still not sufficient to allay the insecurities of slave interests. They also insisted on the three-fifths rule, which stated that in the tabulation of the population for the purposes of apportioning seats in the House of Representatives each slave would count as three-fifths of a free white person. Even with these safeguards it is likely that a majority of slaveholders still opposed ratification of the Constitution because they feared their slave property was not sufficiently protected from the possibility of a hostile federal government.

For their part, Northerners had managed to get slavery banned from the area north of the Ohio River with the passage of the Northwest Ordinance in 1787 and to include a provision in the new Constitution allowing Congress to ban the importation of slaves into the United States after a period of twenty years. In the end, both sides got something out of the bargains struck in setting up the new political framework of the American Constitution. But the process of compromise took its toll, and in the interest of getting a political union in the near term, the delegates accepted language that was deliberately ambiguous with regard to the relation of the federal government and the rights of slaveholders.

For those of us looking back from a distance of more than two centuries, it is easy to exaggerate the extent of disagreement among Americans in 1790. Despite their differences over slavery, residents of both North and South shared a purpose in their efforts to build a new nation. The United States at the end of the eighteenth century was primarily a land of farmers. The "Republican vision" that Thomas Jefferson brought to the presidency in 1800 foresaw a rural society built around family farms extending from the East Coast to the Mississippi River. Slavery might produce political irritation now and then, but the Constitution carefully protected the rights of those who owned property, and most Americans were prepared to accept the idea that slaves were simply a form of property.

Furthermore, to most contemporary observers in both the North and the South, it seemed likely that the slave problem would die of its own accord. Many slaveholders, discouraged by the low prices of slaves throughout the 1780s, supported the ban on slave imports that was approved by Congress in 1809 in the hope that it would increase the value of their slaves. Some even went so far as to hope that without an influx of new slaves, the slave population of the United States would decline over time. Jefferson optimistically predicted that the settlement of Western lands would reduce tensions associated with slavery by spreading the slave population over a larger area. For Jefferson, and for most other Americans, the family farm, whether worked by free or slave labor, was the social and economic core of the new nation. It was this common vision of an agrarian future that made the compromises on slavery surrounding the ratification of the Constitution hold for better than four decades. Not until the late 1840s did those bargains finally begin to unravel into the irrepressible conflict.

The Republican vision of an agrarian society that would expand but not undergo enormous social or economic change seemed plausible at the beginning of the nineteenth century. Even the most imaginative prognosticator of 1790 could not have foreseen that in the next half century:

1. A Yankee visitor to South Carolina in 1790 would invent a cotton gin that made plantations in the American South the most efficient producers of cotton in the world.
2. A revolution that would reshape the social and political contours of Europe would erupt in France.
3. The British economy would experience an Industrial Revolution that would trigger an economic boom in Anglo-American trade that transformed the American economy.

Yet all these happened. In place of the economic malaise and uncertainty that had characterized the American economy during the decade after the peace with Britain in 1783, the United States experienced unprecedented expansion through the first half of the nineteenth century. The territory of the young nation more than doubled with the addition of the Louisiana Purchase, the annexation of Florida and Texas, the acquisition of territories taken from Mexico following the War of 1846–48, and the settlement of the boundary between British Canada and the United States in the Pacific Northwest. At the end of the 1840s "manifest destiny" was the buzzword of the day throughout the land as entrepreneurs in slave and free states hurried to cash in on the gains from economic and territorial growth.

Along with the benefits of expansion and growth came problems. Although both the Northern free economy and the Southern slave economy experienced economic growth, the benefits of that growth were not evenly distributed. Simple demography told much of the tale. At the time of the Constitution the population of the United States was roughly four million people, and they were evenly divided between the slave and free states that formed the Union. In 1850 the population of the United States had grown to twenty-three million people, fourteen million of whom lived in the Northern and Midwestern states. Ten years later the demographic imbalance had reached the point where the free population of the Northern states was almost three times that of the slave states. Despite their cotton prosperity, the Southern states were steadily losing political clout in the national government, and as they contemplated the census returns, these changes were obvious to even the most casual observer.

Equally obvious was the fact that the enormous boom in cotton production had breathed new life into the slave system of the South. Far from dying out, slavery flourished in the years after 1790 as never before. With a growing demand for cotton in Britain and the United States, cultivation of cotton using slave labor pushed steadily westward. Map 1.1 shows the distribution of slaves at the height of the cotton boom just before the Civil War. In 1800 most of the slave population was concentrated in the seaboard areas of Virginia, Maryland, and the Carolinas. From there the slaveholders moved west in three major paths that are clearly evident in the map. The first path was traced by settlers moving into western Kentucky, pushing along the southern bank of the Ohio River, and eventually moving down into western and central Tennessee. A second route of settlement was into the alluvial area of the Mississippi River valley; these planters later pushed westward into Arkansas and Texas. Finally, there was a wide

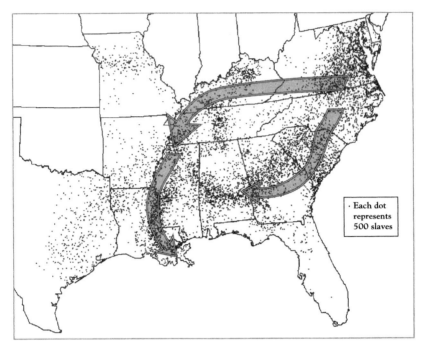

MAP 1.1

DISTRIBUTION OF SLAVE POPULATION IN 1860

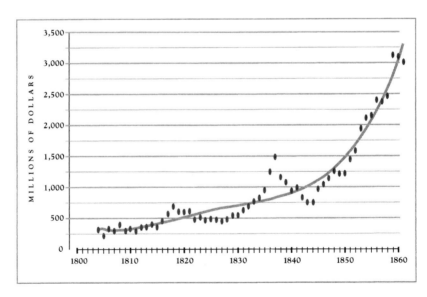

FIGURE 1.1

VALUE OF THE STOCK OF SLAVES
IN THE UNITED STATES, 1805–60

Source: Roger Ransom and Richard Sutch (1988: Table 3)

swath of settlement through the center of Georgia, Alabama, and Mississippi that eventually became known as the Black Belt. The result of this westward expansion of cotton cultivation was a huge investment in slave labor. Figure 1.1 plots the total value of all slaves in the United States from 1805 to 1860. In 1805 there were just over one million slaves whose collective value was worth about three hundred million dollars; fifty-five years later there were four million slaves worth close to three billion dollars, an amount equal to roughly half the total value of all the farms in the slave South. On the eve of the Civil War nearly four out of ten people in the eleven states that were to form the Confederacy were slaves, and they accounted for more than half the agricultural labor in those states.

This huge increase in the value of slaves in the United States came about for two reasons. First was the increase in slave population of over 2 percent per year through the first half of the century—or roughly at the same rate as the native white population. Second was a dramatic increase in the price of slaves. In 1805 the average price of a slave was less than three hundred dollars, by 1850 that had risen to around four hundred dollars, and in the final decade before the war it rose to just under eight hundred dollars.[5]

The economic success of American slavery rested on a legal system of property rights that defined slaves as assets rather than persons. This meant that slaveowners regarded their human chattel as capital rather than as labor. It also meant that slave masters not only could control the labor of their slaves but could buy or sell slaves for whatever price the market might demand. The price that someone would pay for a slave depended on the value of his or her output. For a male slave this was determined by the worth of his labor. The value of a woman, however, depended on not only the value of her labor but also that of any children she might bear. Under American law, children born to a slave woman were the property of the master who owned her. Thus the total return from owning slaves included the gains from an increase in the slave population. This explains why planters growing cotton (and slaves) on the depleted soil of the Southeast in 1859 were still able to earn handsome livings. If a plantation failed to meet its costs through the sale of agricultural output, "necessity" would force the sale of a few slaves.[6] Slave masters of the South invested in slaves the same way that an investor in the North might invest in stocks. They were acutely aware of the profits that resulted from producing both staple crops and slaves. Of course, not all slaveowners had to sell slaves to realize profits. Most slaves—men, women, and children—were put to work in the field so that their master could confiscate the fruits of their labor. In the final analysis, what made the system so successful for those owning slaves in the antebellum period was the enormous boom in the cotton market that began early in the nineteenth century and lasted until the outbreak of the Civil War.

Slaveholders were capitalists without capital. They made good livings from their chattel labor; by one estimate, more than one-quarter of the income of all Southern whites could be attributed to the exploitation of slave labor.[7] To see the extent to which this exploitation of labor produced enormous levels of wealth for slaveholders, one need only look at Map 1.2, which displays the distribution of wealth per free adult reported by households in the 1860 census of population. All the counties in the United States reporting an average per capita wealth of two thousand dollars or more were in the slave areas of the South. We know that the basis of this huge differential in wealth was attributable to slave property because the census reported "personal" wealth (which would include slaves) separately from wealth in property. The map clearly shows why Southerners in 1860 were willing to risk so much to protect the value of their slave assets.

Slaveowners were not the only ones who gained from the rapid expansion of cotton cultivation and exploitation of slave labor in the four decades before the Civil War. The cotton trade created substantial economic opportunities for entrepreneurs in the rest of the country as well. In 1790, when planters were lamenting the economic stagnation of the tobacco market, the value of cotton exports was neg-

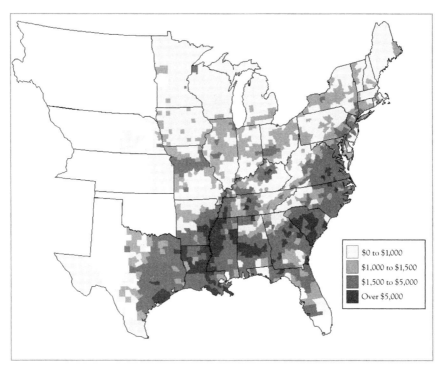

MAP 1.2

REPORTED WEALTH PER FREE ADULT IN 1860

ligible. Only a few areas along the coast of South Carolina and Georgia grew the Sea Island, or long-staple, cotton that could easily be cleaned for use in the textile mills of England. The introduction of the cotton gin in 1790 made it possible to efficiently clean short-staple cotton, which could be grown throughout the South. The result was that by the end of the 1830s cotton accounted for almost two-thirds of *all* exports from the United States. The income from these cotton exports provided a huge stimulus to the economies of states along Atlantic seaboard, a stimulus that soon spilled over into the Old Northwest.

Map 1.3 shows how this network of interregional trade worked in the antebellum period. Southern cotton producers exported their crops to Great Britain and Europe, and with the earnings from this trade, they purchased goods from abroad [A]. The Northeast profited

MAP 1.3
INTERNAL TRADE IN THE
ANTEBELLUM UNITED STATES

from this trade by providing shipping and financial services and by supplying the Southern plantations with cheap manufactures [B]. Southern specialization in staple agriculture also stimulated a demand for foodstuffs in the South that were shipped down the Ohio and Mississippi rivers from farms in the Northwest [C]. Finally, the growth of all three regions promoted a burgeoning trade in foodstuffs and manufactures between the Old Northwest and the Northeast [D]. This network of interregional trade brought substantial benefit to all three regions of the country. However, it was like a three-legged stool: Each region was dependent on the other two, and all three were required to support the expanding national economy.[8] If any one of the three "legs" were pulled away, the stool would topple. Southerners interpreted this dependence of the national economy on the cotton trade as proof that "cotton was King." At least for the first three decades of the nineteenth century, they were probably right.

THIS ANALYSIS of the American economy implies that the North and the South complemented each other nicely in use of resources and markets. Far from being a drag on the national economy, slave labor is clearly seen as a crucial input for the most rapidly expanding sector in the United States. An obvious implication of this line of thinking would be that a political rupture would be very expensive to all three regions of the country. But if this was the case, where did the political crisis that eventually led to war come from? One possibility that was widely discussed when the world was involved in the horrors of the Second World War laid the blame for the crisis of 1861 squarely on the shoulders of leaders whose political cynicism caused them to use sectional rivalry to further their own political fortunes rather than make a serious effort to resolve conflicts that threatened to break up the Union. In place of the Beardian thesis of the Civil War as an irrepressible conflict brought on by inexorable forces of economic and social change, these historians offered a pastiche of diverse "causes" whose only common theme was that war was a tragic mistake.[9]

What's wrong with this picture? An obvious problem with placing the blame on a generation of blundering politicians is that it ignores the extent to which various compromises had worked well for politicians from 1787 to 1850. In 1820 Congress had successfully defused the agitation surrounding the admission of Missouri as a slave state by maintaining the balance between the number of slave and free states and extending the line of demarcation between slave and free territories west of the Mississippi. That compromise held for thirty years. In the 1840s the politicians had managed to steer through the troubled waters created by the annexation and admission of Texas and the war with Mexico. The addition of the Mexican territories in 1848 made the dream of manifest destiny a reality; the nation finally stretched from sea to sea. Despite all the fuss about slavery, the nation in 1850 was seemingly poised on the threshold of another decade of exuberant economic growth. Why did this approach suddenly fail to work for politicians in the 1850s?[10]

One reason was that beneath the façade of compromise and prosperity, the sectional antagonisms over slavery had continued to worsen. Things came to a head when California applied for admission as a free state in 1849. After several stormy debates, Congress finally enacted a series of laws that admitted California as a free state, tightened the Fugitive Slave Act, and created two new territories from the land recently acquired from Mexico. However, the resulting "armistice" was merely the lull before the storm.[11] Within a few years the system of political parties that had governed the country since the time of Andrew Jackson came apart at the seams. The Missouri Compromise was overturned, the Kansas-Nebraska Territory was thrown open to a contest of popular sovereignty to decide whether it was to be free or slave; and by the time of the 1856 presidential election, the Whig Party had ceased to exist as a viable force in national politics.

The crisis of 1850 was a major turning point in the conflict over slavery. Up to then the emphasis on all sides had been on finding some sort of settlement by having everyone stay on the same page, so to speak. But by 1849 it had become clear that Northerners and Southerners were no longer on that page. For the first time there was serious talk of secession on the part of Southern states if California was added to the Union without including some additional safeguards to slavery, and in the North there was a growing feeling that the time had come for the free states to exert their political power and stop making concessions on the question of slavery in the territories. The excitement of the 1848 presidential election had hardly subsided before the more extreme proponents of Southern nationalism began calling for a convention of Southern delegates to gather for the purpose of considering the question of "disunion." By the end of 1849 the legislatures of South Carolina, Georgia, Texas, Virginia, and Mississippi all had agreed to send delegates to a convention that would be held in Nashville, and several other states expressed support for the idea, though they stopped short of agreeing to send delegates.

Nine states eventually sent delegates to the Nashville Convention, which convened in June 1850. Despite a good deal of fiery rhetoric, the gathering served only to underline the fact that Southerners were not yet sufficiently united on the question of disunion to mount an effective threat to leave the Union. When John C. Calhoun, the fiery leader from South Carolina who had championed the Southern cause for more than four decades, died on March 31, 1850, the disunionist movement lost its most forceful spokesman. Nevertheless, the Nashville Convention was not a complete failure for its organizers. By the time the delegates were on their way home, the idea that perhaps the South might be better off outside the Union had been firmly planted in the minds of many Southerners. Shortly before his death Calhoun had circulated a document calling for representatives from the Southern states in Congress to consider secession seriously as an action to counter the threat of political domination by the North. He was disappointed that his proposal, known as the Southern Address, attracted only 48 signatures from the 121 congressional delegates from the slave states.[12] However, numbers can sometimes be deceptive. The fact that such an extreme position could garner signatures from one-fourth of all the U.S. representatives and senators from the South could be seen as an indication of a growing dissatisfaction among Southerners over the political trends in Washington. Moreover, it is likely that Calhoun's plea resonated even more strongly among the common folk of the South.[13] At the very least, the South had served notice that it was prepared to consider the option of leaving the Union if circumstances warranted such a drastic action. Calhoun's Southern Address and the proceedings of the Nashville Convention marked a perceptible escalation in the stakes that Southerners were to bring to the table in the next round of debates over slavery in the territories.

INCREASING SUPPORT among Southerners for disunion was only half the problem confronting those who sought compromise in 1850. Equally important was the growing resentment in the North against any further concessions on the slave question. In August 1846, David Wilmot, a Democratic congressman from Pennsylvania, introduced an amendment to a revenue bill that would prohibit slavery in any of the territories acquired from Mexico during the war. The amendment was eventually quashed by President James Polk and the Democratic leaders in the Senate. But Wilmot and his friends persisted; in January 1847 the Wilmot Proviso was reintroduced and debated at length in the House. Most Democrats favored the war with Mexico and the territorial expansion that would accompany an American victory. However, a growing group of Northern Democratic representatives faced increasing criticism from constituents who demanded that the spread of slavery into the Western territories of the United States be checked. Explaining the reason for the proviso, Wilmot argued that "as a friend of the Union, as a lover of my country, and in no spirit of hostility to the South, I offered my amendment. Viewing slavery as I do, I must resist its further propagation on the North American Continent. It is an evil, the magnitude of which, no man can see."[14] The actions of these dissident Democrats posed a serious threat to the stability of the Democratic Party. From the time of Andrew Jackson's administration, the Democrats had sought to defuse the slave issue by forming a coalition of moderate representatives from all parts of the country who maintained a careful ambivalence on issues of slavery. Though they might have a strong personal distaste for slavery, these Democratic politicians quietly endorsed a party platform that pledged that their party would keep its hands off slavery. Wilmot's resolution represented a crack in the solidarity behind the Democratic pledge not to interfere with the institution of slavery. With antislavery sentiment rising in the North, the Wilmot Proviso provided a litmus test of a politician's commitment for or against slavery. Southerners feared that the actions of Wilmot and his group of renegade Democrats might be an indication of things to come. Events proved them correct in this assessment; all but one of the Democratic supporters of the Wilmot Proviso eventually became members of the Republican Party in the 1850s.

Southern fears of Democratic defections to the antislavery cause in the North were hardly allayed by the actions of Zachary Taylor, the Whig president elected in 1848. Taylor, a Louisianan who owned slaves, hardly seemed a threat in his own right. But when the question of statehood for California became a major issue in 1849, Taylor insisted that it should be admitted without making any concessions to the slave states. It appeared likely that the president would veto any "compromise" legislation that included substantial concessions to the slave interest, a move that would almost surely block any congressional efforts to reach agreement on the issue of slavery in the territories. It appeared that once again Southern dissidents were headed for a showdown with a strong-willed occupant of the Oval Office. However, on July 9, 1850, Taylor unexpectedly died. Vice President Millard Fillmore was more amenable to compromise measures, and with the threat of the veto removed, the Democratic leadership in Congress managed to forge an acceptable compromise that defused the crisis for the time being.

The political crisis of 1849–50 offers us the first opportunity to apply counterfactual analysis to the question of what caused the Civil War. What if Taylor had not suddenly taken ill and died? David Potter is one of the few historians who seriously considered the possibility that the crisis of 1850 could have ended in the dissolution of the Union. According to Potter, Taylor had a "definite and positive position" in response to Southern threats of disunion; he believed the South would back down. If Taylor's assessment of the situation was correct, then "the refusal of Congress to follow his policy cost the republic ten years of avoidable strife ending in a titanic civil war." If Taylor was wrong, then challenging the South in 1850 "would have forced the North to face the supreme test of war for the Union before it had attained the preponderance of strength, or the technological sinews, or the conviction of national unity which enabled it to win the war that finally came in 1861."[15]

Potter's counterfactual regarding Zachary Taylor in 1850 is an interesting case of what-might-be analysis. Taylor's unexpected death meant that neither of the two options postulated by Potter took place. With Fillmore in the White House, Democratic leadership in Congress succeeded in convincing enough representatives and senators that compromise was preferable to either secession or war. But although they had sidestepped the issue of war, the compromisers had not really resolved the underlying issues surrounding slavery. Potter used his counterfactual speculation to raise serious challenges to two contrasting interpretations of the Compromise of 1850:

> Historians sympathizing with the Confederacy have seldom deplored the settlement, even though it caused a fatal ten-year delay in the assertion of southern independence. By 1850, some southerners like Calhoun perceived that time was running against them and they would lose by temporizing. The events of the next two decades showed how realistic they had been. Men like Robert Toombs, who talked so fiercely about secession and then accepted compromise, were setting the stage for Appomattox. The ultimate irony is that prosouthern historians have not been logical enough to condemn Toombs and the other Southern unionists for a compromise that apparently proved ruinous to the South, while antislavery historians have castigated Webster for a compromise that eventually worked to the advantage of the antislavery cause.[16]

Potter's analysis raises an interesting point with regard to the inevitability of the Civil War. Those who argue that the war could have been avoided in 1861 point to the "success" of previous compromises. But as Potter shows, if the compromise fails to address the underlying differences, it will not last. The political settlement in 1850 did not really avert war. The two sides had simply negotiated an armistice that could buy time. "It remained to be seen," writes Potter, "whether the American People, North and South, would, by their actions, convert this settlement into a compromise.[17]

That proved to be no small task. Compromise requires that there be some middle ground around which the more moderate members of each faction can build a viable consensus. Potter's formulation of the counterfactual alternatives in the debates of 1849–50 clearly reveals that those seeking the middle ground in 1850 had been reduced to an argument of simple expediency; averting a nasty confrontation made compromise worthwhile. Later generations called this appeasement and pointed out that there was no powerful vision of the future behind such a course. The groups that articulated clear visions of the future were those who strongly opposed the compromise. The dilemma for the nation as a whole was that these two groups had very different visions of what might be. On the one hand were Southerners who saw the future in terms of a slave society; on the other were Northerners who envisioned the growing commercial and industrial interest of the free states as the dominant theme for the future. Though various leaders articulated both positions in the debates over the Compromise of 1850, neither vision had been sufficiently formulated by that time to appeal to anything approaching a majority of people in the country as a whole. The events of the next decade either would bring these two views of the world together or would sharpen the regional views in a way that made compromise increasingly more difficult. The politicians had reached a fork in the road. They could choose either to follow a path that would continue to accommodate the demands of the "slave power" or to take the path that accommodated the "vision" of the free states demanding a limit to the extension of slavery. The problem was that they could not follow both paths simultaneously.

LET US look first at the path that heads south toward slavery and the cotton culture. The dominant economic feature of Southern society was plantation slavery. The cotton boom of the nineteenth century had brought a level of prosperity to the South unmatched in the colonial era. The per capita income of free Southerners in 1860 was roughly equal to that in other areas of the United States and considerably higher than incomes in all but a handful of countries throughout the world.[18] Wealth was not evenly distributed in this society, and Southerners were highly conscious of class divisions that were based on race and the ownership of slaves and land. At the top of the socioeconomic pyramid were the 394,000 slaveowners. These were the families that controlled the economic and political life of the South.[19] Roughly half of all of them had 10 or more slaves on plantations that produced cash crops that were the lifeblood of the Southern economy. The other half of the slaveholding class, most of whom owned 3 or fewer slaves, owned their own farms, grew a few bales of cotton, and hoped that someday they might acquire additional slaves, allowing them to move up the social ladder and become part of the planter elite. Though they were snubbed by the wealthier planters, it is worth noting that a person who owned even a single slave enjoyed a net worth well above that of most farmers in the Northern states. The largest group of free people in the South were the yeomen farmers who scraped out livings practicing what was called walk-away farming. These families tended to live outside the plantation economy. Most of them owned their own farms, and in a normal year they managed to produce the subsistence needs for their families. In a good year there would be a small surplus that might allow them to improve the condition of their farms. At the bottom of the socioeconomic pyramid were the 4 million African-American slaves who formed the economic foundation upon which the entire cotton economy of the South rested. Lacking any individual rights, they were regarded by all Southerners simply as property. Conspicuous by their absence from this economic hierarchy were the merchants, tradesmen, wage workers, and practitioners of other urban occupations that were common throughout the Northern and Western states.

Economic historians in the late twentieth century have tended to view the South as a prosperous agricultural region spearheaded by the production of cotton and tobacco in the plantation regions.[20] Contemporaries living in the Northern United States who visited the South tended to express a more somber assessment of the region. William Seward, who made several trips to the slave states between 1835 and 1857, offered a view of slave society widely held in the North: "An exhausted soil, old and decaying towns, wretchedly-neglected roads, and, in every respect, an absence of enterprise and improvement, distinguish the region through which we have come, in contrast to that in which we live. Such has been the effect of slavery."[21] Seward was not alone in his tendency to focus on the "poverty" and "backwardness" of the yeomen farmers. Northern visitors blamed these conditions on the detrimental effects of slavery. Most Southerners, they believed, were trapped in a circle of poverty with little hope of escape.

Neither the economic historians nor the contemporary observers are completely wrong. Each presents an incomplete picture. Census data confirm that a considerable disparity in income and wealth did exist between planters and yeomen farmers. The average wealth of a slaveholder in 1860 was almost fifteen times the average wealth of free farmers in the South and nine times that of farmers in the North. Yet while their Northern brethren might look down on the "poor white" farmers of the South, the size of a Southern farm without slaves and the income of most yeomen farmers would have been the envy of most people throughout the world in the middle of the nineteenth century. So long as the cotton boom continued, Southern planters would enjoy a steady flow of income, and the rest of the South could share at least some of that prosperity. What might be seen as an early version of trickle-down economics was particularly true for Southerners in the 1850s; while the average value of slave farms rose by a factor of three over the decade, operators of free farms in the South saw the average value of their farms double over that period.[22] Small wonder that the yeoman farmers regarded King Cotton as a benign ruler whose reign they hoped would extend far into the future.

If plantation slavery was the key to the economic success of the South, it was also a major obstacle to economic development and social change in the region. Part of the problem was the very success of slave agriculture. By the time of the Civil War the system of slave plantations had proved to be an effective engine of growth for more than a century and a half; there seemed little reason to tinker with it. The nature of cotton production on slave plantations had not changed significantly since the turn of the century. Slaves were organized in gangs that planted and harvested the crop; slave labor then ginned the crop, and it was sent off to one of the marketing centers on the coast or along one of the major rivers. The financial details of selling the crop were handled by factors, who saw to it that the cotton was sold either in Europe or the Northern United States. When the transaction was completed, a net balance was credited to the planter's account. Typically the factor also handled the plantation's purchase of goods from areas outside the South.[23] Slaves were an ideal form of labor for plantation agriculture; the field tasks were simple and repetitive, and in the off-season the labor could be used for growing food crops and a myriad of tasks around the farm. The essential element in the success of slave labor on the plantation was the use of coercion by the slaveowner. So long as slaveowners could exercise control over their chattel labor, there was no need to worry about finding new and improved ways of growing cotton.[24]

There was one other aspect of plantation slavery that served to stifle attempts to change the system. This was the question of race. Slaves in the antebellum United States were black, and the system of slavery served not only as a means of production but also as a form of race control. In a society where 40 percent of the population was enslaved and where the concentrations of slave population meant that in many areas of the cotton South slaves outnumbered the free population, the plantation system served as an important means of controlling the slave population. More than just the economics of cotton kept slaves on the plantation and out of the cities of the South. So long as they were isolated in a rural society with limited access to the outside world, the possibilities for escape by enslaved African-American slaves were severely limited. Slave patrollers roamed the rural areas, slaves were not allowed to gather after dark, laws were passed forbidding the teaching of slaves to read, and by the late antebellum period manumission had been severely curtailed in every slave state.

In spite of all these restrictions on the slave population, Southerners had an almost paranoiac fear that slave revolts might violently overthrow their entire social system. This paranoia did more than just create an atmosphere that repressed slaves; it produced a fear throughout the South that bound together all the classes of the free population in a xenophobic reaction to any outside intrusion into their society. One important manifestation of this xenophobia was the absence of either immigrants or settlers from the Northern states to the slave South. In 1860 there were 4.4 million foreign-born residents in the United States, yet fewer than 400,000 of them lived in the South. Map 1.4 clearly shows the extent to which the South did not share in the enormous influx of immigrants from Europe. Apart from a few regions in the lower Mississippi Valley, there were no concentrations of foreign-born residents within the slave states.[25] Native-born migrants from other regions of the United States were hardly more welcome. Examining the place of birth of native-born residents in the western areas of the slave states, we find that almost all of them reported their birthplaces as some other area of the South. In the nonslave areas of the West, by contrast, native-born settlers came from all parts of the United States, including the South.[26] As the map of immigrant settlement clearly shows, the western areas of the United States also

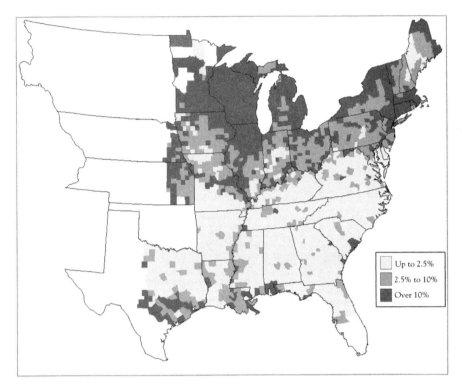

MAP 1.4

FOREIGN-BORN AS A PERCENTAGE OF THE
FREE POPULATION IN 1860

received a substantial influx of foreign-born, again in sharp contrast
with the Southwest. While the free states wrestled with the challenge
of cultural diversity, the South remained largely isolated from the tide
of immigration that came to the United States in the 1850s. Migration
statistics also show that there was a small but steady flow of emigrants
out of the South to free areas of the West in the two decades before the
war. Was this an exodus of people seeking to "escape" the closed society of the South? We have no clear data on the background of these
people, but it is interesting to note that while a significant number of
Southerners left the South to go west, the reverse was not true; neither
immigrants nor Northerners moved into the South in large numbers.

So what was the vision of the future as seen through Southern eyes? Our description of the South at the end of the antebellum period implies that the salient feature of Southern society in the late antebellum period was a fierce resistance to change and particularly to suggestions of change that came from outside the South. The social structure of the South and the values that underlay that social structure had remained essentially unchanged since the time of Jefferson. Northerners characterized the free white population as being held in the grip of poverty by the power of a small oligarchy of slaveowners who were determined to stymie progress. Yet many, perhaps most, Southerners saw their society as a place where the status quo offered ample opportunity for economic growth without having to endure the adjustments that accompanied economic and social change. There were no legal or social restrictions to becoming a slaveowner; all it took was enough capital to buy a slave. Credit markets were more than willing to take slaves as collateral against a loan taken out by a would-be planter, and there was an abundance of cheap land on which the slaves could work. So Southerners borrowed capital and headed west in a steady stream, taking their slaves with them. The Southerners' vision of the future in 1850 was simple: They wanted to extend the past into the future by re-creating the "old South" in the new areas of the West.

The problem with this process was that this westward push by Southern slaveholders onto fresh land in the West was a crucial element in the Southern prosperity. There was a "territorial imperative" that became a persistent source of friction between slave and antislave factions as each competed for the same land. Thanks to the continued availability of territories for settlement, there was enough good land for everyone, so compromises such as those in 1820 and 1850 were able to work things out. But a series of developments outside the Southern states in the 1850s gradually convinced a majority of Southerners that being tied to the Northern states might pose serious threats to their way of life.

We have already noted the first of these threats, the growing demographic imbalance between slave and free states. Simply put, this meant that the safeguards placed in the Constitution in 1790 to protect the South from a national government dominated by powerful Northern interests were no longer sufficient. After the reapportionment of Congress based on the 1850 census, members in the House of Representatives from free states outnumbered those from slave states, 143 to 90; ten years later the Northern representatives outnumbered their Southern counterparts, 155 to 85.[27] In the Senate the admission of California in 1850 broke a thirty to thirty balance between slave and free senators; by the end of the decade two more free states, Minnesota and Oregon, would be added. Still, the specter of domination of the South by a monolithic North was more fear than reality in the early 1850s. Politicians from all regions of the country tended to avoid confrontations over slavery, directing their energies instead to such issues as problems with the banking system, distribution of public lands, protective tariffs, and the need for government expenditures to improve the transportation infrastructure.

On the slave issue there were still a sufficient number of people seeking a middle ground for Congress in 1850 to find a compromise. But the middle ground began to rapidly shrink after passage of the Compromise of 1850. The problems went far beyond the rhetoric about slavery. To understand why sectional differences became increasingly intractable following the settlement of 1850, we need to go back to the fork in the road and take the path that headed north toward New England and the mid-Atlantic states. Here we encounter a society that for the past twenty years has been experiencing what social and economic historians term a market revolution.[28] The rise of a market economy in the northeastern United States dates back to early colonial days. What caused the market revolution suddenly to leap across the Appalachian Mountains in the nineteenth century was the completion of the Erie Canal in 1825. Stretching 365 miles from Albany to Buffalo, the canal provided the first cheap transportation link between frontier farmers in the Ohio Valley and the diversifying economy of the Northeast. Construction of additional canals and improvements in internal waterways continued to reduce transportation costs throughout the 1830s and early 1840s. In the mid-1850s the completion of railroad trunk lines across the Appalachian Mountains accelerated the decline in transport costs to a point where the price of sending a good from New York to a Western city was a tiny fraction of what it had been two decades earlier. The result of these internal improvements was an expansion of interregional trade that eventually dwarfed the traffic between the South and the rest of the country.

What this meant was that the American economy was no longer a three-legged stool. The North and the West now had a solid economic foundation for expanding markets at home and abroad that no longer depended on the flows of trade with the South.

THE MARKET revolution in the Northern states was more than just a phenomenon of economic growth; it manifested itself in a variety of ways that affected the lifestyle of everyone. Among the most visible manifestations were the urban centers that sprang up throughout the North and West. Just over six million Americans, or roughly one out of every five persons, lived in towns or cities large enough to be classified as urban areas by the 1860 census. Map 1.5 charts the counties with urban populations of at least twenty-five hundred in 1860. The concentration of larger cities in the Northeast is immediately apparent. However, while such urban centers as New York, Philadelphia, and Boston were the most visible examples of urban growth, it was the proliferation of smaller cities throughout the Eastern and Western states that illustrated the extent to which the American economy was being transformed into a market society.

Throughout the North, farms increasingly offered their products for the markets created by the growing urban population. The need to market such farm products as grains, corn, dairy products, and meat created an economic base for small towns throughout western New

TABLE 1.1
URBAN COUNTIES IN THE
UNITED STATES, 1860

	Urban Population	Number of Counties	Cumulative Percentage
Northeast[a]			
Over 40,000	2,839.7	15	75.3
10,000 to 40,000	666.8	34	93.0
5,000 to 10,000	187.8	26	98.0
2,500 to 5,000	74.7	21	100.0
Total	3,769.0	96	
South			
Over 40,000	215.0	2	34.1
10,000 to 40,000	213.3	10	67.9
5,000 to 10,000	110.1	15	85.3
2,500 to 5,000	92.7	26	100.0
Total	631.1	53	
West[b]			
Over 40,000	919.8	11	53.2
10,000 to 40,000	231.6	17	66.6
5,000 to 10,000	346.8	48	86.7
2,500 to 5,000	230.8	65	100.0
Total	1,729.0	141	100.0
Total United States	6,129.0	290	

Notes:

    a. Northeast region includes Delaware and Maryland.

    b. West region includes Missouri and Kentucky; also the western parts of New York and Maryland.

Source: Tabulated from U.S. census of 1860 micro data set.

York and Pennsylvania, Ohio, Indiana, Illinois, Iowa, Wisconsin, and Michigan. These towns provided the first step in a complex network that linked the rural producers and the markets for their goods throughout the world. The local merchants, bankers, and other middlemen offered commercial and transportation services to their clients. These farm products eventually reached the major entrepôts on the periphery of the Western economy, like Pittsburgh, Chicago, Cleveland, St. Louis, Detroit, and Milwaukee, all cities along the western rivers and the Great Lakes. These centers were in turn linked to the network of transportation, financial, and credit services of the eastern

· Each dot represents 2,500 persons

MAP 1.5
URBAN COUNTIES IN THE UNITED STATES
IN 1860

seaboard.[29] By the end of the decade American agricultural products were reaching not only the East Coast of the United States but the shores of Europe.

Urban families depended on incomes from wages, and they used those incomes to purchase goods and services in the marketplace. The family production common in rural communities had been replaced by wage labor and trips to the store. The effect of this switch to market activity reached far beyond the city limits. Families living in rural regions were gradually drawn deeper into the market environment as they discovered that even small cities offered opportunities to earn income from wage jobs, although the work was sometimes very seasonal. Most important were the economic opportunities that cities offered in the form of jobs for young people willing to leave the farm. Young adults, who in earlier times were essentially locked into their rural settings, could now break free from the traditional family ties and move to urban areas. The patriarchal control that had dominated rural areas for centuries was slowly eroding away under the pressures of migration to the cities.

The market opportunities offered by urban markets in the West and Northeast went beyond the lure of employment for farm children. Farmers close to a town could depend more on markets and less on home production to provide family needs. A measure of how far this development had progressed by 1860 can be seen by the levels of home manufactures reported by farmers displayed in Map 1.6. Transportation, credit, and other market arrangements had practically eliminated home manufactures on the typical farm in the North. Only a few counties in the North produced as much as five dollars' worth of home manufactures as Northern farmers came to rely on markets rather than family labor to provide the income from their crops with which they could purchase their consumption needs for the farm. On the eve of the Civil War the market society embraced households in every sector of the Northern states.

In the South, with its emphasis on plantation agriculture and the

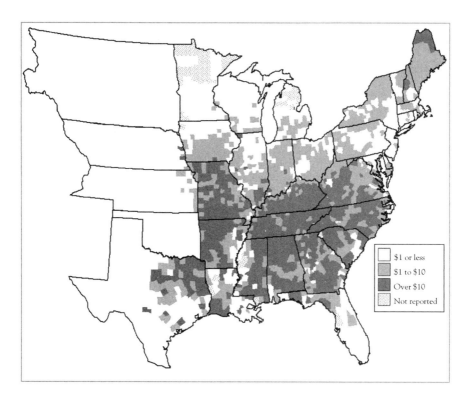

MAP 1.6

VALUE OF HOME MANUFACTURES PER
HOUSEHOLD IN 1860

production of staple crops, we see a very different pattern of urban development. What is particularly striking about urban development in the South was the absence of small towns. Only about 7 percent of Southerners lived in towns or cities of any size, and most of these urban-ites were in the commercial centers on the periphery of the Southern economy.[30] These were the cities where the cotton or tobacco markets that moved Southern staples to markets beyond the South were located. They were the hubs of Southern commerce, but they had little or no direct contact with the everyday lives of Southern farmers. Though they might sell a surplus of cotton or other staples to obtain supplies, Southern farms remained far more self-sufficient than their

Northern counterparts. Almost all counties in the South reported home manufactures of at least fifteen dollars per household. The only areas in the South that reported levels of home manufacture remotely comparable to those of Northern farms were the alluvial cotton regions in Mississippi and Louisiana, some of the tobacco regions of Virginia, where large slave plantations were particularly prevalent, and the cattle areas of western Texas.

How do this growth of a market society and the rise of manufacturing in the North produce a vision of the future that differs from that in the South? The answer lies in the impact of the growth of markets on the social fabric of Northern society. What was taking place was a revolution in family values that changed the way people in the Northern states viewed their world. This new approach, which economic historians call a life cycle transition, placed much greater emphasis on individual decision making, particularly on individual decisions dealing with children and the economic assets of the family. As children grew into young adults, they began to demand the option of making their own decisions regarding their future. In response, older family members had to find ways to deal with the economic uncertainty created by the mobility and increased options available to their children. What emerged was a new breed of acquisitive individualists who relied less on traditional family arrangements for economic security than on market-oriented arrangements to provide for their economic future. Put more succinctly, what we are saying is that the North was taking a large step toward becoming a "modern" society.[31]

Because it was based on a world that was rapidly changing, it is not easy to spell out a succinct Northern vision to contrast with the vision of the future that we have described for the South. The key difference was that while Southerners dealt with a situation that was relatively static, Northerners were forced to adapt to a world that was changing very rapidly. In 1850 the responses to change were still only vaguely understood, and political leaders did not have a well-formed political agenda. Instead, there was a proliferation of parties and ideas that tended to focus on local rather than national issues in the free states. Adding to this uncertainty was the influx of immigrants to the United States after 1847. While the new arrivals gave added impetus to economic growth through their cheap labor and their demands for goods and services, they also brought problems of rivalry for jobs and living spaces, coupled with ethnic and religious beliefs that did not always mix well with those of the native-born. Throughout the 1850s the old political alliances in the Northern states were crumbling in the wake of a myriad of new problems created by the emergence of a market society in the North and the surge of new arrivals from overseas.[32]

Against this background of local turmoil, there were continuing debates in Congress on issues that had dominated political debate throughout the first part of the nineteenth century. These included the land policy of the federal government, government support of internal improvements, the tariff policy, and the organization of banking in the United States. Prior to the 1850s these issues did not create deep divisions along sectional lines. However, the growing influence of markets in the Northern and Western states meant that the political economies of these regions increasingly diverged from those of the South. Legislative battles over these four areas of government intervention generated increasing levels of frustration that reflected the diverging sectional interests. A quick review of the legislative debates on land policy, internal improvements, the tariff, and banking will point out the extent to which Southerners felt an increasing sense of isolation.

Land policy. The manner in which the federal government distributed land to people for settlement had always been a bone of contention between slaveowning planters and free labor farmers. Northerners sought to encourage the creation of "family" farms by having the government offer cheap land in small parcels. Southerners preferred a policy of large tracts of land that would be more suitable for the establishment of plantations. Prior to 1850 the division of territories into slave and free areas largely diffused the tensions over this issue. However, with the creation in 1854 of a huge area of land that could be settled by either slave or free laborers, the question of land policy suddenly became a very hot subject of debate. This all came to a head with the passage in 1860 of the Homestead Act, which was to provide 160 acres of free land to anyone who wanted to settle and farm the land. The bill passed through Congress with the voting following sectional lines but was vetoed by President James Buchanan. The president's actions not only enraged his political opponents but also angered a substantial number of people in his own party.

Internal improvements. We noted earlier the enormous impact of internal improvements on the trade of the Northwest and the Atlantic seaboard. As the transportation projects became more and more ambitious, politicians in the Old Northwest asked Congress for federal aid for canals, river improvements, expanded shipping facilities on the Great Lakes, and a host of lesser projects incorporated into the rivers and harbors bills that were routinely approved with little or no scrutiny. The explosion of new railroad mileage in the 1850s gave added support to those crying for federal subsidies to promote interregional transportation. Southerners did not share the West's insatiable appetite for internal improvements, and they began to balk at the rising costs of these subsidies outside their region. In 1860 a bill proposing a transcontinental railway that would link the Pacific coast to the rest of the country narrowly failed to pass the House. Significantly, no representatives representing districts of the South where there was a significant slave population voted in favor of the measure. To Northerners the bill's defeat was a slap in the face by the slave power.

The tariff. Southerners, with their emphasis on staple agriculture, needed to buy goods produced outside the South, and they strongly objected to the imposition of duties on imported goods. Southerners regarded the tariff as equivalent to a tax on the cotton they exported to Britain. Manufacturers in the Northeast, on the other hand, supported a high tariff as protection against cheap British imports. People in the West were caught in the middle of this controversy. Like Southerners, Western farmers disliked the idea of a high protective tariff that raised the cost of imported goods they wanted to buy for their own consumption. However, the tariff was the main source of federal revenue at the time. Westerners eager for government funds for their internal improvements saw tariff revenues as a source of funding. In 1857 Western and Eastern interests in Congress agreed to support a moderate tariff with duties high enough to offer protection to Northern manufacturers while at the same time generating sufficient revenues to fund internal improvements. Southerners complained that the deal was a blatant example of the willingness of representatives from the West and the North to make economic bargains at the expense of the South.

Money and banking. Getting more involved with markets meant getting more involved with the intricacies of money. The Founding Fathers were so concerned about money that they included in the Constitution a clause stating that only the federal government could print money. The idea was to prevent state governments from recklessly printing money, an action that produced economic chaos. However, innovative entrepreneurs soon found a way around the constitutional limit on the printing of money: They established commercial banks. As private corporations banks could not issue money, but they could print banknotes, and people soon discovered that banknotes could be used to pay for just about anything. Although commercial banks had been around for a long time in Europe, their business had always been primarily concerned with commercial credit and the financing of business enterprises. But by the 1850s banks were serving a wide spectrum of customers throughout the U.S. economy. While the impact of the banks was greatest in the urban centers, farmers became more and more involved with the growing financial network of the North. Banks could provide commercial farmers with loans to buy land, provide credit to tide farms through the growing season, and assist in selling crops. Small businesses and manufacturers throughout the North similarly found banks to be useful institutions for commercial credit and a means of facilitating payments through the use of checks rather than cash.

While banks were clearly a valuable part of the rise of market transactions throughout the country, they were also associated with fraud,
unstable currency, and a monopoly control of credit, all aspects of the
industry that frightened farmers and small businessmen. Financially
conservative Whigs insisted that the answer to this dilemma was a system of nationally chartered banks that were regulated by the federal
government. In the South, where people had far less need for local
banking services, there was little enthusiasm for such a proposal;
Southerners were fearful that a national banking system would be
dominated by Northern interests and that they would reap few benefits from a more centralized system. As with the tariff, Westerners were
caught in the middle. Farmers worried that a system of "national"
banks would be controlled by the already dominant Eastern banking
establishment. At the same time, Western farmers and small businesses
needed reliable local banking services for financing their economic
enterprises, and a national system would offer bank charters for towns
throughout the West together with the financial security of government-
backed banks. By 1860 a growing number of Westerners were inclined
to support the Republican proposal for a banking system in which
banks were chartered by the federal government, not by the states.
Once again Southerners were able to round up enough opposition to
kill the national bank bill that was introduced by Republicans in 1860.
But their success came at a high price; the action alienated many of
their Democratic followers in the free states.

Numerous proposals dealing with each of these issues of political
economy had been hotly debated since the mid-1820s. What changed
in the 1850s was the emergence of a political alliance between the
Northeast and the Old Northwest that gradually tied together all the
pieces of the debates into a loosely defined program that pointedly
ignored the interest of Southern regions. As we have seen, Southerners had successfully blocked this program up to 1860. But the insurgents
were gaining strength at each election. By the end of the decade a political party committed to a platform of political economy that proposed

significant changes in the instructional arrangements of the United States was vying for control of the federal government. After mounting an unsuccessful ticket for the presidency in 1856, the Republican Party made an impressive showing in the 1858 off-year elections, winning ninety-two seats in the House and thirty seats in the Senate. This meant that their seats in Congress equaled or exceeded the number of those from slave states. If they simply consolidated their electoral position in the free states of the Union, Republicans could confidently look forward to controlling Congress and eventually enacting their legislative program by simply ignoring the objections of the South. But to do this, they needed more than a program of political economy promoting market capitalism. Southerners could still count on some support from Northern allies in the Democratic Party on the economic issues. Republicans needed some overarching issue that could unify the Northern electorate around a single cause.

They found it in the one area in which Democrats in the North were most likely to break ranks with their Southern brethren, the disputes over slavery. The problem with slavery was not how it worked in the South. We have seen that—at least from the perspective of white Southerners—it was working very well. The problem was the ways in which the Northern view of free labor and market capitalism posed a threat to slavery. Northern Republicans objected to slavery on several grounds. First, they argued it was immoral. To be sure, abolitionists who argued for the emancipation of all slaves represented a small minority of the Northern electorate. However, a much larger element of the North sympathized with the abolitionists' moral claim that slavery was wrong, even if they were not willing to risk breaking up the Union to free the slaves. In a subtle way, the continual outpouring of moral pronouncements by Northern abolitionists attacking slavery put Southerners in the position of always having to defend the morality of a system that permitted one person to own another. A broader objection to slavery throughout the North was that the institution corrupted the political system of the United States. The core of this objection stemmed from the views of such Northern statesmen as Salmon Chase and William Seward, who argued that the planter elite not only controlled the South but also ran the federal government. As we have seen, this concern had some basis in fact. What Northern critics called the slave power did exert political dominance over the South, and Southern leaders consistently demanded protection for their slave interests from the federal government. The demand that proved to be most galling to Northerners was for the enforcement of the fugitive slave laws, which allowed freelance bounty hunters to track down escaped slaves in the North and seek the aid of federal marshals in getting their quarry back across the Ohio River. Together with the political opposition on the part of Southerners to the programs of political economy outlined above, this obstinate defense of chattel labor produced an overall view of the South in the free states that slavery was a serious obstacle to progress. "Political anti-slavery," notes historian Eric Foner, "was not merely . . . an attack on southern slavery and the society built upon it; it was a reaffirmation of the superiority of the social system of the North.[33]

Finally, it is important to recognize that Northern views of the slave South were heavily colored by the racial prejudice north of the Mason-Dixon Line. The fact that slaves were of African descent produced a considerable antipathy in the North toward the question of emancipation as a solution for the slave problem. On the one hand, many Northerners agreed that slavery was morally wrong. On the other hand, racial prejudice against African-Americans meant that there was little desire on the part of white people in the free states to have large numbers of African-Americans set free—particularly if one worried that the freed slaves might come North. Thus racial prejudice worked to lessen the impact of the moral messages of abolitionists such as William Lloyd Garrison, while at the same time it produced a strong sentiment that slaves should not be set free and made equal to whites. Particularly in the Old Northwest, there were groups, such as the Free-Soilers, that strongly opposed any further incursions of slavery into the Western territories, while also rejecting the idea that African-Americans might be set free. This combination of views is most evident in the Lincoln-Douglas debates of 1858. Lincoln persistently hammered his opponent on the issue of popular sovereignty, which would allow settlers to choose whether or not they wanted slavery in the territories; Douglas responded with the charge that Lincoln was a "friend of the Negro" who would eventually espouse emancipation. Neither candidate could completely escape the charges leveled by the other.[34] In the process of articulating these two themes, the senatorial candidates in Illinois managed to bring the debates of slavery back to the forefront of political discussion throughout the country.

Yet it is clear that for all the agitation against slavery by Northerners, there was still no substantive movement that offered any direct threats to the slave system in the early 1850s. A sizable fraction of Northerners was prepared to support a platform of "containing" slavery within the limits it had reached following the Compromise of 1850. However, economic interests and moral ambivalence produced a strong reluctance to interfere with slavery in a way that might irrevocably alienate the South. The irony of American slavery is that precisely because it was a market institution, slavery could be threatened by a myriad of market or political forces that could not be controlled by either slaveholders or their opponents. A major objective of anti-slave groups in the North was to contain the westward push of slavery. Southerners argued that this was an infringement of a basic property right. Restricting the movement of slaves would almost surely have an adverse effect on the value of slaves. That in turn would threaten slaveholders in the less fertile lands of the Southeast with financial disaster. Disputes over slavery and the West were responsible for the bitterest political conflicts during the first half of the century. Southerners won or at least gained a tie in most of those confrontations. But through it all they worried that the very foundation of capitalist slavery, the right to use slave property in the most profitable endeavors, would be threatened if a powerful antislave coalition of Northerners ever gained control of the government.

Most historians have argued that these fears were largely unfounded.[35] Even the election of Abraham Lincoln did not really threaten the right to own slaves. Lincoln, after all, was a moderate on the slave issue within his own party and went to great lengths to assure his country-men that he had no designs to emancipate slaves. But could Southern-ers trust him? Historian James Huston raises an interesting point when he insists that the question of slave property posed an "irreconcilable problem" to Southerners. "On policy issues," writes Huston, "South-erners could expect to obtain allies; but on the subject of enforcing property rights in slaves the South had no northern allies because northerners did not own slaves and had no direct interest in seeing property rights in slaves enforced." The result, Huston asserts, was that a minority position for the South in the federal government was noth-ing less than "catastrophic."[36] The catastrophe that Huston has in mind, of course, is the loss of millions of dollars in slave capital as a result of a number of possible actions that Northerners in Congress might take to restrict the use of slaves. The point here is not that this what-might-be scenario was in fact very likely in 1860; the problem is that it could happen anytime after the election of Lincoln in 1860.

IT IS clear that a decade after the Compromise of 1850 Americans had moved no closer to finding a solution to their disputes over slav-ery. Indeed, one could argue that they had moved substantially farther away from any solution. The ideological positions that very nearly blocked the Compromise of 1850 had hardened into two radical groups, each of which had gained increasing political support for its position. The events of the 1850s had convinced people on both sides of the Mason-Dixon Line that the other side could not be trusted to keep any agreements that were reached. For six decades politicians had been able to keep slavery off the national agenda save for a few "crises" that were dealt with through an appeal to compromise rather than through destruction of the Union. Yet attempts to finesse the slave issue in the 1850s failed, and the result was disastrous. Was there any way this failure could have been avoided? A counterfactual approach to this question encourages us to ask whether or not there were alternatives that would have made any difference, given how Northerners and Southerners viewed what the future might be in the late 1850s.

No issue had provided a more volatile battleground for competing ideologies than the question of slavery and the settlement of Western lands. By 1850 the only remaining territory that appealed to slave settlers was that directly west of Missouri, an area explicitly set aside as free territory by the Compromise of 1820. In 1854 the Democratic Congress passed the Kansas-Nebraska Act, which effectively overturned the Missouri Compromise by allowing the settlers in the new territory to decide whether or not they wished to permit slavery. This was the first application of what Stephen Douglas termed popular sovereignty. On its face, popular sovereignty looked to be a reasonable way to deal with the question; what could be more democratic than letting the "people" decide an important issue? But looks can be deceptive; in the context of the conflicting visions of North and South, popular sovereignty turned out to be a recipe for disaster.

In June 1857 settlers in the Kansas Territory began a process that they hoped would lead to statehood. From the outset the procedures were beset with difficulties as free and slave factions struggled to gain the upper hand. There were numerous confrontations between competing groups that eventually escalated to the point where the territory became known as Bloody Kansas. The showdown came over the state constitution that was to be forwarded to Washington with the application for statehood. The document that had emerged from the constitutional convention at Lecompton did not provide voters with a choice

over the legality of slavery. Most of the free state voters therefore boy-
cotted the election to approve it. As a result, what became known as
the Lecompton Constitution passed with an overwhelming majority of
those who voted in the election. However, that result was hardly an
accurate reflection of the views held by the population as a whole. By
the time the Kansans' application reached Congress, slave and free factions throughout the country had been polarized into opposing camps.
After much debate, Congress passed a bill approving the admission of
Kansas to statehood. However, the bill stipulated that Kansas voters
must approve the Lecompton Constitution in a new election. Unwilling to accept these terms, Kansans emphatically rejected the constitution, and Kansas was denied admission as a state.[37]

In one sense we could say that popular sovereignty worked. By the
end of 1858 it was clear that a majority of the people in Kansas did not
favor slavery, and thus the decision not to admit Kansas under the
Lecompton Constitution reflected the "people's choice," an outcome
consistent with popular sovereignty. But the process set up to reach
this decision clearly did *not* work. No one "won" the bitter fight over
statehood for Kansas. Statehood was delayed until January 1861.
Stephen Douglas, the man who had developed the concept of popular
sovereignty, was so disenchanted with the irregularities of the electoral
processes that he voted *against* the admission of Kansas as a slave state,
an action that effectively eliminated any hope he had of forging a
coalition of Northern and Southern Democrats around the principle
of popular sovereignty. In any case, he soon found that his party was
irreparably split by the division between free and slave Democrats.
Antislave forces in the Whig Party could momentarily exult that they
had stymied the slave power, but in the process they had alienated
Southern Whigs, who abandoned the party in droves. The immediate
effect of the uproar was therefore the disappearance of the Whig Party
from national politics. Politicians in the North struggled to form a new
party that could be effective at a national level. For the South, the

defeat of the Lecompton Constitution spelled the end of the region's ability to maintain a balance of power in Congress to assure the inviolability of the slave property right. For the first time the South had come away empty-handed in a dispute over slavery.

Most historians who have examined the political machinations from the passage of the Kansas-Nebraska bill through the defeat of the bill to admit Kansas have been highly critical of the politicians who took part in those decisions. Yet those who claim that it was "blunders" on the part of politicians that created the fiasco of Bloody Kansas miss an essential point: Popular sovereignty represented a legitimate attempt to resolve the dispute over slavery in the territories by some form of compromise. It failed. Far from resolving the conflict over slavery, it not only exacerbated the tensions between the two sides but poisoned the air to a degree that made any future compromise even more difficult. The result was a political disaster that, in the opinion of most historians, started the country down the road to civil war. But were there alternatives in 1857 that would have produced different outcomes? When we consider alternatives, it is important that any counterfactual must deal with two powerful historical factors at work here. One was that economic pressures and the push for westward settlement meant that the question of organizing the Kansas Territory could not be put off forever. If Douglas and his allies had not brought it up in 1854, someone else soon would have. The second condition is that any outcome reached by Kansans on the question of slavery had to be ratified by the rest of the nation. Indeed, this is the ultimate reason popular sovereignty failed. It did not matter what the outcome of the vote on slavery in Kansas was, nor did it matter that the vote was honest or dishonest. Whatever the outcome of elections in Kansas might be, there would be a sizable group of people *outside* Kansas who would reject the result of that election. Those people would insist on taking their objections to a higher level of government. Popular sovereignty failed because the conflicting visions of proslave and antislave factions at a national level meant that this was *not* a local decision; it would inevitably touch off a national debate that would escalate sectional rivalries.

Before the final vote on Kansas, politicians thought there were three stands one could take on the slave issue: (1) Slavery should be allowed in all the territories; (2) slavery should be banned in all the territories; or (3) the people should decide the issue. The outcome in Kansas was not some fluke created by political mismanagement; it was dramatic proof that popular sovereignty could not resolve the issue of slavery in the territories. The fact that the two remaining options were opposed to each other meant that there was no way of resolving the issue of slavery in the territories without opening up a national debate on the question. This of course is exactly what politicians throughout the antebellum period sought to avoid. They had good reason to fear the consequences of opening a Pandora's box. Perhaps the greatest cost of the Kansas fiasco was the loss of trust that the dispute engendered. The violence, electoral chicanery, and vituperative rhetoric all pointed to a growing disdain for the ability of the political system of the United States to produce "honest" results. "Popular Sovereignty," observed Senator Charles Sumner of Massachusetts, "which, when truly understood, is a fountain of just power, has ended in Popular Slavery."[38] Sumner's speech was so offensive to Southern interests that Representative Preston Brooks of South Carolina later confronted him on the floor of the Senate and beat him senseless. Sumner, who was unable to return to the Senate for over a year, became something of a martyr for Northern antislavery men; Brooks became a hero to his constituents, many of whom sent him canes to replace the one he had broken over Sumner's head. The attack against Sumner was one of many incidents that reflected the breakdown of civility and trust between the two factions. Governor John Quitman of Mississippi summarized the Southern reaction to the rejection of Kansas when he claimed that the action meant that "the South must regard the plighted faith of the Northern Democracy [as] violated. [It means that] no more reliance can be placed on them to aid us in protecting our rights; that National Democracy is worthless. We must also see in the act, a fixed and inexorable determination on the part of the majority never to admit another slave state, to stop forever the extension of slavery, and thus to bind the South to a triumphant car of an antagonistic majority."[39] In the space of a few short years the Kansas-Nebraska affair had reshaped the political landscape of the United States. It did so by making slavery, the one issue that could instantly inflame regional antagonisms, the primary issue in national electoral campaigns.

AGAINST THIS background of increasing polarization of views in both the North and the South, citizens of the United States prepared to go to the polls in the fall of 1860 to elect a new president. Four candidates were vying for the dubious honor of trying to lead the country out of the impending crisis. Abraham Lincoln was the candidate of the Republican Party. A moderate within his own party, Lincoln had defeated two better-known candidates at the party's convention in Chicago on May 19, 1860. The Democrats had a more difficult time. The favorite for the nomination was Stephen Douglas, but when the Democratic Party convened in Charleston at the end of April, Douglas was unable to gain a majority even after fifty-seven ballots. In July the party reconvened in Baltimore, and this time Douglas prevailed, but only after most of the delegates from the Deep South had left the convention and chosen their own candidate, John Breckinridge of Kentucky, to run on a separate ticket. The fourth candidate was John Bell of Tennessee, who was nominated by the hastily formed Constitutional Union Party in an effort to field a candidate that would represent an alternative to the three major candidates.

On November 6, 1860, Abraham Lincoln was elected president of the United States. He carried seventeen states and won 180 of the 303 electoral votes. His closest competitor was the Southern Democrat John Breckinridge, who carried ten of the fifteen slave states but got only 72 electoral votes. A glance at Map 1.7, which shows the victorious candidate in each county, reveals just how stark the split between North and South had become and how closely the pattern of Republican votes mirrored the economic changes described earlier. The Northeast had always been a bulwark of the Whig Party and was the first region to endorse the nascent Republican political economy in the years leading up to the election of 1860. The key to Lincoln's victory was his success in parts of the Western states where the market revolution had progressed rapidly in the 1850s—particularly the areas around the Great Lakes and the water routes to the East. Though Douglas was able to make a strong showing in the counties just north of the Ohio River and in sections of northeastern Ohio, Lincoln carried the more populous areas to the northwest. While slavery and the threat of secession dominated the rhetoric at the national level, the Republican message of a new political economy was a compelling factor leading voters throughout the free states to come to the Republican banner.

In the final tally, the only nonslave state to give Douglas any votes in the electoral college was New Jersey. His poor showing in the electoral college reveals just how far the support for compromise on the slave issue had sunk in the Northern states. In the presidential election of 1852 the Democratic Party had swept to a stunning victory following the settlement of 1850. But Northern patience was wearing thin, and the message of a progressive political economy and the antislavery of the Republicans struck a resonant chord with the electorate throughout the urban areas of the North. What is striking about the results depicted in Map 1.7 is the extent to which Northern voters not only rejected the compromise message of Douglas but also turned a deaf ear to the pleas of John Bell, who ran on a platform urging the preservation of the Union. Though he outpolled Breckinridge in the popular vote and managed to carry three states in the upper South, including Virginia, Bell did not carry a single county in the free states. His problem was obvious: Northern voters were not attracted by a candidate

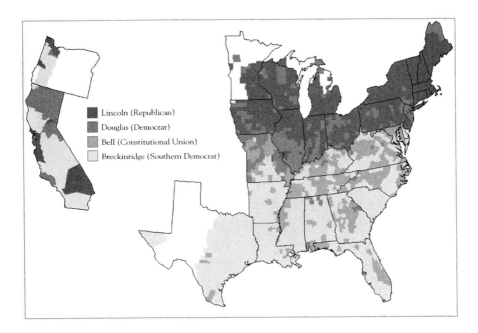

MAP 1.7
ELECTION OF 1860

from a slave state who advocated what was in effect the status quo. Bell's support represented the last gasp of the Southern wing of the Whig Party. These voters were uneasy over the possible breakup of the Union; despite their sympathy for the slave cause, they were unwilling to espouse secession openly.

Just as the events of the 1850s had eroded the influence of the Democrats in the North, so Whigs in the Deep South found themselves between a rock and a hard place. Loyal to the Union, they nevertheless were committed to slavery. In 1850, when Calhoun urged Southerners to leave the Union, Southern Whigs had backed away from so drastic a step, and they had been a powerful enough force to forestall secession. By 1860 their views had crystallized to the point where any threat to slavery was seen as a sufficient threat to warrant the dissolution of the Union. This time a sizable number opted to join the firebrands and vote for the proslave candidate. Breckinridge easily carried all eight states in the Deep South. Calhoun's vision of a unified South had finally been realized. The problem was that this solidarity was no longer enough to carry the day in a national election. Breckinridge's support in the electoral college was less than half that garnered by Lincoln. The question now was how many Southern states would vote to leave the Union after Lincoln's election. The answer was not long in coming. On December 20, 1860, the South Carolina legislature approved an ordinance of secession. By the end of February 1861 the six states from the Deep South had followed South Carolina's lead and voted to leave the Union. On February 4, a month before Lincoln was inaugurated president of the United States, Jefferson Davis was sworn in president of the Confederate States of America. Both sides now waited to see whether or not the upper South would opt to join the newly formed slave republic.

The answer to that question had to await the North's response to southern secession. As he took the oath of office on March 4, 1861, the ball was in Lincoln's court. How would he respond to the threat of rebellion? He had been given ample time to consider his answer. Throughout the period between his election and his inauguration, while politicians in Washington frantically searched for ways to find a last-minute compromise, Lincoln steadfastly urged his supporters not to give in to the pressures of expediency. "Let there be no compromise on the question of extending slavery," he wrote Illinois Representative Lyman Trumbull. "If there be, all our labor is lost and ere long must be done again." Then, in a muted reference that suggests he clearly understood the possibility that inflexibility might lead to armed conflict, he added that "the tug has to come, and better now than any time thereafter."[40]

Early in the morning of April 12 the tug came. Having cleared his decision with Jefferson Davis, General P. T. Beauregard, commanding the Confederate troops in Charleston Harbor, gave the order to fire on the U.S. troops in Fort Sumter. The Civil War had begun.

. . . .

WE HAVE argued that secession was a foregone conclusion if Lincoln was elected. Does this mean that war was inevitable? Obviously, war is never inevitable. Indeed, from an economist's perspective, it is not even rational; a peaceful solution that would be "cheaper" than fighting a major war almost always exists. But as David Potter reminds us, wars do not come about because of a series of rational choices from an ordered list of alternatives. "[I]f we examine the record of modern wars," claims Potter, "it would seem that the way people get into a war is seldom by choosing it; usually it is by choosing a course that leads to it—which is a different thing altogether."[41] Potter's comment brings us back to the consideration of counterfactual worlds in 1861. The underlying conflict that led to secession was a divergence in the vision that Northerners and Southerners had of the future after the election of 1860. Southerners were committed to a way of life that depended on slavery. The solidarity of the Republican victory in the North made it clear that the South was now a minority in the Union. James McPherson sums up the South's problem: "When secessionists protested in 1861 that they were acting to preserve traditional rights and values, they were correct. They fought to preserve their constitutional liberties against the perceived Northern threat to overthrow them. . . . The ascension to power of the Republican Party, with its ideology of competitive, egalitarian, free-labor capitalism, was a signal to the South that the Northern majority had turned irrevocably towards this frightening, revolutionary future."[42] But it is still the case that Southerners did not "choose" war in 1861. What they "chose" was secession. They believed that in order to retain their way of life, compromise with a triumphant Republican Party was no longer a viable option. The events of the 1850s had clearly demonstrated that the North was in a position where it did not need to compromise. Consequently, Southerners found themselves dependent on Northern allies in the Democratic Party to sustain their position in the federal government. But as the defection of the Douglas Democrats on the Lecompton issue demon-strated, support for slavery from Northern Democrats was always a very uncertain thing. It could get only worse for the South. If, as seemed likely, the Republican coalition gained control of the national govern-ment, it could pursue an increasingly hard line on the question of slave expansion. The prevailing Southern vision in 1861 was the one Cal-houn had articulated a decade earlier: Dissolve the Union and estab-lish an independent nation. Southern secessionists, the most ardent of whom were from the Deep South, knew that there were risks attached to this course of action. One risk was the same as it had been in 1850: that the rest of the South might not follow their lead. A bigger risk was that the North would be willing to use force to prevent such action. Looking at the scenario as they saw it, Southerners believed that risk-ing war to get out of the Union seemed worth the gamble.

In the North the options were not so clear. The Northerners' view of the future was that of a market society free from the political and economic obstructions of slavery. To some, secession could accomplish that goal by taking the South out of the picture. A sizable fraction of the Northern electorate was prepared just to let the South go. The Republican majority was not comfortable with this option for two rea-sons. First was the question of whether the Union could survive the shock of having one-third of its population and area simply declare itself free from the obligation of the Constitution. To Lincoln, "Pre-serving the Union" was more than just an empty slogan that could serve as a rallying cry. From the outset of the crisis, he insisted that this was not just a struggle against slavery; it was a test to see if a democra-tic government based on the principles of the Constitution could, as he later put it, "long endure." The rebellion had to be put down, Lin-coln asserted in his First Inaugural Address, because "no State, upon its own mere motion, can lawfully get out of the Union; that *resolves* and *ordinances* to that effect are legally void, and that acts of violence, within any State or States, against the authority of the United States, are insurrectionary or revolutionary according to circumstance."[43]

Scholars have debated at length the legal points in Lincoln's assertion that secession was an insurrection that must be put down by force. Whatever its legal or moral merits, Lincoln was articulating a view that was widely held in the Northern states, and he insisted to the end of the war that preserving the Union was his primary objective in persevering in the conflict. The abolition of slavery was merely a means to that end.

Does that mean that slavery did not enter the decision of whether to fight to preserve the Union? Not exactly. One reason many Northerners were uncomfortable with the idea of an independent South was that it would mean the "problems" of slavery between the two regions would still exist. Over the past decade Northern politicians had struggled to control the slave power. With the election of Lincoln and their growing power in Congress, Republicans were finally in a position to do exactly that. Now the slaveholders were trying to break free from any constraints imposed on them if they were to remain in the Union. Not only would the strength of the United States be sapped by the divisive presence of a slave republic, but slaveholders would also be free to extend their influence over all of the Western Hemisphere. And all of this would be happening right next door! Having insisted that secession was illegal, Lincoln addressed the problem of having two nations competing with each other in the Americas:

> Physically speaking, we cannot separate. We cannot remove our respective sections from each other, nor build an impassable wall between them. A husband and wife may be divorced, and go out of the presence and beyond the reach of each other; but the different parts of our country cannot do this. They cannot but remain face to face; and intercourse, either amicable or hostile, must continue between them. Is it possible, then, to make that intercourse more advantageous or more satisfactory after separation than *before*? Can aliens make treaties easier than friends can make laws? Can treaties be more faithfully enforced between aliens than laws can among

friends? Suppose you go to war, you cannot fight always; and when after much loss on both sides, and no gain on either, you cease fighting, the identical old questions, as to terms of intercourse, are again upon you.[44]

Despite its conciliatory tone in urging peace, Lincoln's speech also laid the groundwork for an argument that it would be better to fight than to allow a slave republic to come into existence along the southern border of the United States. The problem of slavery would not be solved by letting the South go its own way. Indeed, it might make it even harder to deal with.

The two sides projected views of the future that were completely incompatible. Unless one side or the other backed down, the choices they were pursuing would eventually lead to armed conflict. War was the one option that could finally decide the issue. If the South won, it would have its independence; if it lost, the Union would be preserved. Either way, taking the gamble on war would decide the issue for both sides. A gamble on war was the *only* way the South could gain its objective if the North refused to allow it to secede peacefully. Staying in the Union was *not* a viable option for Southerners because that would be tantamount to letting the North "win" through control of the electoral process. The North was willing to take a gamble on war rather than accept a world with an independent slave power because that was the only way to ensure that the Northern vision of a modern society, would persevere. The implicit counterfactual most often invoked by historians discussing what ifs surrounding the crisis of 1861 is "What if the war did not take place?" But keeping the status quo was not an acceptable option to either side. And so, once again to turn to Lincoln, the South *made war* rather than let the Union survive; the North *accepted war* rather than let it perish.

History tells us that the South lost its gamble. Does that mean that its leaders made a tragic error in leading their people to war? With the advantage of twenty-twenty hindsight it is tempting to conclude that it was a tragic error. But there are at least two reasons for suggesting that such a claim is perhaps premature. First is the point that David Potter made concerning the options in 1850. The error of Southern leaders, he noted, was not that they tried to secede; the error was that they waited too long before they tried to break away from the Union. Yet even with the delay, the Confederate effort was almost enough to pull it off. The second problem with saying that the South made a bad decision is that it presumes that the Confederates would lose the war. But what if it had won? Would historians still say it was a tragic error for the South to have seceded? Those are the counterfactual questions we shall address in the remainder of this monograph.

We turn now to assessing what were the chances of that success and what that might have meant for the future of Americans in a world with two nations rather than one.

Chapter Two

· ·

THE SOUTHERN GAMBLE: COULD THE SOUTH HAVE WON?

What [General Lee] surrendered [at Appomattox] was the skeleton, the mere ghost of the Army of Northern Virginia, which had been gradually worn down by the combined agencies of numbers, steam power, railroads, mechanism, and all the resources of physical science. It had, in fact, been engaged in a struggle, not only against the mere brute power of man, but against all the elements of fire, air, earth and water; and even that all-pervading and subtle fluid, whose visible demonstrations the ancients designated "The thunderbolt of the gods," had been led submissive in the path of the opposing army, so as to concentrate with rapidity and make available all the other agencies.

It was . . . the use of these new adjuncts to the science of war, that . . . finally produced that exhaustion of our army and resources, and that accumulation of numbers on the other side, which wrought the final disaster.

—Jubal A. Early (1872)[1]

. . . .

JUBAL EARLY HAD SERVED as a commander with Robert E. Lee in the Army of Northern Virginia during the Civil War. Addressing an audience gathered at Washington & Lee University in January 1872 to honor the memory of the Confederacy's greatest hero, Early sadly recalled his last days with the Army of Northern Virginia. In his speech he sounded a theme he had been expounding for some time. There was, he claimed, no need for Confederate veterans to hang their heads in shame over the outcome of the war. The Southern armies had performed heroically, had persevered for four years against great odds, but had been eventually forced to give way to the force of too many men, too much equipment, and the superior technology of the North. Looking back at events only a few years past, Early concluded that the war had been a magnificent struggle on the part of the Army of Northern Virginia, but it had been a struggle that the South could not have won. In assessing the magnitude of the accomplishments of that army, Early extolled the brilliance of his former commander, Robert E. Lee, who within a few years of his death in 1870 had become the tragic hero in this story of courageous futility. "Our beloved chief," Early intoned, "stands like some lofty column which rears its head amongst the highest, in grandeur, simple, pure and sublime, needing no borrowed luster; and he is all our own."[2] Even in defeat, the Confederates could take some solace from the performance of their noble commander and his embattled army.

Over the next thirty years a dedicated group of former Confederate officers and partisans worked tirelessly to embellish Lee's image as military genius. By the end of the nineteenth century the man who for four years had stymied the forces of the United States at the head of a Rebel army was hailed as the greatest hero of the war—in both the North and the South! Lee's noble infallibility and the inevitability of Confederate defeat were the cornerstones of an "explanation" of Confederate defeat that became known as the Lost Cause.

By the middle of the twentieth century historians were beginning to question the unstinting praise of Lee and his lieutenants that characterized the Lost Cause rhetoric of such men as Jubal Early. Lee's critics pointed out that while he was unquestionably a brilliant field commander, he had made some mistakes during the course of the war, and his aggressive tactics had been very costly to the Confederacy in terms of the casualties that resulted.[3] Moreover, they pointed out, Lee's positive accomplishments could not excuse the inability of the Confederate armies in the West to stem the Union advances into the heartland of the South.[4] This reassessment of Lee's generalship and Confederate leadership in the West raised new issues of why the South lost the war. Could it be that the cause had been not as "lost" as the postwar Southern apologists had claimed?

Present-day advocates of the Lost Cause have stubbornly clung to the theme raised by Early. To be sure, Lee may not have been infallible, and the war obviously did not go well for Southern hopes in the Western theater. However, such caveats do not shake the conviction of the considerable number of historians who insist that the South was doomed to defeat. In a widely viewed PBS documentary on the Civil War filmed in 1990, producer Ken Burns asked historian Shelby Foote whether the South ever had a chance of winning the Civil War. "I think the North fought that war with one hand behind its back," replied Foote. "[I]f there had been more southern victories, and a lot more, the North simply would have brought that other arm out from behind its back. I don't think the South ever had a chance to win that war."[5] Foote's pessimistic assessment of the South's chances represents an updated version of the Lost Cause. Underlying this view is a counterfactual pessimism that pervades the writings of many contemporary military historians who examine the battles that the South fought and lost during the war. Asked if it would have made a difference if the South had won this or that battle, they invariably reply, "Probably not."

These counterfactual pessimists argue that when all is said and done, there was an endless supply of manpower and materials that the

North could feed into its war machine. Consequently, there would always have been battalions of fresh Union troops just around the next bend in the road to confront the beleaguered Confederates and offset the impact of any Confederate victories. The war in this view becomes a Greek tragedy being played out to the bitter—and inevitable—end. In fact historian William C. Davis insists that *all* the military turning points commonly identified as opportunities for the Southern victory are nothing more than "shopworn clichés" that "cloud the realities behind the façade."[6] "The 'turning point' and 'what if' school of Civil War history," writes Davis, "flourishes today, more enthused than informed, and even some of our better historians still take too much for granted without question. A cold, hard look at some of those water-shed moments in the Confederacy's brief life can produce an entirely different outcome."[7]

Davis makes an excellent point when he insists that the time has come to take a "cold hard look" at the counterfactual watersheds in Confederate history. That look, however, must not be colored by either a blinding pessimism that simply rules out the prospect of Confederate victory or the rosy optimism of Confederate partisans who all too often saw success in the war hinging on success in a single battle. We can begin by noting that no single battle was sufficiently important to be a turning point that could have changed the war's outcome by itself. For the Confederacy to prevail in this struggle, several pivotal battles of the war must end in a Southern rather than a Northern victory. These counterfactual victories may not represent the most probable outcome of the war, but as Clausewitz reminds us, war is a game of chance. What we propose to show is that the Confederacy had its chances but was unable to capitalize on them.

THE EVENTUAL outcome of the Civil War was decided by a series of campaigns that took place in three theaters of operations between February 1862 and December 1863. Map 2.1 provides a quick

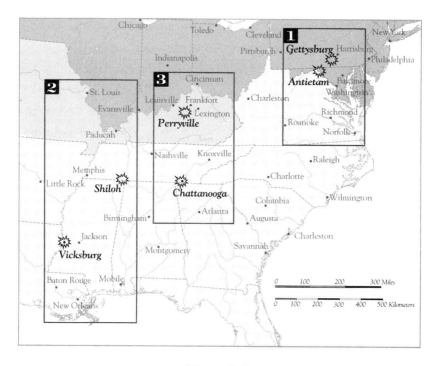

MAP 2.1

MAJOR THEATERS OF WAR

overview of these three theaters of operations and identifies the major
offensive campaigns that took place in each theater.

The Northern Virginia theater (1) is the best-known area of Civil
War battles. This is where Lee's Army of Northern Virginia fought off
repeated attempts by Union forces to capture the Confederate capital
and take the largest state in the Confederacy out of the war. It was also
the setting for two dramatic invasions of the North by Lee's troops in
1862–63. The Mississippi Valley theater (2) encompasses the efforts
by Union army and naval units to occupy the Mississippi River valley
and the waterways of western Tennessee. These objectives had been
successfully met by the end of 1863. Finally, there was the central Tennessee and Kentucky theater (3), which held the key for an invasion
of the heartland of the Confederacy through Georgia in 1864.

While many battles were fought in these theaters, the emphasis of the map is on the offensive operations of each side because in order for either side to win the war, it would be necessary to carry the war to the enemy. This point is obvious enough for Northern military strategy. Lincoln's overall objective was to put down the rebellion, and by the spring of 1862 it was clear that the only way that this could be accomplished was to invade and conquer the rebellious states. The overriding goal for the South was to break away from the Union. While the need to defend their borders was obvious, there was considerable debate within the Confederate high command on whether or not its armies should also take significant offensive actions in order to force the Union to the bargaining table. The map reveals two areas where the Confederates did invade Union territories, and those invasions produced three of the significant battles of the war: Perryville, Antietam, and Gettysburg. The map identifies three other battles that have been considered turning points: Shiloh, Vicksburg, and Chattanooga. All six of these battles were Union victories. These were the pivotal places where the South failed to capitalize on the opportunity to gain a decisive edge. This was where it lost the war.

To place these Confederate defeats in perspective with the rest of the fighting between the spring of 1862 and the end of 1863, we shall briefly review the fighting that took place in each of the three theaters of operations shown in the map.

NORTHERN VIRGINIA

If devotees of the Lost Cause were to construct a highlights film of the Civil War, all but a few of the scenes would come from a series of battles fought in a rather small area in northern Virginia that lies between Washington, D.C., and Richmond. It was here that Robert E. Lee and the Army of Northern Virginia managed to hold at bay the larger and better-equipped armies of the Union. Four times between the spring of 1862 and the summer of 1863 Lee's brilliance and the dogged determination of his soldiers turned back efforts of the Union army to invade Virginia and capture the Confederate capital of Richmond. Their performance over that period stands as one of the great military accomplishments in the annals of modern warfare. Map 2.2 provides the highlights of these invasions, which we shall only briefly describe here.

In April 1862 Union General George McClellan devised what many historians consider the most innovative plan to capture the Confederate capital and perhaps end the war. McClellan brought his army by sea to the Yorktown Peninsula, Virginia, where he planned to capture Richmond from the east. Despite having what Abraham Lincoln referred to as a severe case of "the slows," McClellan very nearly succeeded. Unfortunately for the Union cause, just as the Federal soldiers finally got close enough to see the spires of Richmond, Joseph E. Johnston, the Confederate commander facing McClellan, was wounded at the Battle of Fair Oaks. As a consequence of this wound, President Jefferson Davis decided to give command of the Confederate forces defending Richmond to Robert E. Lee. It was perhaps the most brilliant move the Confederate president made in the entire war.

Realizing that further retreat into the city would lead to a siege that could end only in defeat, Lee decided that the sole hope for the Confederates to protect their capital was to take the offensive. The new commander urged his troops to dig in and hold their position, and when the Union drive had been blunted at Fair Oaks, he ordered a series of relentless counterattacks against the Union army that have become known as the Seven Days' Battle. Engagements at Mechanicsville, Gaines' Mill, Frayser's Farm, and Malvern Hill all were very bloody. Individually, none of these battles were significant victories for the Confederates. But Lee's persistence in attacking his foe, combined with McClellan's timidity and his exaggeration of the forces arrayed against him, resulted in the Confederates steadily driving the Army of the Potomac east toward Harrison's Landing on the James River. The

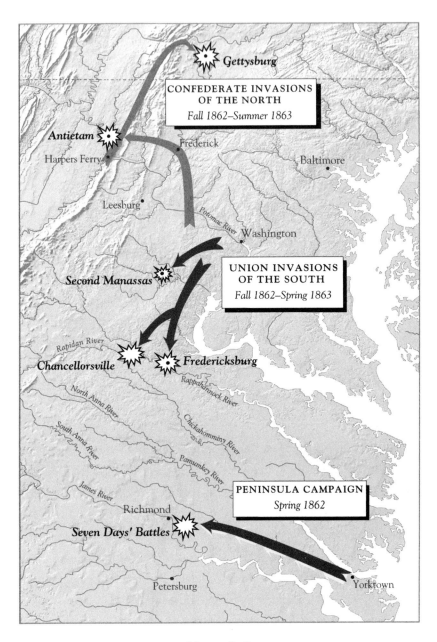

CONFEDERATE INVASIONS
OF THE NORTH
Fall 1862–Summer 1863

UNION INVASIONS
OF THE SOUTH
Fall 1862–Spring 1863

PENINSULA CAMPAIGN
Spring 1862

Gettysburg

Antietam

Harpers Ferry

Frederick

Baltimore

Leesburg

Potomac River

Washington

Second Manassas

Rapidan River

Chancellorsville

Fredericksburg

Rappahannock River

North Anna River

Chickahominy River

South Anna River

Pamunkey River

James River

Richmond

Seven Days' Battles

Petersburg

Yorktown

MAP 2.2
EASTERN THEATER OF OPERATIONS, 1861–63

casualties suffered by the Confederate army during these battles were staggering: Nearly one-fourth of Lee's army was out of commission after the final engagement at Malvern Hill. But the threat to Richmond had been lifted. More important, as events were to prove, the South had found a commander to defend its capital. After the heavy fighting of the Peninsula campaign, Lee reorganized the troops under his command and renamed them the Army of Northern Virginia.

George McClellan, who had arrived at Yorktown with such high hopes only a few months earlier, returned with his army to Washington a thoroughly beaten man. Lincoln had clearly lost faith in the "Little Napoleon," and as the Army of the Potomac returned north from the fight around Richmond, most of the troops were transferred to the Army of Virginia under the command of General John Pope. In mid-July Pope's army moved south into Virginia. Lee sent Stonewall Jackson to keep Pope occupied until he could be sure that McClellan's army was actually leaving the vicinity of Richmond. Jackson, employing his well-known penchant for marching, managed to lure Pope into chasing him over a wide area of northwestern Virginia. When Lee was certain that McClellan's troops were in fact being withdrawn from the Virginia Yorktown Peninsula to the vicinity of Washington, D.C., he sent James Longstreet's corps to join Jackson's troops in the hope that the two Confederate armies could jointly attack Pope before the rest of McClellan's troops could join the Army of Virginia. As fate would have it, Pope played into Lee's plans by attacking Jackson on August 29 near Manassas Junction, where the first battle of the war had been fought in July 1861. Jackson's position seemed precarious, but Pope was unaware that Longstreet was bringing reinforcements from the south. Just as it appeared that the Union forces might gain a significant victory over Jackson, Longstreet's thirty thousand troops arrived and delivered a crushing attack against the unsuspecting left wing of the Federal army. Though the Union forces eventually managed to stem the Confederate onslaught and prevent the Second Battle of Manassas from becoming a repeat of the earlier rout, the Army of Northern Virginia had turned back another Union advance into Virginia.[8]

The third Union invasion of Virginia came in December 1862, when Ambrose Burnside, newly appointed commander of the Army of the Potomac, planned to cross the Rappahannock River and establish a position just south of Fredericksburg that would pose a new threat to Richmond and force Lee to fall back to protect the Confederate capital. The plan was sound, but the execution was faulty. The result was a debacle that was arguably the greatest disaster of the war encountered by any Union army. Knowing that the Confederates had destroyed all the bridges over the Rappahannock, Burnside had arranged for pontoon bridges to be sent by train to Falmouth, Maryland, where they were to meet up with his troops. But the pontoons were late, and it took Federal engineers two weeks to build the bridges. By the time Burnside had his army and bridges in place, the Confederates had been able to assemble a sizable force of infantry and artillery on the hills just outside Fredericksburg. Against the advice of his generals, Burnside proceeded with his original plan and pushed the troops across the river into the town. From there, on December 13, the Union infantry charged up Marye's Heights into the teeth of a withering fire from Confederate soldiers entrenched behind a wall that ran along a sunken road. When darkness finally brought an end to the carnage, more than ten thousand Union soldiers lay fallen on the ground. Witnessing the slaughter from the top of the hill, Lee remarked to Longstreet, "It is well that war is so terrible; men would love it too much."[9] The Federal defeat at Fredericksburg was the low point of the war for the Union troops in the Army of the Potomac. Three times in a single year they had been repulsed by Lee's Army of Northern Virginia. The legend of the invincibility of "Bobbie Lee" was growing.

It grew even larger the following spring. In April 1863 Joseph Hooker, the latest commander of the Army of the Potomac, crossed the Rappahannock at several points north of Fredericksburg in another effort to force Lee to retreat from his trenches on the heights above the city. Having earlier sent Longstreet south to gather supplies in the Carolinas, Lee found himself with fewer than fifty thousand men facing a Union host of more than one hundred thousand. While his position at Fredericksburg was strong enough to withstand a frontal attack by the portion of Hooker's army stationed in the town, the presence of a large body of Union troops south of the Rappahannock to the northwest of the Confederate position spelled potential disaster. In one of the boldest series of maneuvers undertaken by a commander in the war, Lee left a token force at Fredericksburg and took off after Hooker with an army roughly half the size of his opponent. The two armies met in a heavily wooded area near a crossroads known as Chancellorsville.

Though he had begun his campaign aggressively, Hooker suddenly became timid when his troops actually encountered Lee's army. Seizing the opportunity, Lee divided his army once more, this time sending Stonewall Jackson with twenty-five thousand men on a circuitous march around the right wing of Hooker's army. This left only about fifteen thousand men opposite the center of Hooker's line, a situation that would have invited disaster if Hooker had realized what was happening and had taken advantage of Lee's boldness to crush the smaller Confederate force. But Hooker did nothing. At around five in the afternoon of May 2, Jackson's troops charged out of the woods and completely surprised the men of Hooker's right wing as they prepared to eat dinner. The Union troops fell back in disarray. Although the Army of the Potomac eventually regained some semblance of poise and formed a new line of defense that restored order to the battlefield as nightfall arrived, it was too late to counter the Confederate attack effectively. By that time Hooker had become completely unnerved. After a few skirmishes on May 3 he ordered his troops back across the Rappahannock. Another invasion by the Army of the Potomac had been thwarted, this time by an army barely half its size.

Chancellorsville was to be Lee's greatest triumph, but it was also the occasion of his greatest loss. Eager to press his attack on the Federal right wing as daylight was fading, Stonewall Jackson rode ahead of his troops to reconnoiter the territory. Returning to the Confederate lines, he was mistaken for the enemy and was wounded in the arm by his own troops. Though the wound did not seem serious at the time, Jackson died a week after the battle. For Lee, Jackson's death was devastating. Few commanders have formed a better team on the battlefield than Stonewall Jackson and Robert E. Lee. For many who look back on the war, it is no coincidence that the zenith of Lee's career as commander of the Army of Northern Virginia coincides with Stonewall Jackson's death. Jackson's command was filled by A. P. Hill, who was certainly a competent corps commander. But Hill, who had health problems that interfered with his duties on more than one occasion, lacked the verve of the fallen hero. Lee had come to depend heavily on the man he called his "right arm." One of the greatest what ifs debated in the years after the war was the possibility that Stonewall Jackson had survived the Battle of Chancellorsville.[10]

The victories of the Army of Northern Virginia in turning back the Union armies that invaded Virginia in 1862–63 were remarkable achievements. Each represented a possible turning point in the sense that if the Union had won any of those battles, the North might have been able to win the war much sooner. They were not, however, turning points that would provide keys to a Confederate victory. Obviously, the South had to keep the North from overrunning its capital and controlling the largest state in the Confederacy, and with these victories Lee accomplished that. But as Lee realized, simply checking one Federal advance into Virginia after another would not be enough to win the war. What was needed was to take the war to the North, to make "those people" feel the wrath of war. The most significant impact from Lee's successes in repelling the Union invasions was that they opened the way for him to launch counterattacks into Northern territory. He did so on two occasions, and it is the outcome of those two invasions by the Army of Northern Virginia that are crucial to our story of whether the South could have won this war.

In the fall of 1862 Lee was determined to invade the North. It was not an easy decision. His army had taken heavy casualties during the Peninsula campaign and in the victory of Jackson and Longstreet at Second Manassas. A strong case could be made for sitting pat and regrouping, but Lee believed that there were even stronger arguments favoring a move into Maryland and perhaps even as far as Pennsylvania. Despite the toll of the fall's fighting, he noted that the morale of the Army of Northern Virginia was high and that of its opponents extremely low after so many unsuccessful invasions of Virginia. Moreover, there was a question of supplies. Fall was harvesttime, and an invasion of the North would allow Lee's army to live off Northern crops rather than have to be supplied with food from the Shenandoah Valley. It was even possible that Maryland, a slave state, would produce recruits for the Southern cause.

Political considerations also favored an invasion of Northern ground at this time. In November 1862 there would be congressional elections throughout the North. If the Southern armies struck now and were victorious, they might inflict further damage on the already battered morale of the Northern population and damage the Lincoln administration's ability to carry on the war. In the West, Braxton Bragg was urging an invasion of Kentucky that would coincide with Lee's invasion of Maryland. Success of two Southern armies acting in concert might even gain the attention of Britain and France and induce them to intervene on the Confederacy's behalf. Both Lee and President Jefferson Davis agreed, moreover, that time was not on their side. They realized that the relative strength of the two sides was as close to parity in September 1862 as it was ever likely to be. The North had not yet mobilized the full potential of its superior resources. If all went well, the invasions might provide the impetus to force the Union to seek a negotiated peace.[11]

A final inducement for Lee to invade Maryland was that command of the Union Army of the Potomac had been returned to George McClellan. Though "Little Mac" had succeeded in restoring some of the morale in the defeated Union army, Lee was confident that if the

Army of Northern Virginia invaded the North, McClellan would exhibit the same degree of cautiousness in moving to oppose such an invasion that he had displayed outside Richmond the previous spring. Consequently, Lee boldly set his troops in motion, and by September 7 the Army of Northern Virginia had crossed the Potomac and reached Frederick, Maryland. At this point Lee paused long enough to consider his options. One problem facing the Confederates was the Union garrison at Harpers Ferry. While Lee could ignore it, that would leave an enemy force in his rear as the Rebel army moved into enemy territory. Moreover, the arsenal was lightly defended and might yield valuable supplies. Confident that McClellan would not respond quickly to his advance, Lee decided that Harpers Ferry should be taken, and he assigned Jackson's corps to accomplish that chore. As Stonewall's troops moved toward Harpers Ferry, the rest of Lee's army moved northwest out of Frederick, crossed the Blue Ridge Mountains, and fanned out along a front that eventually stretched from Jackson's division at Harpers Ferry to the lead elements of Longstreet's division just outside Hagerstown, Maryland.

By dividing his forces, Lee placed the Army of Northern Virginia in an extremely precarious position. With McClellan's army outnumbering his by almost two to one, Lee's dispersed troops could be attacked piecemeal. Lee was confident that there would be ample time to get the army back together before McClellan and the Army of the Potomac could reach his position. What the Confederate commander did not know was that a copy of the orders describing the deployment of his army had fallen into McClellan's hands on the afternoon of September 13.[12] The Union general therefore knew the disposition of Lee's army and the opportunity it afforded him if he moved quickly. "Here is a paper," he gleefully explained to a fellow officer, "with which, if I cannot whip Bobbie Lee, I will be willing to go home."[13] Still, despite the advantage of both numbers and surprise, McClellan did not move quickly enough to take full advantage of the situation, waiting almost a full day before issuing the orders to break camp and take off after Lee's army. By the time the Union army was getting in motion on the four-teenth, much of the advantage gained by the lost orders had been wasted. Reports from Stuart's Confederate cavalry had apprised Lee of unusual activity in the Army of the Potomac and included a report from a Confederate sympathizer indicating that McClellan had a copy of Lee's orders. Even so, McClellan was moving fast enough to place the Army of Northern Virginia in a tight spot.

At this point Lee had two options: He could gather his army and move south of the Potomac to avoid a conflict with an enemy that greatly outnumbered him, or he could concentrate his army north of the river and invite an attack by McClellan. Lee elected to stay and fight. He posted units along the mountain passes to the east with orders to obstruct the Federal advance while he collected the rest of his army along Antietam Creek, just outside the town of Sharpsburg, Maryland. It was there that the two armies faced each other on the evening of September 16. The Battle of Antietam (or Sharpsburg, as the Confederates prefer to call it) was the bloodiest day of the war. More than six thousand men died, and fifteen thousand were wounded from the day's fighting.[14] The result of all this carnage was indecisive. Lee still had thirty thousand men lined up for battle on the morning of the seventeenth, but McClellan, even though he had at least twenty thousand troops that had not seen action the previous day, declined to engage in any further fighting. The next day the Confederates moved back across the Potomac, and Lee's invasion of Maryland had come to a premature and very costly end.

Antietam was perhaps the single day during the entire war when everything hung in the balance. For the Confederates it was nothing less than a question of survival. Lee's army, still missing Hill's division, which was marching north from Harpers Ferry, had barely gotten in place when the Federal attacks began on the morning of the seven-teenth. Most observers agree that had McClellan simply hurled all his troops in a concerted attack against the enemy, Lee's army would prob-ably have been overwhelmed. As it was, McClellan chose to attack piecemeal, and the Confederates were able to move units around to counter each bloody thrust. Even so, only the timely arrival of Hill's division late in the afternoon provided enough troops for a final Confederate counterattack that blunted a Union offensive that threatened to collapse the Confederate right flank. After the war Lee claimed that Antietam was perhaps his finest moment; he had extricated his army from a desperate situation and avoided what could have been a disastrous defeat. For his part, McClellan claimed that he had won a glorious victory and driven the Rebel army out of Maryland. This he had surely done, but he had also fumbled away what was undoubtedly the best opportunity that any general would have to destroy Lee's army and perhaps to bring about an early end to the war.

Neither side was willing to concede defeat from the day's slaughter. But for Southerners, it was difficult to escape the harsh reality that the Army of Northern Virginia had failed in its mission to inflict damage on the North by invading Maryland. Surprised by the rapid deployment of an enemy that had discovered his plans, Lee had accomplished very little by his brief invasion. Far from gaining new recruits and supplies, he brought his men back to Virginia exhausted by the battle and with their numbers depleted by nearly one-quarter. The cost of the expedition had therefore been considerable, in terms of both men and prestige. For their part, Northerners—and particularly President Lincoln—were disappointed when it became clear that McClellan had wasted an opportunity to destroy Lee's army. Lincoln's impatience with McClellan's caution is apparent from a comment he made to a friend when visiting the army after the battle. "Do you know what this is?" Lincoln asked as the two men viewed the army from a nearby hill. "It is the army of the Potomac," answered his companion. "So it is called," replied Lincoln, "but that is a mistake; it is only McClellan's bodyguard." [15]

Nevertheless, the president was sufficiently encouraged by the battle's outcome to issue a proclamation announcing his intention to free all the slaves in the Confederacy, an action that was to have far-reaching consequences. Across the Atlantic, British supporters of the Confederate cause were dismayed by the outcome. The *Times* of London noted that "the Confederates have suffered their first important check exactly at the period when they might have been thought most assured of victory."[16] For the Confederacy, the problem was that a draw, which is the best face it could put on the outcome at Antietam, was not going to get the South added support abroad. It needed another victory. In the absence of a clear decision favoring the Confederates, the British cabinet elected to take no action for the time being. While he struggled to maintain an optimistic front to the public, Jefferson Davis privately conceded that the opportunity presented at Antietam might not appear again. "Our maximum strength has been mobilized," he told his secretary of war after the battle, "while the enemy was just beginning to put forth his might."[17]

Though the Confederate cause received a very bloody nose at Antietam, the Rebels were hardly ready to throw in the towel. In the spring of 1863 Lee's army rebounded from Antietam by delivering a crushing defeat to Federal hopes at the battle of Chancellorsville. While the Union army once again retreated toward Washington, Lee contemplated a second invasion of the North. The logic was the same as it had been the previous fall: to relieve the pressure on both the Confederate economy and the military situation by carrying the war to the enemy. Lee actually judged the time to be much more propitious than it had been in September 1862. It was still early in the summer, so his army was not yet worn down by a summer of campaigning. Morale in the Army of Northern Virginia had never been higher. "We were all hopeful," noted General Longstreet, "and the army was in good condition."[18] In addition to the advantages an invasion offered his army, Lee knew that time was running out for the Confederate war effort given the situation in the West. It was a gamble, and the stakes were high, but that was not something that had ever daunted Robert E. Lee. After a series of exchanges with Jefferson Davis and his staff in Richmond, Lee won reluctant approval from his superiors again to invade the North, and orders were drafted to set the army in motion. On June 3 Richard Ewell's corps began marching northwest from the Chancellorsville battlefield on a route that would eventually take him across the Blue Ridge Mountains and up the Shenandoah Valley. Meeting only light resistance, Ewell crossed the Potomac River into Maryland at Williamsport on the evening of the fifteenth and continued his northward march through Maryland. Over the next ten days the remainder of Lee's army followed Ewell's corps north toward Pennsylvania. By June 25, Lee's entire army had crossed the Potomac, with the lead units of Ewell's corps as far north as Chambersburg, Pennsylvania.[19] Confederate soldiers foraged for food and animals while the terrified inhabitants of southern Pennsylvania scurried around to find some way of checking the invading army.

The Army of the Potomac was still recovering from the debacle at Chancellorsville. "Fightin' Joe" Hooker remained in command, but he was slow to discern the Confederate army's intentions. When he finally reacted by getting his army in motion on June 13, his primary concern was to keep the Union army between Lee and the Federal capital. It was not until both Hill and Longstreet had their troops across the Potomac on June 24 and 25 that Hooker realized that Lee's immediate objective was Pennsylvania, not Washington, D.C. By this time the Rebels had had several days' head start on their march north, and the Army of the Potomac had to make a series of forced marches just to reach Frederick, Maryland, which was still south of the lead units of Lee's army, by June 28. For the next week both armies moved north along parallel paths on either side of the Blue Ridge Mountains, neither of them fully aware of the exact location or strength of the other. As they marched, the Confederates were roaming over a wide area of southeastern Pennsylvania. Adding to Hooker's uncertainty about their objective, Confederate cavalry under Jeb Stuart executed a daring raid that swept east of the Union army and at one point seemed to threaten Washington.[20]

Meanwhile, the lead units of Lee's army continued to press quickly north toward Harrisburg. By June 27 two divisions of Ewell's corps had reached Carlisle, Pennsylvania, about twenty miles southwest of the state capital. A group of Confederate cavalry under Alfred Jenkins actually reached a bridge that crossed over the Susquehanna River to Harrisburg, but their mission was only to scout, and they returned to the main army without entering the city. The third of Ewell's three divisions, commanded by Jubal Early, occupied the city of York and sent sorties as far as the bridges across the Susquehanna at Wrightsville, some thirty miles downstream from Harrisburg. The advance of Ewell's corps was to be the farthest penetration of the Army of Northern Virginia into Union territory.

On June 28 Lincoln replaced Joe Hooker with General George Meade as commander of the Army of the Potomac. Already concerned that his army might be too widely scattered, Lee used the change in the Union command to reappraise his situation. "General Meade," he remarked to an aide, "will commit no blunder on my front, and if I make one he will make haste to take advantage of it."[21] Not wanting to offer Meade the opportunity to engage the Confederate forces piecemeal, Lee decided it was time to pull together his forces and force the Union to give battle, one that he hoped would produce the decisive victory the Confederacy desperately needed. Accordingly, orders from Lee went out to Ewell on the twenty-ninth, instructing him to move his troops south to join the rest of the army, which was moving east through the Cashtown Gap toward the town of Gettysburg. For his part, George Meade was resolved to catch up with Lee as quickly as possible. Ignoring the temptation to deal with Stuart's cavalry operating to his rear, Meade wrote his wife that his army was "marching as fast as we can to relieve Harrisburg. . . . They have a cavalry force in our rear destroying railroads, etc., with a view of getting me to turn back, but I shall not do it. I am going straight at them and will settle this thing one way or another."[22] As it turned out, all roads led to Gettysburg.

Neither side planned the Battle of Gettysburg, though both were expecting that there would be a major engagement in that area fairly soon. While Confederate forces were converging on Gettysburg from the north, Union cavalry under John Buford got there first and entered the town from the south on June 30. Buford's orders were to establish a position so that the Union infantry commanded by General John Reynolds could take up defensive positions beside his troops before the Confederates arrived. Unfortunately for Buford, it was Confederate soldiers commanded by General Henry Heth who first made contact with the line of dismounted Union troopers just west of the town. Buford's outnumbered force held its ground long enough for the lead units of Reynolds's infantry to arrive. By midmorning troops from both sides were arriving on the scene from every direction, and the fighting expanded as each new unit arrived. When Lee and his staff arrived on the scene around two in the afternoon, the question was whether to disengage Heth's division, whose initial assignment to probe the enemy positions had been completed, or to press the attack forward. While Lee pondered his options, the first units of Ewell's corps arrived on the battlefield from Carlisle. Though he had explicit orders from Lee not to precipitate a "general engagement," Ewell took quick stock of the situation and decided to attack the right flank of the Union troops facing Heth. "It was too late to avoid an engagement without abandoning the position already taken up," Ewell later wrote, "and I determined to push the attack vigorously."[23] Ewell's attack on the Union right flank was successful in helping the Confederates push the Union troops back through Gettysburg, but he did not press on to capture the high ground south of the town, where the disorganized Union troops were eventually able to take up defensive positions.

Ewell's hesitation cost the Confederates a golden opportunity to gain a strong defensive position from which to meet the Army of the Potomac as it arrived from the South. Instead Union troops reaching the battlefield that evening were able to occupy not only Cemetery Hill but nearby Culp's Hill as well. By the morning of July 2 Yankee troops had dug themselves into a strong defensive position that extended from Culp's Hill in a giant fishhook that extended along Cemetery Ridge for a little more than a mile toward the two hills called the Round Tops that eventually formed the southern end of the Union line. Ewell's failure to take Cemetery Hill, which clearly displeased Lee at the time, has become a major point of debate in later years. Had the Confederates taken the position, it would have been the Confederate army, not the Union army, that occupied the strong defensive position as the remaining units of the two armies arrived during the night. "If Ewell had attacked Cemetery Hill on July 1," asks historian James McPherson, "could he have taken it, and if he had, would the outcome of the battle and the war have been the same?"[24] Most observers believe that Ewell probably could have taken the weakly held position and that such a move would have given the Confederates a considerable advantage in the subsequent fighting.

Still, the afternoon's fighting on July 1 had gone well for the Confederates. They had managed to get more men into action than had their foe, and their troops had badly mauled several of the enemy's army corps and pushed them back through the town of Gettysburg, which was now occupied by the Confederates. As evening fell, though he was disappointed by Ewell's lack of initiative in pressing the attack on the Federal right wing, Lee was sufficiently encouraged that he decided to maintain the offensive and attack the Union position the following day. As he reported after the battle, "Encouraged by the successful issue of the engagement of the first day, and in view of the valuable results that would ensue from the defeat of the army of General Meade, it was thought advisable to renew the attack."[25] These comments highlight one of the most important elements of the Confederate defeat at Gettysburg: Lee's unwavering belief in the necessity of achieving a decisive victory over his opponent and his consequent determination to press the attack even in the face of marked reluctance on the part of his subordinates. Both Hill and Ewell had argued against Lee's suggestion that their troops assault the Union position on Cemetery Hill late in the afternoon of the first day. Whether or not their reluctance was justified by the situation at hand is a judgment that is easier to make after the fact than it was at the time. After the war debates raged on whom to blame for a decision that most historians concede was a serious mistake. Alan Nolan, one of the few historians to exonerate Ewell for not making the attack, claims that whatever blame there is for error lies with Lee, who did not issue a "preemptory order" to attack, thus leaving the final decision to Ewell.[26]

Having lost the opportunity to gain the high ground south of the town on the evening of the first, Lee was confronted with the problem of how to attack the strong defensive positions the Federal army had taken in front of Ewell. His solution was to direct Ewell to make a "demonstration" against the Union right flank while the troops commanded by Longstreet, most of whom had not seen action on the first day, would attack the left wing of the Union army. This time it was Longstreet who strongly opposed the plan. He insisted that it would be far more prudent for the Army of Northern Virginia to break off the current engagement and move south around the left wing of the Union army, thus placing itself between the Army of the Potomac and Washington. Given political pressures in Washington, this would surely force Meade to initiate an attack on Confederate defensive positions, an option that Longstreet believed would offer a far better chance of success than the present positions of the Army of Northern Virginia. Lee demurred and directed Longstreet to move his men into position to attack the far left of the Union position as soon as possible on the afternoon of the second. Longstreet did as he was ordered but clearly lacked enthusiasm for the plan. It took his troops most of the following day just to get into position for an attack, so that the initial assault against the Union lines was not launched until around four o'clock in the afternoon. Even so, Longstreet's confident veterans very nearly carried the day. In some of the fiercest fighting of the war, the Union defenders were pressed almost to the breaking point, but their line held—partly because Meade was able to rush a steady stream of reinforcements to the point of Longstreet's attacks. Meanwhile Ewell's corps waited for Longstreet's troops to make their attack before taking any action against the Union troops on Culp's Hill on the north end of the Union line. This time the Confederates actually punched a hole in the Federal defenses, but there were no reserves to exploit the advantage, and they were forced to pull back. By the end of the second day all that Lee had to show for the efforts of his men were ten thousand casualties that the army could ill afford. The positions of the two armies remained essentially unchanged.

The fact that the Confederates had on several occasions during the second day come close—oh, so close!—to breaking through the Union lines suggests that Lee's decision to press the offensive may not have been the wrong decision. Numerous writers have pointed out that while the right and center of the Union army were strong defensive positions, the left wing was, as Lee suspected, initially exposed and susceptible to attack. Moreover, as we have already noted, Lee believed that the opportunity offered by the successes of the previous day, incomplete though they were, could not be passed up. One account of the battle goes so far as to claim that attacking on the second day was the "only *realistic* decision" that Lee could have made.[27] Another points out that if the Confederate attack had been successful—and it almost was—Lee's critics would have been quickly silenced.[28] The failure of Longstreet's effort marks the second major what if of the Battle of Gettysburg.

The problem facing Lee on the night of July 2 was what to do next. One could still argue that at this point the battle had gone favorably for the Confederates. Though the enemy lines had held, Lee knew that their troops had taken a severe punishment during the day's fighting. Reviewing his options, he made what appears to be one of the great blunders of the war. Rather than break off the engagement with his army still relatively intact after giving the Army of the Potomac another very bloody nose, Lee elected to use his last fresh group of troops, Pickett's division of Longstreet's corps, to launch a massive assault against the center of the Union line on the afternoon of the third day of battle. The result was a catastrophic disaster for the Confederates. Meade anticipated Lee's move, and the Confederates found themselves marching into the teeth of Federal artillery and troops stationed behind fences and stone walls. Pickett's men were cut down before they ever reached the Federal lines. The Union soldiers, recalling an equally futile charge of their own seven months earlier, began to shout, "Fredericksburg! Fredericksburg!" as they poured volley after volley of shot into the advancing troops in gray. At the end of the day Pickett's division had suffered more than seven thousand casualties, and the Battle of Gettysburg was finally over.

Gettysburg was a disastrous defeat for the Southern cause. For more than two years the Army of Northern Virginia had been more than able to hold its own against a numerically superior opponent. Much of the credit for its success goes to the audacity and tactical brilliance of its commander, Robert E. Lee. At Gettysburg Lee's presence once again towered over the battlefield. It was his decision to press the attacks on all three days, and responsibility for the final disaster rests squarely on Lee's shoulders.[29] "Gettysburg," notes historian Shelby Foote, "was the price the South paid for having R. E. Lee."[30]

Notwithstanding the bloody reverse at Gettysburg, Lee and his Army of Northern Virginia had managed to create a stalemate in the Eastern theater of the war by the end of 1863. Moreover, they had created an identity for the Army of Northern Virginia that made it a symbol of Confederate resistance to the Union, a symbol that continued to frustrate Northern military hopes for another year and a half. Had the Confederate troops in the Western theater been able to do the same, Lee's efforts might have been enough to break the Confederacy free from the Union's grasp. Unfortunately for the hopes of Southerners, that was not to be the case.

THE MISSISSIPPI VALLEY

From the outset of the war, Lincoln and his advisers sought to gain control of the Mississippi River and to push the Confederates out of Tennessee. Map 2.3 depicts the major offensive campaigns in the Mississippi theater of the war in 1862 and 1863. The Union push into Confederate territory began when Ulysses S. Grant, using the combined resources of the Union navy and his own troops, moved swiftly along the Tennessee and Cumberland rivers to capture Forts Donelson and Henry in early February 1862. Following these successes, Grant pushed farther south along the two rivers, and by the end of March his army was threatening Corinth, Mississippi, a major transportation hub for Confederate forces in the Mississippi Valley. At the same time that Grant's forces were gaining these victories, Union forces under General Pope and Admiral Andrew Foote were advancing down the Mississippi River with the intent of capturing Memphis. Though the territory occupied by Union troops was relatively small, these advances along the western rivers posed a major threat to the supply lines of Confederate forces operating throughout the Western theater of the war. The problem could get much worse if the troops of Union General Don Carlos Buell, which were stationed in Louisville, Kentucky, were to join Grant's army at Pittsburg Landing, Tennessee.

The Confederate commander in charge of the West, Albert Sidney Johnston, responded to this threat by concentrating as many Confederate troops as possible at Corinth, Mississippi, by the end of February. Johnston and his second-in-command, P. T. Beauregard, hoped to surprise Grant's force before Buell's army could arrive on the scene. Early on the morning of April 6, 1862, the lead units of Johnston's army charged into the right wing of the Union army that had camped on the southern side of the Tennessee River around Shiloh Church. The Confederate attack took the Union troops by surprise and drove them back in disarray. For a while it seemed likely that the Confederate attacks would succeed in pinning a major portion of Grant's army against the

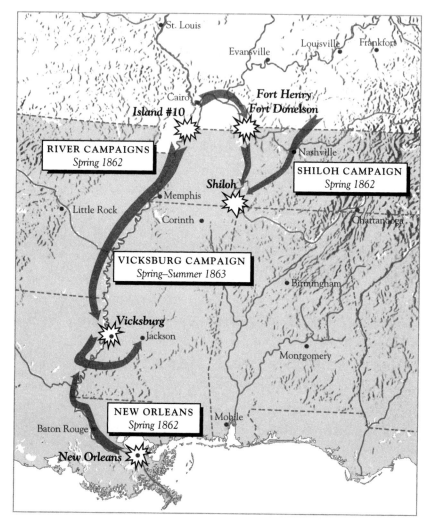

MAP 2.3

MISSISSIPPI THEATER OF OPERATIONS, 1861–63

bank of the Tennessee River with few avenues of escape. But this was
not to be. The inexperience of Confederate troops in their first battle,
together with stubborn resistance from troops in the center of the
Union position, slowed the Confederate advance long enough for the
Union troops to regroup and form a defensive line near the river. Nev-

ertheless, nightfall found Grant's army in a precarious position, and the Confederates waited to renew their attack successfully in the morning.

Unfortunately for the Southern cause, the first units of Buell's army had arrived on the scene early that evening, and with these reinforcements Grant had gained a significant numerical superiority. He wasted no time taking advantage of his reinforcements; early on the morning of the seventh the Union troops launched a massive counterattack against the Confederate lines. To make matters worse for the Confederates, Johnston had suffered a fatal wound the day before. Confronted with the reinforced Union army, Beauregard ordered a retreat back to Corinth. Eventually the Confederates were forced to abandon Corinth and retreat another fifty miles south to Tupelo, Mississippi. The first major battle of the war had ended in a Union victory. But the cost had been high. Though people on both sides eventually came to expect such slaughters after major battles of the war, the casualty lists for Shiloh staggered them. Just over thirteen thousand Union troops and about eleven thousand Confederates were killed, wounded, or missing after the battle. Nor was there much cause to celebrate on either side after the fight. Grant's army had been surprised, and the fight could easily have been a Union disaster rather than a somewhat tarnished victory. Thanks to the Confederate withdrawal, Grant's river campaign had been successful—but by the narrowest of margins. It took another year for the Union to capitalize on this success.

As we look back from our present vantage point, it is clear that Shiloh was a lost opportunity on the part of the Southern commanders. By failing to check Grant's advance down the Tennessee River, Johnston and Beauregard lost a golden opportunity to change the momentum in the Western theater of the war. The war in the West had not gone well for the Confederacy before Shiloh, and it soon got even worse. In the same month Union forces captured Island No. 10 in the Mississippi River, and by the end of June the Confederates had been forced to evacuate Memphis. An even more staggering blow was dealt to the Rebel forces when a Union fleet under David Farragut captured New Orleans on April 25, 1862. Within the space of two months the Union offensives of early 1862 had all but sealed the fate of the Mississippi Valley for the Confederacy. Rebel forces continued to harass Union forces in the area throughout the war. In September 1862 they tried to recapture Corinth at the battles of Corinth and Iuka. However, Union forces repulsed the attacks and were poised to renew their advance down the Mississippi River.

By the spring of 1863 Grant was again poised to push his troops south toward Vicksburg in an effort to secure the Mississippi River for Union forces. After several efforts to approach the city from the eastern side of the Mississippi River, Admiral David Porter came up with a daring plan. If Grant marched along the west bank of the river to the town of Bruinsburg, south of Vicksburg, Porter would have supply ships run past the Vicksburg batteries and rendezvous with Grant at Bruinsburg. Porter's plan worked, and after the Union navy had ferried Grant's troops across the river, he proceeded to march east to the state capital at Jackson. There he repulsed a force commanded by General Joseph Johnston that hoped to relieve Vicksburg. Having deflected Johnston's relief army, Grant turned west toward Vicksburg and surrounded the city and its garrison of thirty thousand. The city eventually surrendered on July 4, 1863. "Glory hallelujah," exulted William Sherman, who thought this was "the best Fourth of July since 1776."[31] The Vicksburg campaign was an excellent example of Grant's talent as a general who favored movement in warfare.[32] His successes were not lost on one interested observer; Abraham Lincoln made plans to appoint Grant commander of all the Union armies in the West.

Though the situation stabilized somewhat after Shiloh as the Union armies became bogged down deep in enemy territory, Southern commanders were never able to regain the initiative in the Mississippi Valley. Following Shiloh, Union troops occupied Tennessee as far east as Nashville, and by the end of 1862 they had pressed into the northern corner of Alabama and Georgia west of Chattanooga. Nevertheless, the amount of territory actually occupied by the Union forces as a result of their offensives along the Western rivers was fairly limited. To be effective in an area where Confederate cavalry still roamed freely, Union commanders found that they needed to stay near water transportation to maintain supply routes in hostile territory. Grant sent Sherman back to Jackson after Vicksburg had been secured; however, the main purpose of that mission was to destroy the rail connections, not to occupy territory.[33] The eventual fall of Vicksburg was symbolically devastating to the Confederate cause, but as Herman Hattaway and Archer Jones point out in their analysis of the Western campaigns, the Confederate high command had largely written off Vicksburg well before the actual surrender. Apart from the loss of men involved in the surrender, it was not of enormous military significance.[34] At the end of 1863, much of Mississippi and Louisiana still remained under Confederate control. The failure to defeat Grant at Shiloh was a lost opportunity for the South that we shall consider in greater detail in chapter 3, but it hardly meant the end of Confederate resistance in the West. So long as the South could hang on to eastern Tennessee, the heartland of the Confederacy remained beyond the reach of Union troops.

KENTUCKY AND CENTRAL TENNESSEE

The struggle for Vicksburg overshadowed the efforts of the Union to control Tennessee. Map 2.4 shows the activities in this theater of action. By the middle of 1862 the success of the Union navy in controlling the Tennessee and Cumberland rivers had allowed Don Carlos Buell to move the Union Army of Ohio into Alabama with the intent of attacking Chattanooga. Rather than wait for Buell to attack, Braxton Bragg, the newly appointed commander of the Confederate Army of Tennessee, elected to go on the offensive. Bragg planned to invade Kentucky. This would not only draw Buell out of Tennessee but also offered the possibility of gaining supplies and recruits from a border state with strong proslave sympathies.

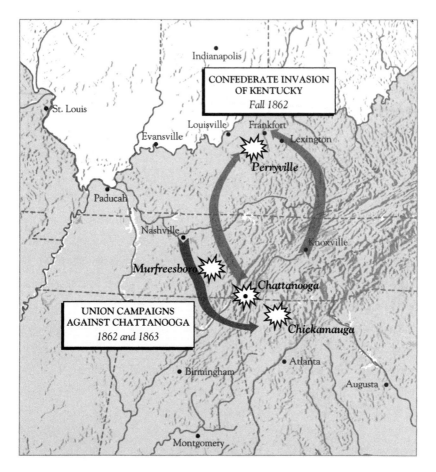

MAP 2.4

TENNESSEE THEATER OF OPERATIONS, 1861–63

Gathering troops from armies throughout the western Confederacy, Bragg managed to amass a force of more than thirty thousand at
Chattanooga without the Federal high command's noticing what was
going on. In mid-August these troops, together with ten thousand
under Edmund Kirby Smith at Knoxville, moved north through eastern Tennessee in two columns and crossed into Kentucky. As Bragg
had hoped, the Confederate invasion of Kentucky forced Buell to
move northward, first to Nashville and then on to Bowling Green,

Kentucky, where he paused, expecting Bragg to attack him. But Bragg stayed east of the Union army; he captured a Union force at Mumsfordville and was now in a position to threaten Buell's line of supply to the North. Buell therefore retreated to Louisville, which he prepared to defend from attack.

Once again the Confederates had other ideas. While Bragg was keeping Buell's force off-balance, Smith moved north from Knoxville and reached the Kentucky capital, Frankfort. Bragg took leave from his army long enough to join Smith there, and on October 2 the two generals proclaimed Richard Hawes, a strong secessionist before the war, the Confederate governor of Kentucky.[35] At this point the invasion seemed to be going well, and Southern hopes for success were high. But things soon began to unravel for the Confederates. It gradually became apparent that Bragg had no plan for what to do once he invaded Kentucky. He had hoped to attract recruits, but the response of Kentuckians to his plea for volunteers was unenthusiastic, to say the least. With his army scattered over a wide area of northern Kentucky, the "invasion" had turned into little more than a disorganized raid into unfriendly territory.

Compounding his problems was Bragg's deteriorating relations with his fellow commanders, including Smith, which made coordination among various units of the Confederate army difficult. When Buell finally moved southeast from Louisville, the two armies engaged each other at Perryville on October 8. The resulting battle was bloody but inconclusive. Most observers credit Bragg with achieving a tactical victory in the sense that his army retained the initiative against the overly cautious Buell. But the Rebels' logistical situation continued to deteriorate. Without a clear plan of action, the invading force found itself far from its bases of supply in Tennessee, while Buell's troops retained interior lines to Louisville and the Ohio River. With the prospect of more Union reinforcements on the way, the bickering Confederate generals decided to march back to Tennessee. They reached Chattanooga and Knoxville by the end of October.

Relieved to see the Confederates leave Kentucky, Buell set up shop once more in Nashville, awaiting his next move. But Lincoln had lost his patience with his overly cautious commander. In November 1862 the president replaced Buell with William Rosecrans. The new Union commander promptly renewed the Federal effort to capture Chattanooga, but his army's advance was checked by the Confederates at Stones River (or Murfreesboro), southeast of Nashville, on December 30. In a battle in which both sides lost roughly a third of the men engaged, the Confederates managed to hold their position against superior numbers, so that Bragg could again claim a tactical success. But when Rosecrans renewed the fight on January 2, Bragg decided to withdraw rather than incur additional casualties. Relative to the number of soldiers involved, the losses in this battle were the heaviest of any in the war.[36] Though he had succeeded in occupying Murfreesboro, it would be six months before Rosecrans believed that his army was sufficiently recovered to resume the offensive against the Confederate Army of Tennessee.

When all was said and done, neither side had much to show for what had been an autumn of heavy fighting in Tennessee and Kentucky. Three months after Bragg had launched his invasion into Kentucky, the Confederates were back where they had started and the Union army was still stationed in Nashville, regrouping for its next attempt to capture Chattanooga. Kentucky, which up to that point had been treated by both sides as neutral territory, was now occupied by Union forces. On the other hand, the Confederates retained control of eastern Tennessee and the transportation hubs at Chattanooga and Knoxville. Although Bragg's excursion into Kentucky had not accomplished all that the Confederate high command had hoped for, it had forced the Union to pull back its forces in Tennessee and had reestablished a small degree of stability in the Confederate defensive position in the West. Grant's army was still bogged down trying to capture Vicksburg, and the Union successes in the West up to then had been confined to areas served by waterways that the Union navy could use to provide logistical support to the troops in the field. Areas away from the rivers remained in Confederate hands. If they could hold on to eastern Tennessee, the interior of the Confederacy would stay secure. The key was Chattanooga.

The situation in the West remained stabilized for the Confederates through the early fall of 1863. This was, to be sure, more a result of the dispersal of commands among the Union armies in the West than any actions on the part of the Confederates. At the time of Vicksburg's fall, there were five independent Union commands in the West: Rosecrans' Army of the Cumberland in middle Tennessee; Ambrose Burnside's Army of the Ohio in Kentucky; Grant's Army of the Tennessee at Vicksburg; Nathaniel Banks's force in the lower Mississippi Valley; and John Schofield's army in Missouri. Of the five, it was Rosecrans's Army of the Cumberland that posed the most immediate threat to the security of the western defenses of the Confederacy. In early June Rosecrans finally left Murfreesboro (where he had been nursing his army back to health after the casualties suffered six months earlier) and moved south in an effort to dislodge Bragg's army from Chattanooga. This flanking maneuver was eventually successful; by early September Union troops had moved far enough into northern Georgia that Bragg was forced to abandon Chattanooga on September 9. Once again the South faced a dire situation in the West.

The Confederate high command reacted to this latest crisis by concentrating troops at the point of Union attack. This time, in addition to gathering as many troops as he could pry free from various parts of the Western departments, Bragg received help in the form of two veteran divisions from the Army of Northern Virginia, commanded by General James Longstreet. While the Federals mistakenly took Bragg's retreat from Chattanooga as a sign that he was retreating back into Georgia, Bragg in fact was planning to attack the left wing of Rosecrans's army at Chickamauga. Reinforced and energized by the infusion of new troops, the Confederates were able to gain a stunning victory and force the Union troops into a disorganized retreat back to Chattanooga. Longstreet and several other commanders urged Bragg to press the attack and drive the Federals out of Chattanooga, but the commander in chief demurred. By the time he finally decided to move, the Federal army had regrouped, and an attack on the city was no longer deemed feasible.

Although Bragg had missed a chance to exploit his victory by pushing the retreating Union army back into central Tennessee, he was able to cut off virtually all the supply routes into Chattanooga. With only a single sixty-mile road open to the outside, the Army of the Ohio was trapped in the city. Indeed, it appeared possible that the Confederates might even be in a position to force Rosecrans to surrender. But again bickering among the generals in the Confederate Army of Tennessee came to the Union's rescue. In the months following the invasion of Kentucky, Bragg had totally alienated the commanders in his army. The situation got so bad that Jefferson Davis had to intervene by calling Bragg to Richmond to confer about the complaints of his subordinates. When this failed to quell the complaints, Davis made a personal visit to Murfreesboro to try to restore the peace. However, he obstinately refused to take the obvious step of replacing Bragg. Kirby Smith insisted on a transfer to the Western Department to escape having to work with Bragg. Longstreet soon joined the chorus of voices urging that Bragg be replaced after Chickamauga—preferably by no less a personage than Robert E. Lee. G. Moxley Sorrel, Longstreet's chief of staff, was appalled by the situation. "Bragg," he noted, "was the subject of hatred and contempt, and it was almost openly so expressed. His great officers gave him no confidence as a general-in-chief."[37] When Davis still refused to replace Bragg, Longstreet succeeded in getting approval for the twelve thousand troops in his corps, together with five thousand cavalry under Joseph Wheeler, to be detached from Bragg's army and sent on a diversionary campaign to recapture

Knoxville from Federal control. This decision proved to be disastrous. Longstreet's campaign against the Union army at Knoxville was not successful, and the removal of seventeen thousand men from Bragg's army further weakened the army besieging Chattanooga. At the very time the Confederates needed to concentrate their troops in an effort to crush the army trapped in Chattanooga, Longstreet's departure scattered Confederate forces and ultimately gave the initiative back to the Union commanders.

While Jefferson Davis anguished but did nothing to clear up the command mess in his Western theater, Lincoln took decisive steps to stabilize the situation on the Union side. The most significant of these was a series of orders issued in mid-October that created a Military Department of the Mississippi and placed General U. S. Grant in command of the three armies commanded by Rosecrans and Burnside, together with his own Army of the Tennessee. Grant was further given discretion to replace Rosecrans with George Thomas, credited with having saved the Union forces at Chickamauga from complete disaster, as commander of the Army of the Cumberland at Chattanooga. Lincoln ordered Hooker's corps from the Army of the Potomac to reinforce the troops at Chattanooga, and he approved the transfer of Sherman's corps from the Union Army of the Tennessee. This meant an addition of roughly thirty-six thousand men to the garrison at Chattanooga. Armed with his new authority and with substantial reinforcements on the way, Grant set out for Chattanooga on October 20. Lincoln's decision to place Grant in charge not only of the troops at Chattanooga but of the entire area between the Mississippi and the Appalachian Mountains reveals the difference between the Union and Confederate presidents. While Davis waffled in the face of Bragg's obvious shortcomings and wound up leaving an incompetent general in command and scattering the Confederate forces in eastern Tennessee, Lincoln and his secretary of war, Edwin Stanton, acted quickly to place their most successful general in command of all forces in the area and to reinforce the army at the crisis point of the war.

The Union leaders were soon rewarded for their efforts. Grant arrived in Chattanooga, reorganized the army, and got to work opening supply lines to the outside. By the end of November 1863 he had stabilized the situation to a point where he was ready to take the offensive against the demoralized and now-outnumbered Confederates.[38] Grant's plan was simple enough. While Hooker's and Thomas's men advanced against the left wing and center of the Confederate position to draw the Rebels' attention, Sherman would attack the Confederate right wing with four corps of the Union army. However, events did not go exactly as planned. When Sherman attacked the right wing of the Confederate army on November 25, he made very slow progress. Worrying that the Confederates were moving reinforcements to their beleaguered right wing, Grant ordered Thomas to have his men advance against the Rebel positions on Missionary Ridge. To everyone's astonishment, Thomas's men kept advancing all the way to the top of the ridge. In a war where charges against strongly held positions almost invariably resulted in bloody repulses, the Union troops broke through the Confederate line after suffering very light casualties.

The defeat of the Army of Tennessee at Chattanooga spelled the beginning of the end for the Confederacy. The gateway to the heart of the Confederacy was now open to invasion by Union troops. Chattanooga also confirmed what many were already beginning to believe: Lincoln had found a general who could finally lead the Union armies to victory. In fact, what he had found was a *team* of generals that could crush the Confederacy. In December 1863 the president appointed Grant lieutenant general in charge of all the armies of the United States. Over the next few months, Grant, Lincoln, and Stanton put together a chain of command that was to coordinate the movements of Union armies. George Meade, who had defeated Lee at Gettysburg and started the momentum that eventually led to the defeat of the Army of Northern Virginia, remained in command of the Army of the

Potomac, though Grant would be with his army most of the time, look-ing over his shoulder. William Tecumseh Sherman would take overall command of the Western armies with the responsibility of capturing Atlanta and defeating the only other Rebel army of any consequence still in the field, the Confederate Army of Tennessee, now commanded by Joseph E. Johnston. Under these men was a cadre of experienced commanders leading one of the best-equipped armies the world had ever seen.

By this time the Confederates had no more answers: Their cause was indeed lost. They put up a stout resistance for another fifteen months, but the eventual outcome of the war was no longer in doubt. Map 2.5 shows the territory occupied by Union armies at the end of 1863 and the two principal offensives of the last year of the war. When Sherman finally occupied Atlanta in September 1864, he recalled the success that Grant's troops had experienced living off the land in the Vicks-burg campaign. Leaving George Thomas with the task of taking care of the remnants of the Confederate forces in Tennessee, Sherman set out from Atlanta at the head of seventy-five thousand men and marched across the state of Georgia in one of the most celebrated "raids" in military history. Intending to "make Georgia howl," Sher-man succeeded beyond his wildest expectations. By the time he reached the coast at Savannah, his name had become identified with a new kind of warfare, war against the enemy population as well as its armies.[39]

To the north, Grant and Meade led the Army of the Potomac south one more time. Rebuffed by Lee's stubborn resistance at the Wilder-ness and Spotsylvania Courthouse, Grant simply stepped back and ordered his troops to march farther south. He knew that he had more men than Lee, and although Lee seemed to have the advantage of inte-rior lines, Grant could make use of the ports along the coast of Virginia to sustain supply lines to his army. Though he had failed to break through Lee's lines by the end of July, the Army of the Potomac had

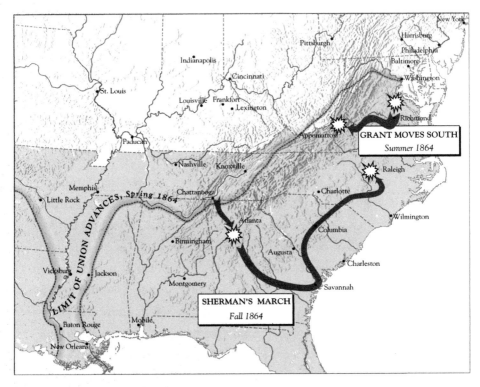

MAP 2.5

UNION OFFENSIVES IN 1864

stretched the Confederate lines from Richmond to Petersburg. While Lee's troops still defiantly stood their ground in elaborately fortified trenches, Grant knew that he had accomplished what no other Union general had been able to do: He had finally brought "Bobbie Lee" to bay. The Confederate leader had nowhere to go. His army had exacted a heavy enough toll of casualties to discourage further attacks by Grant while he rested his exhausted troops. But with the commencement of operations in the spring of 1865 the Confederate resistance quickly collapsed. Hoping to join up with the remnants of Johnston's Confederate army as it retreated through the Carolinas under the pressure of Sherman's troops, Lee gambled one last time and tried to break free of

Grant's grip around Petersburg by retreating west. It was a futile gesture that ended with the weary Confederates surrounded at Appomattox. On April 9, 1865, almost exactly four years after the Confederate guns had opened fire on Fort Sumter, Robert E. Lee surrendered the Army of Northern Virginia. It took a few more weeks for the rest of the Confederacy to surrender, but to all intents and purposes, the Civil War was over. The North had won.

OUR REVIEW of the fighting between early 1862 and 1863 reinforces what we already suspected: The South was facing heavy odds. Yet we were able to identify several battles, all of them Union victories, where a Confederate victory could have substantially improved their chances of winning the war. Our summary of the fighting also reinforces the argument that the Civil War was not going to be won or lost as a result of a single battle that might eventually determine the outcome of the war. Before we reexamine specific battles in a counterfactual light to see how they might have made a difference, it will be useful to consider if the South's loss was a result of faulty strategy. If it was faulty, had there been alternative strategies and tactics that might have produced a very different result?

Historians debating these issues have tended to identify two major shortcomings in Southern strategy and tactics. First was the penchant of Confederate commanders to favor offensive tactics that resulted in substantial casualties without producing decisive victories. As a result of these casualties, these critics argue, the South no longer had the manpower to prolong the stalemate beyond the spring of 1864 and force the North to the negotiating table. The second major criticism is that the Confederate leadership pursued a strategy of trying to protect extended lines of defense that could not be sustained with their limited manpower. In so doing, Jefferson Davis and his generals ignored the opportunities offered by a Fabian strategy of retreating into the interior of the South in order to stretch Northern supply lines to a point where the Southerners could successfully counterattack and defeat the overextended enemy.[40]

We begin by addressing the claim that Lee and other Confederate generals wasted manpower through their unremitting commitment to the tactical offensive, what Grady McWhiney and Perry Jamieson call the attack and die approach to warfare. This argument is based on an analysis of casualty rates suffered by the two sides in the major battles of the war. McWhiney and Jamieson present statistics on the "losses" suffered by both sides in the first twelve major campaigns of the war—from Shiloh through Chickamauga. By their count, the Confederates suffered losses totaling 153,000 over this period, compared with only 113,000 men lost to the Federal armies fighting them. Since the Union forces engaged in these campaigns outnumbered their foe by a ratio of 4:3, the disparity in casualty *rates* was greater still; the Southern armies had an aggregate loss rate of nearly 25 percent while the Northerners lost only 14 percent of their men.[41] Summarizing these data, McWhiney and Jamieson conclude that "the South simply bled itself to death in the first three years of the war by taking the tactical offensive in nearly 70 percent of the major actions."[42] At the head of the list of generals who were accused of squandering lives was none other than Robert E. Lee. The Army of Northern Virginia lost approximately 121,000 men, or roughly 20 percent of those engaged, while fighting with Lee as their commander. No other Confederate general matched this rate of attrition.[43]

Does this mean Southern generals bled their armies to death through the reckless use of the tactical offensive? There is no doubt that Confederate armies suffered horrendous casualties in these battles. But before we simply accept the argument that the South squandered its manpower in unnecessary offensive actions, we should note several points that have been raised in response to these criticisms. To begin with, there is considerable ambiguity regarding the construction and interpretation of statistics on casualties in the war. Table 2.1 presents our "best guess" of the "total losses" incurred by each side in the key battles between Shiloh and Chattanooga. The data are organized into three categories: men killed, men wounded, and men missing. The estimates in all three categories suffer from problems in the collection of data and the resulting estimates; Appendix 1 discusses the methodology used to construct the estimates.

Critics claim that what appear to be disproportionately high Confederate casualties were the result of an eagerness to take the tactical offensive too often. Yet it is not clear that these tactics explain the high casualties in most battles. One of the compelling facts to emerge from an examination of Table 2.1 is that with few exceptions, both the attacker and the defender suffered high losses in almost every major battle. Even at Fredericksburg, where the Union army lost 12,700 men, many of them squandered in fruitless charges against an entrenched enemy, the Confederate defenders still lost 5,300 men. And this was surely not a typical battle. As Confederate General Joseph E. Johnston noted when he heard of Lee's victory at Fredericksburg, "What luck some people have, nobody will come to attack me in such a place."[44] Lee's other victories came at a much higher price. In the Peninsula campaign against McClellan, which was the largest army that Lee commanded during the war, the Confederates lost more than 30,000 men. This was one of the few cases in which the Confederate losses actually exceeded the losses sustained by the Army of the Potomac. At Chancellorsville, widely regarded to be Lee's most brilliant victory, his army lost 13,500 men, or almost a quarter of the men engaged. At Second Manassas, Jackson and Longstreet lost more than 9,000 men, or roughly a fifth of their army while routing Pope's Army of Virginia. Even though he usually imposed heavier losses on his foe in absolute numbers, Lee was depleting his own manpower faster than he was draining the strength of "those people" on the other side. But was this simply a blind adherence to offensive tactics? What were his alternatives? In defense of Lee's tactics and strategy, historians have stated that his boldness not only blunted the military advances of the Union into the South but was a crucial element in building morale throughout the South. By the

TABLE 2.1

LOSSES IN MAJOR CIVIL WAR

BATTLES, 1862–63

Theater of Action	Union	
	Total Losses	Losses as % of Men Engaged
Virginia		
Peninsula campaign	25,400	14.6
Second Manassas	16,000	25.9
Antietam	12,400	16.5
Fredericksburg	12,700	12.7
Chancellorsville	17,300	17.8
Gettysburg	22,800	26.6
Total[a]	112,400	16.1
Tennessee/Kentucky		
Perryville	4,200	18.3
Murfreesboro	12,900	31.2
Chickamauga	16,200	27.8
Chattanooga	5,000	10.3
Total[a]	44,500	24.0
Mississippi Valley		
Shiloh	13,000	20.8
River campaigns[b]	16,600	9.6
Total[a]	29,700	12.6
Total, all campaigns	186,562	16.6

a. Totals include additional battles listed in Table A.1 (see Appendix 1).

b. Totals do not include men surrendering at Vicksburg and Fort Donelson.

Confederate		Confederate Losses as a Fraction of Union Losses	
Total Losses	Losses as % of Men Engaged	Total Losses	Losses as % of Men Engaged
30,500	18.0	1.20	1.23
9,200	19.0	0.57	0.73
13,700	26.5	1.11	1.61
5,300	7.3	0.42	0.58
13,500	23.5	0.78	1.32
28,000	37.2	1.23	1.40
105,000	18.8	0.93	1.17
3,400	22.6	0.81	1.24
11,700	33.8	0.91	1.08
18,500	27.8	1.14	1.00
6,700	14.4	1.14	1.40
40,700	24.1	0.92	1.00
10,700	26.5	0.82	1.27
24,000	20.7	1.44	2.15
34,700	22.2	1.17	1.76
180,400	20.4	0.97	1.23

Source: Ratios computed from data in Table A.1 (see Appendix 1). Loss totals have been rounded to the nearest 100 persons.

time Lee headed north on the Gettysburg campaign in the summer of 1863, his army had become the symbol of the Southern rebellion. Until the Northern armies were able to catch and defeat Lee, the rebellion would continue.[45]

This leads us to the second criticism of Southern strategy in the war: Why didn't the South pursue a policy of conserving its own strength by avoiding pitched battles and wearing down its foes? Numerous writers have raised this possibility. They note that Southern armies seldom suffered from a deficiency of weapons or supply, that at the outset of the war Southern generals could often take advantage of their interior lines and utilize the tactical offensive, that the South was a large and thinly settled region that the North had to conquer. With competent Confederate military leadership, the advantages of being on the defensive should have been able to offset northern numerical superiority.[46] While it may seem obvious that a Fabian strategy would make sense for the South, a closer look at the implications of a strategy of withdrawal to the center of the Confederacy reveals some serious drawbacks to such an approach to the Southern war effort.[47]

To begin with, we have already said that our statistics on Civil War casualties clearly demonstrate that there was no such thing as a "cheap" fight in terms of casualties. Although a Fabian defensive strategy eschews costly offensive operations, the enemy must be engaged to some extent in order to harass and disrupt its supply lines and gradually wear down its forces. In fact, in many instances a Fabian strategy is associated with relatively high casualties because retreating armies often suffer substantial losses. Hannibal imposed huge casualties on the Romans, but his own losses were so great that he was finally forced to withdraw. The Russians suffered heavy losses against Napoleon in 1812 and against the Germans in World War II when they withdrew into the interior of Russia.

The examples where the Confederates took a somewhat Fabian approach to strategy turned out to be quite costly in terms of losses. Lee's defensive experience in the final year of the war is often cited as evidence of what might have been had the Confederates chosen not to press their attacks earlier in the war. But such reasoning ignores the fact that Lee suffered very high casualties, particularly in relation to the reduced size of his army, in the summer of 1864, when he tried to block Grant's advance. In his unsuccessful attempt to defend Atlanta in 1864, Joseph Johnston, a Confederate general who is often criticized for preferring to retreat rather than engage in bloody battles, lost as many men as Sherman's attacking army. Moreover, unlike Lee, who at least had some positive results to show for his willingness to fight, Johnston was responsible for the steady erosion of morale among his troops because of his penchant for pulling back. Those who defend Lee's aggressive strategy assert that his victories boosted morale in his army and among the civilian population of the Confederacy, which otherwise showed the demoralizing effects of a strategy calling for constant withdrawal.

Finally, the Confederacy faced a serious problem with its slave population if it allowed Union troops to occupy areas of the South where slaves lived. Retreat by Confederate forces into the interior of the South threatened to erode the very foundation of the Confederacy by undermining slavery. As Union armies advanced into the South, blacks were quick to recognize the opportunity afforded them by invading troops. "Whether in the loyal slave states of the Union or in the heart of the Confederacy," historian Barbara Fields writes, "the slaves themselves had to make their freedom real."[48] They did so by enlisting for military service, by defecting with their families to the Union lines, or by refusing to accompany their owners when they fled at the approach of Union troops. Still, refugees were not always met with open arms by Union troops. Early in the war the flow of refugee slaves posed an awkward question of emancipation for the Union commanders. Slavery was still legal in the United States, and the Union government was reluctant to "free" escaped slaves. But what were the commanders to do with the African-Americans who flocked to their camps? It made no sense to return them to their owners, who would put them back to work supporting the rebellion. General Benjamin Butler came up with a brilliant way to temporize on the question by confiscating the bondsmen as "contraband property" and refusing to return them to their owners. But this was only a temporary solution. As the number of contrabands increased, the problem of the South was not only a loss of valuable labor but the growing conviction among slaves that their hour had come and that this was confirmed by the presence of Yankee troops. It was crucial to the South that the Union troops be kept out of the areas of the South where the slaves lived.

All these considerations point to a situation in which the Confederate high command had no choice but to do everything possible to protect as much territory as possible. To lose territory was to lose the war. Not surprisingly, President Davis worked to implement strategies that would forestall invasions into the South by Union forces. He called his approach an offensive-defensive strategy that sought to hold as much territory as possible with defensive maneuvers, while looking for opportunities to take offensive action to throw the invaders off-balance or even to carry the war to the North. While this might have been Davis's intent, it was seldom obvious how this policy was to be implemented. Adding to the problem was the absence of a system of command to ensure that a given strategy would be followed by commanders in the field even if Davis were to dictate one. The result was that the strategy actually followed by Confederate armies in the field was not apparent at the time, nor has it proved obvious to historians who have sought to examine it after the fact.

Whatever the underlying strategy that Davis and the military leaders of the Confederacy followed, it did not prevent a Union victory. As the leader of the South Davis has received much of the blame for its defeat. Devotees of the Lost Cause have been particularly hard on the president, insisting that his system of military departments hindered efforts to defend the western perimeter of the Confederacy, that he made poor appointments and quarreled with the generals he did appoint, and that he stubbornly ignored advice from his generals. Historians have charged that both Davis and Lee tended to concentrate so much attention on the Virginia theater of the war that Confederate fortunes in the West suffered. This is a theme that a group of generals, led by Joe Johnston and P. T. Beauregard, vociferously articulated during and immediately after the war. Recent work by a diverse group of historians suggests that much of this criticism may have been misplaced. They have defended Jefferson Davis,[49] arguing that the joint efforts of Davis and Lee in carrying out a strategy to keep the North at bay was quite successful,[50] and at a more general level concluded that the South did a reasonably successful job of concentrating troops at points of attack while pressing offensive actions against the Union when the opportunity presented itself.[51]

Yet, for all the ink spent detailing the strategic shortcomings of the Confederate command, too little attention has been directed toward a simpler explanation for the South's failure. Perhaps the South lost the war because it was unable to find commanders comparable to those who eventually emerged in the North. Our review of the actual course of fighting during the war points to three specific areas where Confederate forces failed to implement strategies that were basically sound. First, while it seems unlikely that Confederate forces could have prevented the Union push down the Western rivers by late 1863, they could have done a more effective job of impeding that advance, and they could have avoided losing the thousands of men who were captured in river strongholds such as Vicksburg. Second, if they had succeeded in at least slowing the Union advance down the Mississippi, Confederate forces would have been able to hang on to Chattanooga and eastern Tennessee until after the Northern election in 1864. Had these two areas been stabilized, and if Lee had avoided the catastrophic losses at Antietam and Gettysburg, then there would have been a stalemate in the Eastern theater of the war that would have forced the Union government to ask for an armistice after the presidential election of 1864.

To have all this come to pass admittedly stretches the imagination.

Yet as we have argued above, war is a gamble, and imagination is an important ingredient in the making of counterfactual history. With that in mind, we turn once more to the question that we opened this chapter with: Could the South have won this war? One way to answer that question is to construct an actual counterfactual scenario that has the South win the war. It is time to add some imagination to our counterfactual pudding.

Chapter Three

. . . .

AGAINST ALL ODDS: THE ANATOMY OF A SOUTHERN VICTORY

If we can break up the enemy's arrangement early and throw him back, he will not be able to recover his position or his morale until the presidential election. And then we shall have a new president to treat with.

—General James Longstreet (Spring 1864)

LONGSTREET'S ASSESSMENT OF THE South's military and political situation in 1864 proved far too optimistic. By the spring of 1864 the Confederacy was hanging by a thread of hope that the Army of Northern Virginia could somehow perform one more miracle and throw the Yankees back over the Mason-Dixon Line. It was not to be. If, however, the military fortunes of the Confederacy had followed a more favorable course leading up to 1864, a dissatisfied Northern electorate just might have voted in a new president who would have been willing to extend overtures to end the war. Our argument to date has been that there *were* opportunities for Southern armies to produce a stalemate that might have forced the Union to the negotiating table.

As we have identified those possibilities, our counterfactual speculations have been limited to focusing on individual situations that actually took place but could have turned out differently. We have resisted
the temptation to cut free from the record of what actually happened
and launch ourselves into a world of what might have been. Yet the
basic ingredients for our counterfactual Civil War have been assembled. In the last chapter we mixed a heavy dose of historical plausibility with common sense to see if the South could have won the war. The
next step is to add imagination and pour our counterfactual pudding
into the historical mold of the American Civil War and construct a
counterfactual scenario in which the South prevails.

The war described in this chapter is one of many possible scenarios
in which the South might have triumphed. If the story seems strangely
familiar, that is because I have made a conscious effort to place the
counterfactual changes outlined earlier into the historical mold of the
war as it actually took place. Thus the time period for the duration of
the war is roughly the same: spring 1861 to spring 1865. Most of the
battles occur in the same places at roughly the same times as those
reported in chapter 2. Up until the last year of the counterfactual war
many of them have the same outcomes. The changes that I introduce
in constructing the counterfactual scenario all are based on suggestions
developed in chapter 2. The result, as we shall see, is a war that looks
familiar in many ways but has a very different ending. While a healthy
dose of imagination is important to make our story interesting, we
must be careful not to let our imaginations run wild. To remind us that
the changes I make to the actual course of events are in fact reasonable, I have occasionally inserted footnotes that are "reality checks" to
support my counterfactual events.

THE WESTERN THEATERS

In the first week of February 1862, Union General Ulysses Grant with
an army of roughly twenty thousand men, supported by a flotilla of

gunboats commanded by Flag Officer Andrew Foote, moved south along the Tennessee and Cumberland rivers toward the Confederate outposts of Fort Donelson and Fort Henry. Concerned that the loss of both forts would represent a disastrous breach of the Confederate lines, Albert Sidney Johnston reinforced Fort Henry with an additional twelve thousand troops in the hope that Grant's advance could be checked. Unfortunately for the Confederates this was a case of too little too late. Grant's troops were able to surround the fort, and only the insistence of General Nathan Bedford Forrest that the Confederates should fight their way out of the Union encirclement prevented the fort's capture from becoming an even greater disaster for the Southern forces. On the afternoon of February 15 Forrest's men managed to open a gap in the Yankee lines that allowed thirteen thousand Confederate troops to escape capture and rejoin the Confederate forces at Bowling Green.[1] Even so, the surrender of the fort the next day put the Confederate military in a precarious situation and forced Johnston to reevaluate his options. He realized that only a bold move would stop Grant's advance down the Tennessee River, and he knew that he must act quickly.

By the end of March, Grant's army, now numbering some forty thousand, was camped along the west bank of the Tennessee River at a place called Pittsburg Landing. The Union commander had persuaded his reluctant superior, Henry Halleck, to allow him to move quickly into the heart of the Confederacy. A. S. Johnston realized that Grant's aggressiveness offered the Confederates an opportunity to regain the initiative. Johnston's hope was that Rebel troops could surprise Grant and engage him before additional troops could arrive from farther north. Accordingly, the Confederates gathered roughly forty thousand troops at Corinth, Mississippi. The success of the Confederates' plan depended on their ability to surprise Grant's unsuspecting troops before Union General Don Carlos Buell could join Grant's army with an additional twenty thousand men. On the morning of April 6 the Confederate troops under Johnston and P. T. Beauregard attacked the Union position at Shiloh and completely surprised the Union right wing, commanded by General William T. Sherman. Sherman sustained a serious wound in the early phases of the action and was taken to the rear. His absence contributed to the panic that spread from his troops to the entire right wing of the Union army.[2]

When Grant, who had been staying at Savannah, about nine miles north of Pittsburg Landing, arrived on the scene, pandemonium reigned. Men had abandoned their gear and were cowering along the riverbank; officers were nowhere in sight. When he asked where Sherman was, Grant was told that his friend had been seriously wounded and taken to safety across the river. A group of Union soldiers had been holding out in what became known as the hornets' nest, but by late afternoon it was learned that their position had finally been overrun. Their efforts had brought Grant a brief respite, but his army was still in dire straits. Only a supreme effort by their commander, and the confusion of the untested Confederate troops on the other side of the lines, kept the Union forces from complete collapse. If Don Carlos Buell arrived in time to join the fray the following morning, the battle might yet be won.

As he desperately sought to rally his panicked troops, Grant learned that Buell would not arrive in time to assist him. To ensure that his army would not have to deal with both Union armies at once, A. S. Johnston had dispatched a detachment of cavalry under Bedford Forrest to intercept Buell and take whatever steps he felt necessary to delay Buell's march. Displaying his usual flair, Forrest took advantage of the element of surprise and attacked the supply wagons at the rear of Buell's army as they moved to join Grant at Pittsburg Landing. The resulting melee threw the entire Union column into disarray. Buell and his staff frantically tried to find out what had happened. Unable to determine the size of the attacking force, the Union commander gave orders to halt. Once some sense of order had been restored, Buell took stock and decided the prudent thing was to have his army camp for the night and protect against any further depredations by enemy forces in the area. Buell deployed his troops to ward off any subsequent attacks. He also sent word of his predicament to Grant late on the evening of the fifth and waited for orders before proceeding farther south. Forrest's raid had succeeded beyond all expectations. By the time the courier carrying Grant's message ordering Buell to "press ahead with all speed" reached the beleaguered general amid the confusion of battle on the following day, the bulk of Buell's army was still encamped thirty-five miles away from the action.

Though he received some help when Lew Wallace's division arrived late in the afternoon, Grant realized that he faced a serious risk of creating a major disaster if he did not evacuate his disorganized men quickly. Fortunately for him, the Confederates were almost as disorganized in victory as the Union troops were in defeat. Around six in the evening the Rebel attacks on the Union lines finally came to a halt. As darkness came, Grant reluctantly took advantage of it and gave orders for the Union troops to be ferried back across the river. By morning all but Wallace's division had embarked. Covered by the cannons of the Union gunboats, Wallace's men retreated north toward Crump's Landing, where they too were ferried to safety across the river.

The Confederates were in no condition to pursue the retreating troops. Though they had succeeded in driving the Yankee invaders back, they had suffered horrendous casualties, and their commanding general had been seriously wounded. A command structure that had been imperfect to begin with now became almost completely dysfunctional as Beauregard sought to establish some sort of order in his disorganized army. Since the Union navy still controlled the river, there was still a possibility that Union forces would launch a counterattack, and Beauregard devoted his efforts to making sure that his troops were in position to ward off any new offensive by the Yankees.

However much Grant might wish to resume the offensive, neither he nor his troops were in any position to do so. His primary concern at this time was to reorganize his demoralized army and determine the position of Buell's army, which was still recovering from Forrest's successful raid. Moreover, Grant's own command of the Union forces was at best uncertain. Within hours of learning of the Union defeat, Henry Halleck had boarded a boat at St. Louis and was rushing to the scene. His orders, telegraphed ahead of his arrival, were that Grant do nothing until he arrived. Upon his arrival, Halleck, who had never had much admiration for Grant's abilities, immediately relieved him of his command.[3] Unaware that the Confederate army was probably as disorganized as his own and worried about the presence of a Confederate force that could be threatening to cut the lines from Buell's army to Nashville, Halleck ordered Buell to retrace his steps back to his base at Nashville. A short inspection of Grant's troops convinced Halleck that they too should withdraw, and he made arrangements for the army to move back to Cairo, Illinois, where it could reinforce the army of John Pope, which was preparing to move down the Mississippi and the Confederate positions at Island No. 10.

The first major thrust by Union forces down the Mississippi Valley had ended with a very bloody nose.

THE REPERCUSSIONS of the Union defeat at Shiloh echoed through the Western theater of the war for another year. There were, to be sure, still plenty of Union troops in the region that could be marshaled to form a new invasion force. But who would lead them? Grant, whose reputation was shattered by the defeat, had been replaced by Halleck. Sherman, who was Grant's friend and had commanded the right wing of the Union army at Shiloh, was recuperating from his wounds and would not see action for another ten months. His reputation had also been damaged by the Confederate success in surprising his unprepared troops. Neither Halleck nor Buell was prone to be aggressive, so the removal of Grant from a position of command took the teeth out of the Union offensive in the Mississippi Valley. Union forces did capture Island No. 10 in June 1862, and Grant's performance in that action allowed him to regain some of his stature as one of the army's best field officers. But there were no further offensive actions in the summer and fall of that year. At the end of 1862 the Confederates still held Corinth and Pope's army had yet to occupy Memphis.

As Albert Sidney Johnston lay recuperating in a hospital from an operation that removed his leg, he could take some solace from the fact that the theater of operations under his command at least had been stabilized for the time being. However, the loss of Forts Henry and Donelson and the costly victory at Shiloh caused him to rethink his ideas of how to best defend the Western states of the Confederacy. The retreat of Union forces after Shiloh had bought the South some time by delaying the advance of those forces and throwing the Union high command into confusion. But Johnston knew that the defeat of Union troops would not indefinitely forestall the Union thrust down the Mississippi River. The inescapable fact was that the South had no effective answer to Federal naval power. Counties along the banks of the Mississippi, Cumberland, and Tennessee rivers all were vulnerable to a coordinated attack by Northern naval and land forces. Should he try to contest these naval advances? Johnston did not doubt the political value of holding on to strongholds along the Western rivers in terms of civilian morale. But such efforts were almost surely doomed to failure in the face of Union naval power, and if the cost was more battles like Shiloh, Johnston doubted that the Confederacy could continue to pay the bill. Above all, the Confederacy must avoid a contest of sieges that eventually lost both men and matériel without inflicting a high cost on the enemy.

As he discussed the merits of pursuing a strategy of delaying tactics against an invading enemy, it occurred to Johnston that the experience of the battles for the forts and the battle at Shiloh had revealed one general who appeared to be perfectly suited to implement a strategy of harassment and withdrawal. Nathan Bedford Forrest had managed to escape from the encirclement of Fort Henry, and his raid on Buell's army at Shiloh had demonstrated audacity as well as skill in evading the subsequent efforts to capture his force. Shortly after Shiloh, Johnston approached Forrest about taking command of the Confederate cavalry units in the Mississippi Valley. The choice proved to be a good one; by the end of the war Forrest's exploits in harassing Federal units along the Western rivers rivaled those of Lee's cavalry commander with the Army of Northern Virginia, Jeb Stuart. There remained the question of who could command the troops that would resist the Union armies as they moved down the Mississippi. For this Johnston eventually turned to his namesake from the Eastern theater of the war, Joseph E. Johnston. J. E. Johnston was a cautious commander who had a reputation for avoiding pitched battles and high casualties, which, as long as he did not carry it to an extreme, suited A. S. Johnston's proposed strategy quite well.

All that was needed now was for the Union to cooperate with the Confederate plan. For a time the war went rather well. Halleck, who replaced Grant as the head of the Union Army of the Tennessee, was the perfect foil. Cautious by nature and fearful of the consequences of advances into enemy territory, Halleck tended to move at a snail's pace and halt at the slightest evidence of action on the part of the enemy. He had limited experience in the field, and he was anxious not to repeat Grant's error at Shiloh. Even though Union forces substantially outnumbered their opponents, they had moved only as far as Jackson, Tennessee, fifty miles north of the Shiloh battlefield, by the end of July 1862. Following a policy of obstructing but not fighting pitched battles, Joe Johnston evacuated Jackson and pulled back toward Corinth, Mississippi, where he hoped to put up stronger resistance.

At this point Halleck was called to Washington, and Grant again took command of the Union forces in the Department of Tennessee. Grant immediately stepped up the advance, and by the end of October Union troops had finally returned to the Shiloh battlefield. Gathering his army together, Grant prepared to assault Corinth. In two days of bloody fighting the Union forces finally succeeded in driving the Confederates out of the town. Hoping to secure his base for the eventual attack on Vicksburg, Grant pushed his tired troops farther east and occupied the town of Iuka. The important east-west rail terminus at Corinth was now in Federal hands.[4] With the rail connections to the interior severed, the Confederates could no longer hold their position in Memphis, which was evacuated in early November.

At the end of 1862 both sides could take some satisfaction from the year's fighting in the Mississippi Valley. In spite of the initial setback at Shiloh, Grant had regained the initiative and was poised to invade Mississippi in the spring of 1863. On the Confederate side, the victory at Shiloh had provided a huge boost in morale, and Confederate forces had exacted a heavy toll on Halleck's and Grant's troops as they sought to regain the lost ground in eastern Tennessee. The casualties suffered at Shiloh and Corinth had a pronounced effect on the commanders of both armies. Grant began to rely more on a war of movement rather than on pitched battles—particularly assaults against fortified positions. J. E. Johnston, already criticized for being too timid in resisting the Yankee invaders, would be even more reluctant to offer battle.

Grant resumed his offensive in the spring of 1863, moving south toward Vicksburg in two columns, one on either side of the river. He immediately ran into problems. Raids by Forrest and Earl Van Dorn destroyed his supply depots at Holly Springs and Jackson, Tennessee. Because of the difficulty of maintaining his supply lines and the terrain on the east bank of the Missisippi, Grant focused his attention on the west side of the river. Progress was slow, but by the end of July the Union forces had finally reached the proximity of Vicksburg. On August 3 Sherman's division assaulted the Confederate position at Chickasaw Bluffs, just north of Vicksburg. It was repulsed with heavy losses, and Grant realized that additional assaults would fare no better. Consequently, Grant determined to move his army south of the Confederate stronghold, to cross the river and approach the city from the east. At the end of August a Union force of about forty thousand troops reached the town of Hard Times. After running gunboats and supply ships past the Confederate shore batteries, the Union navy was able to ferry Grant's army across the river to Bruinsburg on October 5, and he wasted no time heading northeast toward the state capital, Jackson.

Grant's intent was to get between John Pemberton's garrison in Vicksburg and J. E. Johnston's army at Jackson. However, Johnston did not wait for Grant to attack his forces piecemeal. He ordered Pemberton to move all but a token force out of Vicksburg and march quickly to join the main Confederate force just east of the state capital. Knowing that he would be able to collect more troops from the west side of the Mississippi if he occupied the east bank of the river at Vicksburg, Grant altered his route of march and surrounded the city. When it finally became apparent that Johnston was not going to move against the Union troops, the garrison of fifty-seven hundred men surrendered. On November 2 Grant entered Vicksburg.[5] With the fall of Port Hudson, Louisiana, a few weeks later, the Mississippi River was now completely in Union hands.

All this represented a stunning victory for the Union forces in the Mississippi Valley. The Christmas party for Union officers hosted by Grant in 1863 was a far happier affair than that hosted by General Halleck a year ago. But as the Union officers savored their triumph, their commanding general sat in a corner of the room, sipping cider and pondering the fact that their job was not yet finished. That same week Joe Johnston was giving a Christmas party for his officers in Jackson. Reflecting on the past twelve months, Johnston was forced to conclude that 1863 had not been a good year for the Confederate forces in Mississippi. Ulysses Grant was determined to see that 1864 would be no better.

WHILE THE armies struggled for control of the Mississippi throughout 1862 and 1863, the war for Kentucky and Tennessee raged on. Two years of fierce fighting had settled nothing. In the fall of 1862 Braxton Bragg and Edmund Kirby Smith had launched an invasion of Kentucky. Though Smith's army reached the state capital, Frankfort, long enough to proclaim a secessionist governor of the state, the Confederates were soon forced to withdraw following the Battle of Perryville. At the end of 1862 Bragg's army fought an inconclusive but very bloody battle with General William Rosecrans's forces at Murfreesboro, Tennessee. The year ended with the two armies situated about where they had been at the beginning of the year, Bragg with his headquarters in Chattanooga and Rosecrans operating out of Nashville. In the spring of 1863 Rosecrans took the offensive and eventually managed to maneuver Bragg out of Chattanooga and invade northern Georgia. But the Union forces lost the initiative when Jefferson Davis reinforced Bragg with Longstreet's corps from the Army of Northern Virginia, and the Confederates succeeded in driving Rosecrans back to Chattanooga following the Battle of Chickamauga in late September.[6]

President Lincoln was alarmed at the plight of the Union forces at Chattanooga, but there was little he could do. Union resources were simply stretched to the limit. Grant still faced a sizable Confederate force not far from Vicksburg, and Lincoln was reluctant to take troops away from his best general. The war was fairly quiet in the East at this point, so the president finally decided to send Hooker's corps west as reinforcements for the beleaguered garrison. He also issued orders for George Thomas, who had performed well at Chickamauga, to replace Rosecrans. Having done what he could, Lincoln could only hope that with the reinforcements Thomas would find a way to hang on through the spring.

Jefferson Davis was also struggling with questions posed by the situation in the West. Grant's victory at Vicksburg did not sit well with the Confederate president. In his view, either J. E. Johnston should have used his forces to attack Grant while his army was exposed without strong support on the east side of the river, or Pemberton should have been given enough troops to resist the Union attack on the city. To be sure, Johnston had successfully carried out a strategy of withdrawal in the face of superior Union naval power on the rivers, and his decision to pull Pemberton out of Vicksburg had greatly reduced the overall damage associated with the eventual loss of that city. Nonetheless, Davis found Johnston to be something of a whining fussbudget who was a little too eager to retreat into the interior, and the Confederacy could ill afford any further loss of territory. He would have preferred a more aggressive general in command at Jackson.

For the moment Davis did nothing partly because the situation in eastern Tennessee required more immediate attention. Bragg was one of those generals who, even when they succeeded, managed to alien-ate their men thoroughly. His failure to follow up on the victory at Chattanooga and occupy the city was the last straw. Convinced that leaving Bragg in command would cripple the Army of Tennessee's actions in the coming year, A. S. Johnston insisted that a change had to be made. The problem, of course, was who would replace Bragg. The two senior generals in the West were Joe Johnston, who already had an independent command in Mississippi, and P. T. Beauregard, who was intensely disliked by President Davis. An obvious solution would have been to appoint Albert Sidney Johnston himself; however, Johnston's wound at Shiloh had never completely healed, and he was unable to handle the physical duress of a field command. So Davis turned to Longstreet, who had served well in the Virginia campaigns, who had the confidence of officers in the Army of Tennessee, and had played a major role in the Confederate victory at Chickamauga. Not the least of the factors in Davis's decision was a strong recommendation from the one person he trusted above all others, Robert E. Lee.[7]

After three years of fierce fighting, all either side had to show for its efforts were an enormous number of casualties and a tenuous stalemate in the Western theater of operations. In Mississippi and western Ten-nessee the Union forces seemed to have the upper hand. They con-trolled the major rivers in the area, and the commander was eager to resume the fight. "I want Johnston broken up as effectually as possible, and roads destroyed," Grant told Sherman as they sat down to plan the coming campaign.[8] Of course Johnston was not the only problem; Union forces in the region were continually harassed by Confederate

cavalry led by Forrest, Van Dorn, and Joe Wheeler. The Union foothold in eastern Tennessee was less secure; though the Union army had
a firm grip on Nashville, Thomas's army in Chattanooga was in danger
of being forced to evacuate because of the pressure from the Confederate forces under Longstreet. Thomas could probably hold out through
the spring of 1864, but he would pose little threat to the heart of the
Confederacy that still lay untouched by Union arms.

The coming year promised to be busy in the West. But it was in the
East, where Robert E. Lee, and his Army of Northern Virginia continued to defy the odds and hold the North's Army of the Potomac at bay,
that this war would ultimately be decided.

THE EASTERN THEATER

From the moment he took command of the Confederate army outside
Richmond and renamed it the Army of Northern Virginia, Robert E.
Lee was able to infuse his troops with an élan that produced a string of
victories seldom equaled in the annals of warfare. His army successfully
turned back invasions of Virginia by Union armies substantially larger
than his own with victories on the Yorktown Peninsula (May–June
1862), Second Manassas (August 1862), Fredericksburg (December
1862), and Chancellorsville (May 1863). Lee's heroics kept the Southern cause alive for the first two years of the war. By the end of 1863 Lee
and his colleague Thomas "Stonewall" Jackson had become the scourge
of the North.[9]

Lee knew that simply keeping the North at bay was not enough.
Victory for the South required that the Confederates take the war to
the North. Twice in the first two years of the war the Army of Northern Virginia invaded the North. While these raids carried considerable
risks, they also offered the possibility of considerable gains. The Antietam campaign came on the heels of a stunning success of Confederate
forces with the victories in the Peninsula campaign and the rout of
Pope's army at Second Manassas. Confederate armies under Bragg

were advancing north into Kentucky, causing the Union armies to withdraw from Tennessee. The Union army in Mississippi was stalled after the defeat at Shiloh. Finally, Lee's decision to go north in the fall of 1862 came at a time when the North's huge advantage in manpower and matériel had not yet been fully mobilized. Another victory over the Union armies would also have given a boost to those in Britain and France who were pressing their governments to intervene and mediate a peace between the warring factions in America.

No one knows exactly what Lee had in mind when the campaign started; it is likely that the Confederate commander left his plans deliberately fluid. After crossing into Maryland on September 4, the army moved on to the town of Frederick. Here Lee decided that the lightly defended Federal arsenal at Harpers Ferry was too good a prize to pass up. Accordingly, he issued orders for Jackson's corps to attack the arsenal while the rest of the army moved northwest into Maryland. Harpers Ferry fell to Jackson's troops on the fifteenth, and by the morning of the seventeenth his corps had rejoined Lee at Sharpsburg with a large booty of supplies from the Federal arsenal. Lee had already ordered his army to spread out and scour the Maryland countryside for supplies. The Army of Northern Virginia eagerly took to the task of collecting a huge stash of foodstuffs, horses, mules, cattle, hogs, and even some former slaves. For the next week supply wagons rumbled through Sharpsburg on the way back to Virginia with the fruits of their efforts. Lee was taking a huge gamble by dispersing his troops so widely, but he was confident that his army could reunite before the Union army arrived to threaten his position. The payoff in terms of supplies and increased morale of his troops, together with the demoralizing effect his invasion had on the Northern population, was well worth the risk.

Where was the Union army all this time? When Lee started north, George McClellan, who had been reappointed commander of the Army of the Potomac, was still trying to piece his army back together after the fiasco at Second Manassas. "Little Mac," who was not known for precipitate action, remained true to form. Alerted by scouts who reported when Lee crossed the Potomac, McClellan nevertheless waited until Lee had left Frederick and moved west to Sharpsburg before issuing orders for his army to break camp and take out after the rebels. Part of McClellan's problem was that he was getting conflicting reports about where the Rebels were. Reports claimed there were concentrations of Confederate troops at Harpers Ferry (Jackson), at Williamsport (Jackson), at Hagerstown (Longstreet), and in the passes through South Mountain (Lafayette McLaws and D. H. Hill). On the seventeenth, McClellan finally decided that he would move against Lee's position at Sharpsburg. The lead units of the Army of the Potomac finally engaged the troops of McLaws and D. H. Hill at Turner's Gap and South Mountain on the eighteenth. Lee had hoped that those troops would be able to hold the Federals long enough to allow his army to regroup. But the Union troops broke through the Confederate defenses, and Lee realized he was going to have to fight in order to buy time for his army to withdraw. By the evening of the twentieth, McClellan's troops were finally in position to engage the hastily regrouped forces of the Army of Northern Virginia.

The Southerners were not in a favorable position. McClellan had close to eighty thousand troops to Lee's fifty-five thousand, some of whom were still arriving as the Union attacks began early on the morning of September 21. The battle that ensued was the bloodiest single day of fighting during the entire war. As was often the case, the outcome was indecisive. McClellan squandered his numerical advantage by attacking piecemeal in three distinct assaults on the Confederate line. The Confederate lines held, but not without severe casualties, and by the end of the day both armies still occupied their initial positions. At that point the initiative should have swung over to McClellan, who still had troops in reserve to throw into a fresh offensive. However, the Union general had no stomach for further bloodshed, and after a day of uneasy skirmishing, the Army of Northern Virginia was able to withdraw across the Potomac without further damage from the enemy on September 23.[10]

For a Northern populace eager to hear of any success in dealing with Robert E. Lee, the Battle of Antietam was hailed as a major victory. The Rebels, after all, had been driven back across the Potomac with heavy losses. McClellan declared that his army had "thoroughly whipped" the Rebels. Lincoln knew otherwise. Lee's foray into Maryland had in fact been a stunning success. He had demonstrated the Union's inability to prevent such raids, and the Rebel commander had escaped not only with his army intact but with his quartermaster able to inventory a huge cache of captured supplies, animals, and equipment. Nor did it escape Lincoln's notice that similar raids by the Army of Northern Virginia in the future could have disastrous consequences on Northern morale. In this, Lincoln proved to be prescient indeed.

Lee was not celebrating either. Although he was satisfied that he had seriously embarrassed the Union military and pleased that his army had captured a large store of supplies, he had hoped for more. He had wanted a decisive victory over McClellan's army, one that would have sent a clear message to "those people" in Washington, D.C., that they should end this war, and end it quickly. Instead, Lincoln had defiantly issued an Emancipation Proclamation, freeing all the slaves in the rebellious states. Like many others, Lee viewed the proclamation as an empty gesture to gain support from the strong antislave groups both abroad and in the United States and perhaps at the same time to undermine the morale of white Southerners. Whether or not it was just an empty gesture, Lincoln's decision to release his proclamation meant that the Northern president had no intention of easing up in his efforts to crush the rebellion in the South. As he mulled over his next move, Lee made a mental note that the *next* time he invaded Northern territory, the Army of Northern Virginia would deal "those people" a blow from which they would not so easily recover.

. . . .

BEFORE LEE could seriously consider another venture onto Northern soil, he had to deal with the renewed efforts of the Union army to come south and capture Richmond. In December 1862 the Army of Northern Virginia turned back the Army of the Potomac at Fredericksburg with huge losses on the Northern side. Five months later Lee and Jackson combined for a stunning victory at Chancellorsville.[11] As the dispirited Union troops straggled back to Washington, D.C., Lee saw his chance. On June 1 he wired Jefferson Davis that he was once again going to invade the North. Only one thing caused him a twinge of uncertainty: Stonewall Jackson had been wounded at Chancellorsville. Jackson would recover from his wound, but he would not be able to accompany Lee on the upcoming invasion, and his command was turned over to A. P. Hill. Hill was a competent commander, but he was not Jackson.

Lee spent the next two weeks putting the finishing touches on the plans for his second invasion of the North. This time he had a clear set of objectives. He would march north toward Harrisburg, Pennsylvania, collecting supplies and spreading panic as he went. If Hooker and the Army of the Potomac came after him, as Lee was sure they would, the Confederates would wait for an opportune moment to turn and offer battle. That battle would offer Lee the opportunity to inflict a disastrous defeat on the principal army of the United States. Lincoln would then have no choice but to sue for peace. The countryside of southern Pennsylvania was well suited to Lee's plan. A series of parallel valleys run north from Harpers Ferry toward Harrisburg on the Susquehanna River. By staying west of South Mountain, Lee would be able to shield effectively his line of march from any pursuing Federals. Once his forces got to Harrisburg, they could turn around to face the approaching Union forces at a place of their choosing. Jackson's absence caused him to juggle his command structure slightly, but other than that, the Army of Northern Virginia was in its best condition of the war.[12]

On June 23 seventy thousand Confederate troops crossed the Potomac River and moved quickly north through the town of Sharpsburg, where Lee's veterans had fought only a few months earlier. Everything went according to plan. By June 25 lead elements of Ewell's corps had reached the bridges across the Susquehanna at Harrisburg and slid south along the river to Wrightsville. Following Lee's explicit orders, Ewell's troops did not attempt to cross the river. Ewell set up his headquarters in Carlisle and awaited further orders from Lee. The other two corps of the Confederate army were strung out in a series of long columns that stretched back to Chambersburg, where Lee had set up his headquarters. The stage was set for the battle Lee so desperately wanted.

The plan that Lee had finalized just a few days earlier was for the Confederate army to regroup in the vicinity of the town of Gettysburg. Just south of that town were some hills and ridges that seemed to offer the Confederates an excellent defensive position to meet the Union army as it marched north to meet the invaders. On June 28—the same day that Ewell's troops reached the bridge over the Susquehanna at Harrisburg—Lee learned that Joe Hooker had been replaced by George Meade. More alarming than the challenge of a new opponent was the news that the Union army was rapidly moving north on a course that would soon bring it exactly where Lee's men were heading, Gettysburg. Lee sent out orders to gather the Confederate forces at Gettysburg. Events did not go exactly as planned: On the afternoon of June 30 the lead units of Confederate infantry approaching the town encountered Union cavalry commanded by John Buford. Throughout the rest of the afternoon, troops from both sides poured into the countryside around the town. By midafternoon, when Lee arrived on the scene, the Union troops were falling back to a site known as Cemetery Hill, just south of town. Lee had hoped to occupy this position *before* the Union troops arrived, and he sent General Isaac Trimble with orders for General Ewell to "take the high ground south of the town." Unfortunately for the Confederates, Winfield Scott Hancock, the

Union general in command on the scene, had also recognized the significance of these hills and moved troops and artillery into position to defend them. Efforts to dislodge the Federal troops from Cemetery Hill were unsuccessful.

Lee's plan was in danger of falling apart. However, Trimble, who had stayed with Ewell during the unsuccessful attacks on Cemetery Hill, learned that Culp's Hill, just to the east of Cemetery Hill, had been left unguarded by the Federals. When Ewell refused to order any troops to occupy the two hills on the ground that he was supposed to "avoid a general engagement," Trimble took matters into his own hands. Storming out of Ewell's headquarters, he came across a brigade of North Carolinians waiting for orders. Informing the officer in command that he had direct orders from General Lee, Trimble convinced the brigade commander to move his men onto the hill. Trimble thereupon galloped back to Lee's headquarters with the news that although Cemetery Hill was still in Federal hands, Culp's Hill had been secured for the moment. Realizing the importance of Trimble's actions, Lee immediately sent orders to reinforce the troops on Culp's Hill "at once." By midnight additional troops from Early's and from Johnston's corps, together with some of Johnston's artillery, had occupied Culp's Hill.[13]

Lee was annoyed that Ewell had not prevented the Union soldiers from digging in on Cemetery Ridge, but thanks to Trimble's initiative in occupying Culp's Hill, it was the Yankees—particularly O. O. Howard's XI Corps—who were in the most precarious situation. Map 3.1 shows the disposition of troops at the end of the first day of fighting. While the Confederates were digging in on Culp's Hill [1], Howard's men from the Union corps were digging in on Cemetery Hill [2]. The Confederate position curved around behind the Union right flank, so that the entire right wing of the Union army was exposed to a potential attack from two sides. Meade quickly realized the precarious position of Howard's corps. The problem for the Union army was how to effect the withdrawal of troops from Cemetery Hill without exposing the entire army to an attack by the Confederates from Culp's

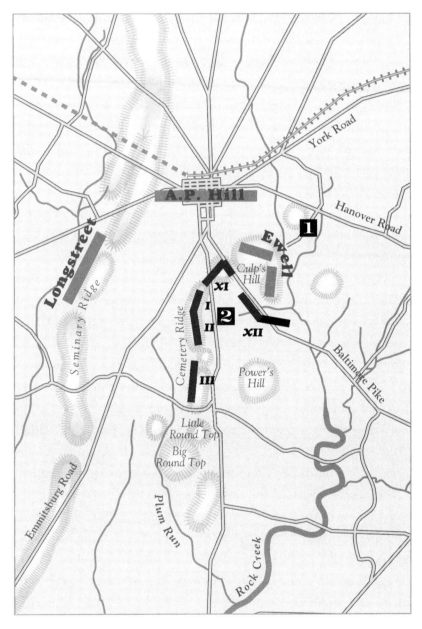

MAP 3.1
THE COUNTERFACTUAL BATTLE OF GETTYSBURG,
DAY 1

Hill. Meade decided that H. W. Slocum's XII Corps would make a "strong demonstration" to convince the Rebels that the Federals were trying to take Culp's Hill early the following morning. The task of protecting the right flank of the Union army from a possible Confederate attack fell to Daniel Sickles's III Corps. Sickles was ordered to occupy the Round Tops as an anchor for the retreating Union army.

A few miles away Lee pondered his options. The day had gone rather well. The Confederates were in a strong position vis-à-vis the Union right wing, and reports from scouts indicated that Sickles had not yet secured the Union left. Lee determined to attack the Union forces on Cemetery Hill before they could be withdrawn. He therefore ordered both Ewell and A. P. Hill to concentrate as many troops as possible in an assault against the exposed right flank of the Federal army. At the same time, Lee planned to cut off the Federal line of retreat by sending Longstreet's corps on a wide flanking movement around the south end of the Union line.

As the sun rose on July 2, the Confederate attacks swept over Cemetery Hill and threw the retreating Union troops into total confusion. Map 3.2 depicts the fighting on the second day of the battle. Two Union corps—Howard's XI and Abner Doubleday's I—were enveloped so quickly that most of the troops either fled the field or surrendered [1]. By ten o'clock the charging Confederates had driven the Union forces back roughly a mile [2]. Here the Rebel advance was stalled by a combination of factors. The three corps in the center of the Union line— Sykes's V, Slocum's XII, and Hancock's II—rallied to form a line along Rock Creek, and Henry Hunt, the Union artillery commander, managed to get enough guns on Power's Hill to deliver a devastating barrage of artillery on the advancing Confederates. Moreover, there was growing confusion behind the Confederate lines created by the speed of the advance and the need to deal with the sudden collapse of Howard's and Doubleday's corps. In early afternoon the Confederate troops paused to catch their breath and re-form their ranks. At this moment John Sedgwick's VI Corps arrived along the Baltimore Pike

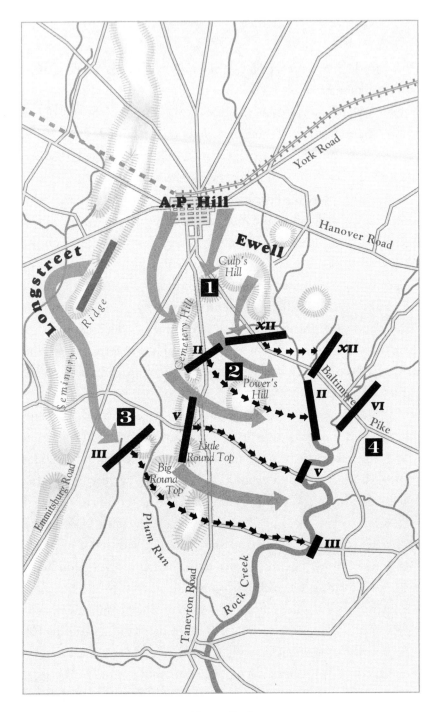

MAP 3.2
THE COUNTERFACTUAL BATTLE OF GETTYSBURG,
DAY 2

with reinforcements for the beleaguered Union troops. Sedgwick's presence bought precious moments for hard-pressed men who had initially met the Confederate onslaught to make a more orderly withdrawal.

While all this was going on, Hood's and McLaw's divisions reached the Emmitsburg Road in their effort to sweep around the left flank of the Union army. For reasons that have never been fully explained, the Union III Corps under Sickles, which was supposed to be dug in along Cemetery Ridge as far as the Round Tops, had been stationed out near the Emmitsburg Road. These troops were half to three-quarters of a mile west of the rest of the Union army stationed along Cemetery Ridge. When McLaw's Confederates encountered Sickles's men around one o'clock in the afternoon, they were unsure what to do. Their orders were to not engage the enemy. After a brief conference with Longstreet, the decision was made to attack the exposed Federal position [3]. The attack was successful, and Sickles's troops were driven back toward Cemetery Ridge and the Round Tops.[14] However, this decision to attack Sickles ultimately disrupted Lee's plan to have Longstreet's men in the rear of the Union army by the late afternoon. Longstreet now decided to push forward with the attack on the Union position, hoping to take the high ground on Little Round Top. However, Union General Gouverneur Warren also recognized the danger if the Confederates gained the high ground, and he rushed two brigades from Sykes's corps to reinforce the position on Little Round Top. The crisis for the Union came late in the afternoon. While two brigades of Union troops desperately clung to Little Round Top, the remainder of Sykes's and Hancock's corps completed their move to the east side of Rock Creek to set up a line that would allow the Army of the Potomac to retreat down the Baltimore Pike toward Littlestown [4].[15]

By the end of the second day of fighting it was clear that Lee had gained an enormous victory. The Army of Northern Virginia had once again routed the Army of the Potomac, this time on Northern soil. To put it simply, the Union army was in headlong retreat, leaving the Confederates in command of the battlefield south of Gettysburg. Of the seven corps that constituted Meade's command on the morning of July 2, one—Howard's XI—had simply ceased to exist, and three others—Doubleday's I, Hancock's II, and Sickles's III—were so badly mauled that they were in no shape for fighting the next day. The rest of the army was streaming down the Baltimore Pike as quickly as it could. In their efforts to escape, the troops left behind food, guns, ammunition, and wagons that eventually fell into the hands of the pursuing Confederates. Retreating units clogged the principal route of escape, adding to the confusion. However, the Confederates also experienced logistical problems. In addition to congested roads, the supplies left behind by Union soldiers hindered Confederate efforts to quickly pursue their foe. Stores of food and clothing proved too alluring for the Rebel troops to pass up. Consequently, despite the efforts of Lee and his officers to maintain order, the Confederate pursuit had temporarily ground to a halt by early evening of July 2. Throughout the evening and night Union troops continued to push doggedly on toward Littlestown, where Meade hoped to establish a new defensive position and await Lee's next move.[16]

Lee was unhappy that a large segment of the Union army escaped from the Gettysburg battlefield. Map 3.3 shows the disposition of troops on the morning of July 3. Meade's troops were still arriving in the area around Littlestown [1]. Recognizing the disorganized state of his own army after the melee on the second day, Lee finally allowed his exhausted troops to rest and consolidate their gains. But not for long; Lee was anxious to ensure that the beaten Federal army did not turn west in its retreat and place itself between his army and the routes back to Virginia. He therefore ordered George Pickett's division, which had not seen action on July 2, together with Stuart's cavalry, to move quickly to occupy Taneytown. They were then to move toward the Union supply depot at Westminster, Maryland. Additional units from Longstreet's and Hill's corps would then move down the Taneytown road to reinforce the Confederate position. With the Union forces in disarray, Stuart's and Pickett's men occupied Taneytown after a brief,

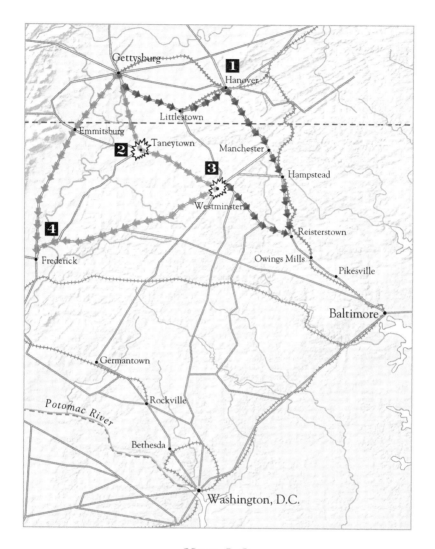

MAP 3.3
THE COUNTERFACTUAL BATTLE OF GETTYSBURG,
THE RETREAT

albeit fierce, fight. The Union garrison at Westminster put up a more spirited fight, but they were also no match for the Confederates, who occupied that town as well, seizing a huge store of arms and ammunition left by the retreating Union troops [3].

Despite the extent of his victory, Lee faced serious problems in deciding what to do next. As was the case with every major battle of the Civil War, the fighting took almost as heavy a toll on the victors as it did on those defeated. As the reports of casualties came in, Lee began to realize just how costly his triumph had been. The Confederates lost almost twenty thousand men killed, missing, or wounded. The Union army had taken an even worse beating; counting the twelve thousand Yankees taken prisoner, the losses totaled well over thirty thousand men, and many of the surviving units were in no condition to fight. Several of Lee's generals were eager to pursue the retreating Union forces. But this was more easily said than done, and it was not clear what would be gained from such a move. As he pursued his defeated foe farther east, Lee would be moving his army into hostile territory that was more populous. Even in their disorganized state, Union forces could make Confederate efforts to attack a city the size of Baltimore or Washington, D.C., costly in terms of further casualties. The Army of Northern Virginia had delivered a stunning blow to the Army of the Potomac, one so serious that it would take the U.S. military many months to recover—if, indeed it could ever completely recover from the trauma of such a devastating defeat. Lee's decision therefore was to have Stuart's cavalry discourage any further offensive actions on the part of the Federals while the Army of Northern Virginia retired south to Frederick, Maryland [4]. There Lee could refurbish his army, inquire about the condition of Stonewall Jackson, and hope that the North would soon come to its senses and accept the reality of Southern independence.

Gettysburg was clearly the turning point of the war. Morale in the North plummeted to new lows. Antiwar Democrats in Congress denounced the conduct of the war and asked how much longer the Lincoln administration intended to pursue this ruinous conflict. When Lincoln responded by calling for more troops, riots against the draft broke out in cities and towns across the North. In New York City disturbances continued for almost a week before three regiments that had fought at Gettysburg arrived to assist civil authorities in restoring order.

Across the Atlantic the news of Lee's victory spurred new efforts on the part of pro-Southern factions in Britain and France to have those countries recognize the Confederate States of America.

No one recognized the significance of Lee's victory more than Abraham Lincoln. These were, the president observed at a cabinet meeting shortly after the battle, "the darkest days of the United States Republic since Washington's army struggled to survive at Valley Forge." One of the most pressing problems facing the president was who should take command of the defeated Northern army. Winfield Scott Hancock, one of the few heroes of the battle, was a likely candidate, but he had been seriously wounded rallying his forces during the retreat. If Lincoln were to go outside the Army of the Potomac, his first choice would have been Ulysses Grant. But Grant was still fighting to take Vicksburg, and if he could gain a major victory, it would be the one small ray of hope in an otherwise depressing summer. Moreover, Lincoln might need Grant to deal with the deteriorating situation in Tennessee.

So Grant stayed at Vicksburg. Eventually Lincoln and his secretary of war, Edwin Stanton, swallowed their pride and offered command of the shattered Army of the Potomac to the one man they hoped might be able to revitalize it. On July 23, to the cheers of his men, George McClellan again took command of the army he had led twice before. Neither Lincoln nor McClellan had any illusions that the partnership would last very long. McClellan had not hidden either his disdain for the president's mishandling of the war or his own political ambition to take Lincoln's place in the White House. That was a risk that Lincoln was willing to take. McClellan's greatest skill was organization, and he was still popular among the rank and file troops. Lincoln needed an army to save the country, and McClellan needed a victory to save his political career. It was an uneasy marriage, to say the least, but it might work in the short run.

Lincoln hoped that the short run might be long enough. There was, after all, the possibility that when Grant was finished at Vicksburg, he could come east and take command of the newly refurbished Army of the Potomac.

Three years into the rebellion the military situation was hardly encouraging for the Union. Map 3.4 summarizes the situation. In the Eastern theater of operations, not only had the Army of Northern Virginia successfully protected the Confederacy's capital, but Lee's army had demonstrated at Gettysburg that the Union forces were helpless to prevent forays into their territory by the Rebels. Lee did finally break camp and return to Virginia, but not before the Army of Northern Virginia had enjoyed the fruits of Northern cuisine for the better part of three months [1]. How soon the Army of the Potomac would be ready to challenge Lee again was unclear. Reviewing the requests for men and equipment that flowed into his office in the aftermath of Gettysburg, Lincoln ruefully commented: "Now that we have supplied the rebels with enough provisions for the coming year, we must turn our attention to supplying our own armies." In the West the war was going somewhat better for the Union. Vicksburg was now in Northern hands, and there was some hope that in the spring of 1864 Grant would quickly defeat Joe Johnston's Confederate forces and finally secure the Mississippi Valley for the Union [2]. In Tennessee, Thomas's troops clung to their tenuous position at Chattanooga. However, it was not at all clear how long his army could stay in the city if he did not receive some help [3].

Against all odds, the South had managed to produce a stalemate by the end of 1863. The only question was whether or not it could hang on long enough to influence the elections in November of 1864.

1864: THE YEAR OF DECISION

The spring of 1864 started well enough for the Union. With his usual energy, Grant moved on the city of Jackson, Mississippi, in early March. With his usual temerity, J. E. Johnston abandoned the city after only token resistance. Exasperated, President Davis relieved Johnston

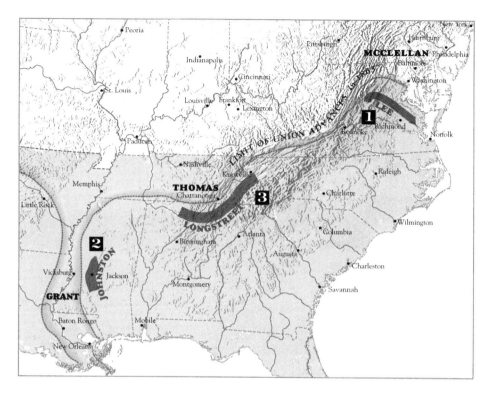

MAP 3.4
COUNTERFACTUAL SITUATION AT THE END
OF 1863

of his command and put in his place the more aggressive John B. Hood, who promptly took the offensive and decided to goad Grant into an attack by placing his forces at Champion's Hill, between the Union army at Jackson and his base at Vicksburg. The tactic backfired terribly when Grant attacked Hood's army on April 6 and drove it back toward Sherman's corps advancing from the West. Caught in a vise between the two Union forces, Hood's army barely escaped total disaster. The Battle of Champion's Hill effectively eliminated the Confederate Army of Mississippi as an effective fighting force. The only Rebel forces remaining in the region were cavalry units commanded by Van Dorn and Sterling Price. With little hope of inflicting substantive damage to Union forces in the area these units were either moved to the west side of the Mississippi River or sent to join Bedford Forrest in harassing the Union supply lines in Tennessee.

With the Mississippi secured for the Union, attention shifted to the plight of Thomas's troops in eastern Tennessee. Here the situation facing the Union was not as good. The Confederates held the high ground south of the city, severely limiting the ability of the Federal army to supply its troops in Chattanooga. In early January Thomas received reports that Longstreet was about to be reinforced by troops from Lee's army. Thomas knew that in their weakened condition, his troops were in no position to challenge a Rebel attack if they chose to force the issue, and rather than risk being surrounded by the Confederates, he abandoned the city and withdrew to Murfreesboro at the end of January. The loss of Chattanooga was one more blow to the Union's already sagging morale and one more hurdle to overcome before a serious challenge could be mounted against the center of the Confederacy in Georgia later in the year. Grant was furious over Thomas's decision to retreat, but he conceded that he was too busy with his own problems to offer much help.

In the East, George McClellan was doing what he did best, restoring the morale of the Army of the Potomac and worrying that he did not have enough men to launch an offensive against a foe that greatly outnumbered him. It was not until mid-May that McClellan finally announced that he was ready to begin what he termed "the campaign that will finally end this war." Map 3.5 shows the situation in the East at the time. The Army of the Potomac was camped outside Washington, while Lee had stationed his army between Warrenton and Culpeper, patiently waiting for McClellan's first move. McClellan's plan was simple: He proposed to move south along the west bank of the Potomac River toward the city of Falmouth, a few miles northwest of Fredericksburg. If all went according to plan, the Union army would cross the Rappahannock at Falmouth and move on Richmond.

Lee was determined to see that everything did not go according to

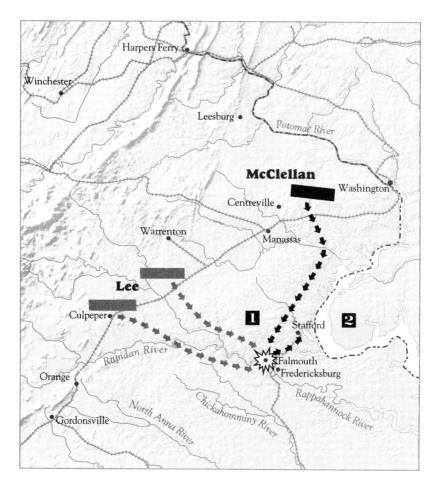

MAP 3.5
MCCLELLAN'S COUNTERFACTUAL OFFENSIVE,
JULY 1864

plan. Once it became clear where McClellan planned to strike, Lee put his own army in motion. He ordered Hill and Ewell, stationed near Culpeper, to move as quickly as possible along the south bank of the Rappahannock toward Fredericksburg, with orders to delay any attempt by the Federals to cross at that point. His third corps, Jackson's, he ordered to move more slowly and to keep north of the Rappahannock. Stuart was ordered to provide a screen to mask Jackson's movement from the Federals. Thanks to McClellan's well-known propensity to move cautiously, the Army of Northern Virginia was able to position itself on the south bank of the river before the Union forces arrived on June 5 just west of Falmouth. Lee did not attack the Union forces until roughly a third of the army had crossed over to the south bank on the afternoon of the sixth. At that point the Confederates struck at the exposed flank of the Union troops that had crossed the river [1]. The Union troops held their ground and were on the verge of forcing the Rebels to give way and allow the Army of the Potomac to establish a position on the south bank of the Rappahannock when the rest of Lee's army struck the Union forces on the other side of the river. Only a determined stand by Hancock's II Corps prevented the Union army from total collapse. As it was, McClellan's army suffered heavy casualties, and the Rebels took five thousand prisoners on the south side of the river. The remainder of the Federal forces retreated to Stafford, where support from Union gunships stationed in the Potomac offered them a sanctuary from further attack [2].

The Battle of Falmouth was a stunning Confederate victory, but it was obtained at the price of more than eight thousand casualties. Lee knew that the Confederacy could not afford many more "victories" that were this costly. For the time being McClellan was content to lick his wounds at Stafford. But Lee feared that when they got reorganized, the Federals would resume the offensive. Next time he might not be as fortunate; he needed to plan something dramatic that would finally force the Northern government to throw in the towel.

For the moment Lee did not need to do anything at all. Shortly after the battle at Falmouth, McClellan traveled to Washington to demand reinforcements. It soon became clear to Lincoln and his advisers that political considerations, as much as the military situation in Virginia, were responsible for McClellan's lack of aggressiveness in resuming the fight against Lee. The defeat at Falmouth had raised the outcry against the war to where it was obvious to the most casual observer of the political scene in the United States that Lincoln's government might not survive the presidential election in November. Members of his own cabinet—notably Secretary of the Treasury Salmon Chase—were sending out feelers that they would be willing to replace Lincoln on the November ticket. At the Republican National Convention, which convened in Baltimore two weeks after the Battle of Falmouth, angry radicals called for a change in leadership of the government and a greater voice in conduct of the war. Though Lincoln's nomination prevailed on the first ballot, the acrimonious debates at the convention revealed deep divisions in the party, divisions that would be exacerbated if there were further setbacks on the battlefield.

One of the fiercest targets of the Republican ire was McClellan, a Democratic general who many radicals believed had presidential ambitions of his own. Lincoln did not disagree with this assessment, but he hoped to put off McClellan's resignation long enough to appoint his one successful general, Ulysses S. Grant, the new commander in chief of the Union armies. Grant was currently in the midst of a campaign to recapture Chattanooga from the Confederates. He had succeeded in driving Longstreet's men out of the city, but the Rebels now held the high ground south of the city and were effectively blocking Grant's efforts to open a pathway into central Georgia. The first two attacks on the Confederate position were repulsed with heavy casualties. Finally, after receiving reinforcements from McClellan's idle army in Virginia, Grant's troops succeeded in breaching the Confederate line and forcing Longstreet's army to fall back toward Dalton, Georgia. On July 26 Grant wired Lincoln: "Chattanooga is now securely in our hands. Making plans to move on Atlanta." Lincoln wired back: "Excellent news. Congratulations on a brilliant victory. I have a new job for you. Please report to me at once." Three days earlier McClellan had tendered his resignation to Lincoln, who accepted it without comment. On July 27 U. S. Grant was offered command of all Union forces, and Winfield Scott Hancock was appointed to replace McClellan as commander of the Army of the Potomac. Grant and Hancock would make one last effort to win the war in Virginia.

Grant would have preferred to draw up his own plan for the invasion, but time was running short for the Union high command. Sherman was stalled well north of Atlanta, and the election was only three months away. There seemed little prospect that Atlanta would fall soon. Grant and Lincoln decided to gamble everything on one final roll of the dice. The Army of the Potomac would push into Virginia, destroy Lee's army, and capture Richmond before the November election. Both men knew that the continuation of the Lincoln administration—and of the nation itself—depended on the success of the Army of the Potomac. If Grant failed, the election would be lost, and a new government would almost surely sue for peace from the Confederates.

Pressed for time, Grant had to work with what McClellan had left him. Together with Chief of Staff Halleck and Secretary of War Stanton, Grant gathered all available soldiers in the Eastern theater and sent them to the army camped at Stafford. He ordered Sherman to return Hooker's corps to the Army of the Potomac, which by the end of August had swelled to 130,000 men and was ready to move south (see Map 3.6.) Past experience had shown that Fredericksburg was not a good spot to attempt a forced crossing of the Rappahannock, so Grant moved his massive army westward, looking for an opportunity to cross into Virginia. Lee vigilantly moved along a parallel path on the south bank of the river. The first clash came at United States Ford, just north of the Chancellorsville battleground. Here Grant ordered Hancock and Warren to try to establish a bridgehead on the other side [1]. The Confederates were ready to resist, and the result was a great deal of blood in the river, but after two days of hard fighting Union troops held only a small bridgehead on the south bank. Leaving two corps to continue the attempt to expand the bridgehead at United States Ford, Grant ordered the rest of his forces to press on toward Kelly's Ford, where another attempt was made to cross the Rappahannock. Once again, Lee's men were prepared, and the Federals had little success in establishing a bridgehead on the south side [2].

Well before Grant began his offensive, Lee realized that the Army

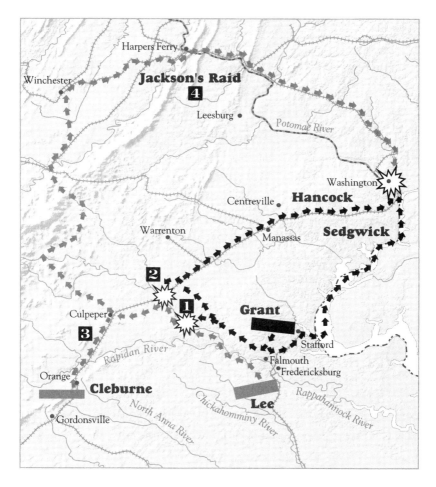

MAP 3.6
GRANT'S COUNTERFACTUAL OFFENSIVE AND
JACKSON'S RAID, AUGUST 1864

of Northern Virginia could not hold a line along the Rappahannock if
Grant chose to continue to probe at every bridge or crossing. Eventually Lee's troops would have to fall back toward the Rapidan River and
perhaps as far as the North Anna River. The problem facing the Confederates was simple: They could delay Grant, but could they delay
him long enough to affect the outcome of the election by contesting
every crossing? Lee decided his outnumbered army would be over-

whelmed if he simply tried to slug it out with Grant's troops. He therefore decided on a plan that would divert some of Grant's men and
create confusion among the Northern populace. Conferring with Jefferson Davis on August 26, Lee decided that Longstreet should send
Patrick Cleburne's division from Tennessee to the Eastern theater. Cleburne was to join Stonewall Jackson's division at Culpeper, Virginia
[3]. The combined force, totaling around twenty-five thousand infantry and five thousand cavalry, would then march north through the
Shenandoah Valley and turn east toward Washington [4]. While Jackson roamed through Maryland toward Washington, Lee would pull his
forces back from the Rappahannock and dig in along the Rapidan. If
Jackson were successful, Grant would be forced to respond by releasing
forces to protect the capital of the United States, and Lee was prepared
to gamble that his forces would be able to fend off what remained of
Grant's army [4].

Seldom has a plan so daring proved to be so spectacularly successful. Leaving Culpeper on September 3, Jackson's army, augmented
by Cleburne's men, marched north to Winchester, Virginia, and on
September 10 reached the outskirts of Harpers Ferry. From there the
Confederates turned east toward Frederick, Maryland, where they
encountered the first serious resistance from a Union force of about
twelve thousand hurriedly gathered together by General Lew Wallace.
A few of Wallace's men were veterans who had been rushed up from
Grant's army, but most had never seen action in battle. They were
hardly a match for Stonewall's veterans, who quickly sent them scur-
rying back to Washington. With no remaining enemy troops to block
his path, Jackson moved toward Washington, cutting telegraph lines
and spreading panic as he advanced. On September 19 Wade Hampton's cavalry reached Fort Stevens, on the outskirts of Washington.
The following day the remainder of Jackson's army arrived on the
scene.[17]

As Jackson's exhausted troops rested at the northern edge of the
capital, the lead units of Sedgwick's VI Corps were unloading from

ships in the southern part of the city and were greeted by President
Lincoln, who had refused the entreaties of his cabinet to leave the city.
When news that Union reinforcements were arriving in the city got
back to Jackson, he faced the decision of whether or not he should
actually try to occupy the Union capital. Lee had made it clear that
this operation was a "demonstration" designed to draw troops away
from Grant's forces in Richmond. The reports that several corps of
Union troops were arriving in the city confirmed that the raid was
clearly having the desired effect on Grant. If they simply stayed on the
outskirts of the city for another day or so, Jackson's troops could draw
additional units away from Grant. Stonewall decided to stand pat. The
strategy proved effective; over the next three days, a total of three
Union corps were detached from Grant's army on the Rappahannock
and sent north to relieve the threat to the capital. By the evening of
the twenty-second the Federal force in Washington had grown to
more than thirty thousand men under Hancock's command. Stonewall
decided it was time to pull back. Having accomplished his primary
objective, he fired several volleys of artillery fire in the direction of the
center of the city. On the morning of the September 23 the Confederate army began its withdrawal into Virginia. A week later Jackson
crossed the Potomac and set up camp in Leesburg, Virginia.

Jackson's raid caused a huge sensation in the Northern press. The
New York Times proclaimed: CONFEDERATE GUNS SHELL NATION'S CAPI-
TAL. Dailies in other cities amplified rumors that several shells had hit
the White House; some went so far as to report that President Lincoln
and several cabinet members had been seriously wounded or perhaps
even killed. (A shell had hit the White House, but neither Lincoln nor
his cabinet was there at the time.) Southern newspapers were jubilant,
declaring: STONEWALL SACKS WASHINGTON! Editorials throughout the
South exulted: YANKEE GOVERNMENT FLEES CAPITAL! For the next week
newspapers on both sides of the Potomac followed the unsuccessful
attempts of the Union army to bring Jackson to bay as he retreated to
Virginia. When the news of Jackson's "sack" of Washington reached

Great Britain, Foreign Secretary John Russell drew up a draft resolution calling for an end to hostilities and offering British assistance in mediating a peace between the warring parties. On October 20 Prime Minister Palmerston met with his advisers and suggested that while Russell's idea had merit, Her Majesty's government should wait until after the upcoming election before making such overtures.

For Grant and Lincoln, the success of Jackson's raid was a stunning setback to their summer offensive. Apart from the propaganda value of the raid, Grant now found his army split in two, and he was confronted with a serious threat from the rear should Jackson capture the rail connection that headed south out of Manassas. Despite pleas from Lincoln that he resume his offensive now that Jackson was back in Virginia, Grant felt compelled to pull the right flank of his army east toward Fredericksburg so that he would not be dependent on the rail route to Manassas for supplies. No amount of explaining that this action was a strategically sound move could convince those opposing the war that this was not yet another defeat. Map 3.7 shows the positions of armies at the time of the November election.

It now seemed obvious to everyone that the stalemate in the East could be broken only at an enormous cost of lives. Neither side was anxious to initiate another bloodbath. Civil unrest protesting the continuation of the war swept through the North. Slogans that would have been regarded as treasonous two years earlier were now greeted with cheers. Clement Vallandigham, the Copperhead leader who had been exiled from the United States by the Lincoln administration the previous year for treasonous remarks, was now welcomed back and regarded by many antiwar Democrats as a serious presidential candidate. At the end of August the Democratic Party had gathered in Chicago to select its candidate to run against Lincoln. George McClellan, who had resigned from the Union army after Falmouth, was the early favorite. But the defeat of "little Mac" at Falmouth had considerably diminished his popular appeal, and although he had strong support on the early ballots, it soon became clear that the general would

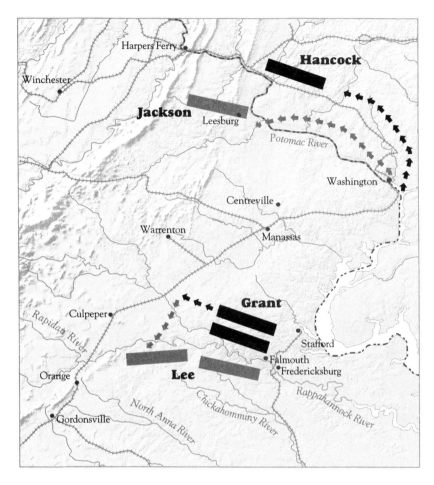

MAP 3.7
THE COUNTERFACTUAL STALEMATE IN THE EAST,
NOVEMBER 1864

not be able to garner the votes necessary for the nomination. Two other candidates vied for the position: Vallandigham and Horatio Seymour, the governor of New York. On the tenth ballot Vallandigham threw his support to Seymour, and the New Yorker went on to become the Democratic nominee. A bitter fight then developed between McClellan and Vallandigham for the vice presidential candidate. Anxious to avoid a split between the two factions, Seymour prevailed upon the leaders in both camps to accept Congressman George Pendleton as a compromise choice on the ticket. Already in serious trouble because of the military setbacks, the Republican cause was further damaged when a band of disaffected Republicans announced their support for John C. Frémont, who had been the party's candidate in the 1856 election. Frémont had no chance to win the election, but every vote he received reduced Lincoln's total.

On November 8, 1864, Americans went to the polls and elected Horatio Seymour to be the seventeenth president of the United States.[18] The new president-elect asked for a meeting with Abraham Lincoln. The two men met on November 23, and Seymour pressed Lincoln to join him in requesting a cease-fire from Confederate President Davis. Lincoln asked Seymour to give him a few days to consult further with his cabinet. The next evening Lord Richard Lyons, the British ambassador to the United States, called on the president with a note saying that in the event of a Democratic victory in the presidential election, he had been instructed to tell Lincoln that Her Majesty's government was now prepared to recognize the Confederate States of America. On November 25 Lincoln met with the cabinet to discuss Seymour's request and the British note. The mood was tense, but the outcome was inevitable. That evening Lincoln summoned Seymour to the White House and told him that he was prepared to co-operate with the president-elect in establishing a cease-fire with the Confederacy.

IF ALL this came to pass, then by the time the new president took office in March 1865 in our counterfactual world, the guns would be silent for the first time in four years. An armistice would end the fighting, but the war would not yet be over. The Confederates had managed a stalemate in the war; now they needed to forge an agreement that would ensure the peace. That, as we shall see, would be no small challenge. An even more daunting challenge would be the building of a new country.

Chapter Four

. . . .

THE KING IS DEAD, LONG LIVE THE KING: THE FUTURE OF THE SLAVE SOUTH

> *Jefferson Davis and other leaders of the South have made an army; they are making, it appears, a navy; and they have made what is more than either, they have made a nation. . . . We may anticipate with certainty the success of the Southern States so far as regards their separation from the North.*
>
> —William Gladstone (October 7, 1862)

IN THE FALL OF 1862 the British chancellor of the exchequer confidently predicted to an after-dinner audience at Newcastle that the Confederate States of America was on the brink of success in its effort to break free from the United States. William Gladstone's confidence stemmed from a string of reports reaching Britain describing the victories of the Army of Northern Virginia in the spring and summer of 1862. Now, as the leaves were just beginning to turn in the Shenandoah Valley, Lee's forces had launched their first invasion of the North, an action that promised to put the finishing touch on the Army of the Potomac. Unfortunately for the Confederate cause, the British minister's prediction of Southern success, which was shared by his colleague in the cabinet Foreign Secretary Russell, proved premature. Unbeknownst to Gladstone, Lee's invasion of the North had ended in a bloody repulse at the Battle of Antietam three weeks earlier. When news of the Confederate defeat finally reached Britain, Viscount Palmerston, the British prime minister, who only a few weeks earlier had voiced support for a proposal by his two ministers that Britain should intervene in the American conflict if Lee's invasion was a success, became very cool to the idea of intervention. "I am inclined," Palmerston wrote his ministers on October 22, "to change the opinion I wrote you when the Confederates seemed to be carrying all before them." He was now convinced that the British government "must continue to be merely lookers-on till the war shall have taken a more decided turn."[1] So the British waited. As weeks turned into months, the opportunity to act never again appeared so bright. The weeks just before Antietam turned out to be the high-water mark of Confederate hopes for cooperation from abroad.

Much has been written on the "lost" opportunity for foreign intervention in the fall of 1862. From the outset of the war Confederate strategy had counted on some form of European intervention. The leaders of the Confederacy were confident that King Cotton would force the Europeans to take some action to break the Northern blockade of Southern ports that President Lincoln announced in early 1861. Europe, they reasoned, would not be able to stand the effects from a loss of cotton shipments from the American South. To this end the Confederate government instituted an embargo on all cotton exports in the spring of 1861. The embargo succeeded in blocking cotton exports for the remainder of the year. Unfortunately for the South's plans to "starve" European textile manufacturers of raw cotton, British and French manufacturers had been stockpiling cotton in anticipation of hostilities in America, and their inventories were at record levels.

Consequently, all the Confederate embargo of cotton did was to deny planters the opportunity to ship their cotton abroad before the Northern blockade had begun to close Southern ports by spring 1862. The failure of cotton diplomacy was more than a matter of bad timing. From the beginning of the war the Rebels' policy was founded on a simplistic view of the impact that an interruption of cotton shipments would have on foreign economies. The policy was aimed primarily at Great Britain, where a disruption of cotton imports was sure to create problems for the textile industry.[2] The Confederate embargo and the Union blockade eventually did produce that outcome, but the reaction to the cotton famine was not what Southerners expected.

British policy toward the two belligerents in the American Civil War was based on several considerations. One of these influences, which the Confederates consistently overlooked, was the extent to which Britain's importation of grains from the Northern states was as important as the cotton trade. To the dismay of Southern diplomats, the British working class seemed to understand that bread was more important to their welfare than cotton. The working class also perceived that the Northern cause was the one championing liberty and the demise of slavery. The British had eliminated slavery in the British Empire in the 1830s, and antislavery sentiment was now focused on the suppression of the slave trade.

As if jobs, food, and antislavery ideology were not enough to complicate the debates over which side Her Majesty's government should support in the American war, there were also serious doubts whether Britain had the military might to carry on a war in America. With their naval and manpower resources already stretched to the limit by the requirements of the empire, British military leaders were leery of undertaking any major operations in America. Adding to these concerns was the threat of an American invasion of Canada in the event of hostilities. Palmerston's ambivalence on the question of military intervention in America mirrored a very real split in the British government. Unless the Southerners could provide strong evidence that they were actually winning the war, British intervention in the American Civil War was unlikely.[3]

If the British were unwilling to back military intervention, the other major European powers were hardly likely to do anything by themselves. This meant that unless the Confederacy could muster clear evidence of military success against the Union, armed intervention from abroad was unlikely. If Southern diplomacy could not convince the European states to intervene directly in the war, a less ambitious objective would be to get them to recognize the Confederacy as an independent nation. Such recognition would, among other things, permit the Confederate government to enter alliances and negotiate treaties with other nations dealing with everything from military affairs to commercial relations. The United States took this threat very seriously. As early as April 1861 Secretary of State Seward wrote to Charles Francis Adams, the American ambassador in London, that recognition of Southern independence by any European power would be regarded as a casus belli.[4] Seward maintained this stance throughout the war with sufficient determination that no European country was willing to risk war by recognizing the South. For all the rhetoric and diplomatic posturing that went on during the war, the British government steadfastly maintained a carefully balanced neutrality between the warring factions in America, and other European governments followed suit.[5]

A final way in which the European powers might influence the outcome of the war in America would be through offers by the great powers to mediate a settlement to end the fighting. In the fall of 1862 there was a flurry of letters and communiqués among Palmerston, Gladstone, and Russell agreeing that the best way for their government to become involved in the American war would be to offer to arrange an armistice, followed by a conference in which the British, French, and Russians would act as the mediators. However, mediation would be practical only if both parties had some incentive to accept a cease-fire long enough to talk things over. As the *Times* of London pointed out in an

1862 editorial comment, this was hardly the case in the American situation. "What hope would we have that the Federal Government would submit to a suspension of arms by sea and land for six months?" the *Times* asked its readers. Such an armistice would be "very convenient" for the South as well as for Britain and France. "But what would the North get by it?" the *Times* continued. "To her it would be a request to allow us to tie up her right arm."[6] Foreign Minister Russell, one of the staunchest supporters of intervention in the British cabinet, went a step farther when he observed that even if the United States agreed to an armistice, the British government "must be prepared to answer the question on what basis [is our government] willing to negotiate?"[7] None of the ministers could provide an effective answer to that question.

The fundamental problem facing the Confederacy in its attempt to gain recognition—and it hoped military assistance—from the European powers was its inability to convince the world that it was capable of winning its independence through an armed rebellion against the United States government. On the eve of Antietam it appeared that it might be able to do so. Lee's defeat, coupled with the astute action of Lincoln in issuing the Proclamation of Emancipation, meant that the South was never again in a position where one could reasonably expect it to force the North to accept any form of cease-fire or mediation.

The arguments of the last chapter provide a basis for asserting that the South could have created a stalemate by the end of 1864. That counterfactual outcome now becomes the basis for addressing the question of how the South could have turned the military stalemate into a situation in which it could have forged a meaningful peace treaty with the United States. To do this, we must construct the historical mold into which the counterfactual "pudding" of chapter 3 can be poured. We do have some fairly firm historical evidence upon which to base our analysis of what would have happened to the South in a world in which there were two "American" states rather than one. However great its impact on the United States and the Confederacy, the fighting in North America would have had only a very limited impact on the world at large. We shall therefore use the global situation as it actually existed in the last third of the nineteenth century as our "mold" for constructing a counterfactual future of the Confederate States of America.

WE KNOW that mediation by European powers was an option favored by Palmerston's government in Britain as well as the government of Emperor Louis Napoleon in France. Both leaders believed that the major obstacle to mediation was the North's unwillingness to accept an armistice so long as it seemingly maintained the upper hand in the fighting. Though the Southern military effort had stymied Northern efforts to conquer its territory for four long years, the Confederacy was in a precarious position. An armistice would provide both sides with a welcome break in the fighting. The war had stretched to the limit Southern resources, not to mention the South's luck on the battlefield. The Richmond government faced a situation in which every week its bargaining position vis-à-vis the North became weaker as the pressure from the Northern naval blockade continued to exacerbate the shortages of imported goods throughout the Confederacy.

By 1864 the Union navy had succeeded in curtailing the seaborne trade of the Confederacy to a tiny fraction of its prewar level. While blockade-runners had managed to get enough essential military goods through the cordon of Union ships to sustain the South's military needs, the coastal trade, which had been an important avenue of commerce before the war, had been completely eliminated. There is no reason to suppose that the Union government would lift the blockade just because an armistice was agreed to by both parties.[8] Southerners needed to seize the window of opportunity at the beginning of 1865 to negotiate a peace treaty as expeditiously as possible. They would readily accept assistance from the international community in pressuring the North to negotiate. But what could the British or French do that might encourage the North to come to a negotiating table and discuss the terms of a lasting peace? One answer might be to grant unilateral recognition of the Confederate government unless the North agreed to arbitration in resolving the dispute. This, as we have already noted, is exactly what Northerners feared. Recognition of the Confederate government by Britain, France, and Russia would enable those governments to enter alliances that would protect the fledgling nation from subsequent retaliation by its more powerful neighbor to the north. A threat of recognition of the Confederate government would put pressure on the United States to open negotiations.

Although the North had adamantly opposed any form of international recognition for the Rebel government while the fighting went on, the South had won de facto recognition by forcing the United States to accept a formal cease-fire agreement. If the United States now rejected an offer of mediation by the major powers, it ran the risk of leaving its country isolated in our counterfactual world. Moreover, the British had one final card in their hand to play if the Northern government stalled too long. Though its resources were stretched across a wide expanse, Britain was the one country that possessed the means to challenge the Union blockade. By 1865 the British navy had two vessels, the *Warrior* and the *Black Prince*, that were steam-powered ironclads mounting rifled guns. The British Admiralty had little enthusiasm for a naval war with the United States in 1865; however, by themselves the *Warrior* and the *Black Prince* could probably have caused serious problems with the U.S. naval units blockading the Southern ports.[9] A threat of British naval intervention would be a powerful enough incentive for the United States to come to the negotiating table.

Let us quickly review the counterfactual situation as it has unfolded to this point. The Confederate successes in the field would have produced a bloody stalemate in the fighting by late 1864. Abraham Lincoln would be defeated in November 1864 by the Democratic candidate, Horatio Seymour, who ran on a platform pledging to end the war. Lincoln thus becomes a lame-duck president faced with the dilemma of whether or not he should continue the war. After reviewing his options, he would decide to cooperate with the incoming president-elect and negotiate a cease-fire with the Confederacy. Sometime in the early spring of 1865 the Union and Confederate governments would have reached an agreement to attend a conference at a neutral site for the purpose of ending the American war. We shall assume that the site chosen is Toronto, Canada.

We turn now to the question of how the two sides might eventually reach agreement on a treaty that would end the war. This, it should be noted, would be no mean feat. There were many issues that must be dealt with; we shall focus on the most significant challenges confronting the negotiating teams as they arrived in Toronto.

1. RECOGNITION OF THE CONFEDERATE STATES OF AMERICA AS AN INDEPENDENT NATION BY THE UNITED STATES OF AMERICA

For the Confederates, simply getting the North to recognize secession would be enough of a victory for the Confederate negotiators to go home to an exultant populace. The remaining issues of the Toronto Conference would be primarily concerned with ensuring that the South's sovereignty could be sustained over time. For the Union, admitting that the rebellion had been a success would be a bitter pill to swallow. But they had no alternative. If they refused to recognize the South, then they would be confronted with the prospect that war would go on—with European recognition of the Confederacy. The voters of the United States had made it clear that they were weary of the war by electing a new president in November 1864. The task of the Union negotiators would be to do everything in their power to see that the terms of the peace treaty offered the Union some hope of keeping the slave republic in check.

2. TERRITORIAL CLAIMS BY THE
TWO COUNTRIES

In any war that involves a division of territory between the contesting parties there will be areas that both sides covet. In the case of the American Civil War, the most hotly contested areas would include the four slave states—Missouri, Maryland, Kentucky, and Delaware—that had not joined the Confederacy in 1861, as well as the newly formed state of West Virginia and the Western territories that had been at the center of so many antebellum crises. The founders of the Confederacy had hoped that all four border states would join the effort to secede from the Union. Maryland, Missouri, and Kentucky had been allotted representation in the Confederate Congress; however, none had accepted the offer.[10] All three states had experienced fighting in the course of the war, and each had contributed a substantial number of recruits to both sides.

Would the Confederacy succeed in getting them as part of the new nation? Several factors mitigated against such a move. First, the three states had been occupied by Union troops when our counterfactual armistice was declared in 1864. To withdraw those troops would represent a major concession from the United States at a time when it had already agreed to give away one-third of the territory it had governed before the war. Second is the fact that with the exception of Kentucky, the slaves in these states were a relatively small fraction of their populations. Moreover, despite their commitment to slave property rights, Missouri and Maryland had strong economic ties to the North; each had urban areas that were tied to the commercial network throughout the United States. Their economic and demographic patterns more closely mirrored those of the market society of the North than of the slave society of the South. Finally, geographical considerations would mandate that the United States strongly resist any efforts to push the Confederacy so far north. Letting Missouri become a Confederate state would place an enormous obstacle in the way of projected transportation routes through Kansas and Nebraska and on to the Pacific coast. Giving Maryland to the Confederacy would mean that the District of Columbia would be isolated. For their part, the Confederates had little reason to press hard for these territories, both of which would have been a source of persistent irritation with their Northern neighbor.

It might be willing to let Maryland, Missouri, and Delaware stay in the United States, but the South had powerful reasons for wanting Kentucky to be part of the Confederacy. Kentuckians, who had elected to remain "neutral" at the outset of the war, would be split on the question of where they should go in 1864. Of all the border states, Kentucky had the largest commitment to slavery, and its economy was closely tied to that of the cotton South. Moreover, its geographical position made it a vital territory for the South to incorporate within its borders. The Ohio River, which forms the northern border of Kentucky, would represent a natural barrier between the Confederacy and the United States. The importance of this natural boundary was not just for purposes of national defense. The Ohio was also a very convenient "fence" in the way of slaves seeking escape to freedom in the Northern states. Having given way on letting Missouri and Maryland stay in the Union, the Southern negotiators would hold the line and insist that Kentucky become a Confederate state.

The Southern negotiators would love to have West Virginia returned to the Confederacy. But this would be a very difficult request to get the Union, not to mention the people of West Virginia, to accept. Western Virginia was admitted to the Union in 1863 as the state of West Virginia. This action, together with the fact that West Virginia had been occupied by Federal troops since late 1861, would make it very hard for the Confederates to pry it away from the Union.

In 1860 more than one-third the territory of the United States consisted of unsettled land between the tier of states along the west bank of the Mississippi River and the states along the Pacific coast. What would come of this land as a result of the breakup of the Union? Here we have very little on which to base our counterfactual conjecture.

The most likely result would be that the Confederacy would show little interest in acquiring part of what was referred to as the great American desert. The Confederates would insist on the Indian Territory north of Texas that borders the Red River, an area that was a potential farming area for both cotton and cattle. They would also covet Arizona and New Mexico. We shall assume that in return for the Confederates' dropping all claims for any other Western territories belonging to the United States in 1860, the Union would acquiesce in an arrangement whereby all three of these territories would be ceded to the Confederacy.

Another territorial issue to be worked out would involve river traffic on the Ohio and Mississippi rivers. At a time when water transportation was still the primary means of conveying goods over long distances, these rivers were essential transportation routes for the upper South and the lower Midwest. A few years earlier the possibility that a foreign power might control the mouth of the Mississippi at New Orleans would have been unthinkable to people in the Old Northwest. However, by 1860 the opening of the Erie Canal and the rapid construction of other internal waterways had greatly reduced the West's dependence on access to the ocean through New Orleans. Rail construction in the 1850s further cemented the availability of land routes to the East Coast. Despite these improvements in the transportation network, the Mississippi River was still an important avenue of commerce, and the United States would insist on guarantees that traffic from the United States could still travel to the Gulf of Mexico. A protocol for policing the river traffic would be worked out.[11]

The situation we have just described would mean that geographical boundaries of the two North American nations after the Treaty of Toronto would look like Map 4.1. One can imagine that the Confederacy might convince the Union to cede the desert areas of New Mexico and Arizona to the South, but the United States would retain the southern part of California, with its access to the Pacific Ocean.

MAP 4.1

TERRITORIAL SETTLEMENTS OF THE PEACE OF TORONTO, 1865

THE UNITED STATES OF AMERICA

THE CONFEDERATE STATES OF AMERICA

Seattle
Portland
Sacramento
San Francisco
Los Angeles
Salt Lake City
Denver
Phoenix
Tucson
Albuquerque
Minneapolis
Omaha
Des Moines
Kansas City
Jefferson City
St. Louis
Milwaukee
Chicago
Indianapolis
Detroit
Cleveland
Cincinnati
Louisville
Buffalo
Albany
Boston
New York
Philadelphia
Baltimore
Pittsburgh
Washington
Richmond
Norfolk
Raleigh
Charlotte
Wilmington
Columbia
Charleston
Savannah
Jacksonville
St. Petersburg
Miami
Tallahassee
Mobile
Montgomery
Birmingham
Atlanta
Macon
Chattanooga
Knoxville
Nashville
Memphis
Jackson
Little Rock
Baton Rouge
New Orleans
Houston
Galveston
San Antonio
Abilene
Dallas

3. WHAT TO DO WITH SLAVE PROPERTY?

Next to the issue of boundaries, the thorniest problem facing the negotiators would be to determine what should be done about maintaining
slave property rights. The most pressing problem would be what to do
with slaves who had left their masters for the safety of the Union lines
during the war. From the outset of the fighting, slaves were eager to
take advantage of the advance of Union troops into Confederate territory. The number of slaves who would have become contraband—
enemy property that had been "seized" during the rebellion—in our
counterfactual war is difficult to estimate. As we noted in chapter 3,
Union troops occupied significant areas along the western rivers of the
Confederacy over the course of the war. (See Map 3.7.) A crucial question is whether or not slaves in these areas would have fled north prior
to the armistice in the hope that they might gain their freedom. If substantial numbers did flee Confederate control, the issue of runaway
slaves would be a central point of discussion in Toronto.

Would these slaves be returned to their masters at the end of hostilities? The answer is not obvious. There would be little sentiment in
Northerners for them to stay in the North. They would be homeless
refugees in a society with widespread racial prejudice. Already burdened with the task of taking care of men who had been crippled during the war, white Americans would surely balk at the added costs of
caring for homeless black freedmen and their families. On the other
hand, a substantial number of the escaped slaves would have enlisted
in the Union army and fought against the Rebels. Turning these men
back to their Confederate owners would be seen as an unconscionable
betrayal of trust. To complicate matters further, many refugees had
left family members behind in the Confederacy in the hope that the
Union would eventually free them at the end of the war. At the very
least, it is likely that the Confederate government would demand some
compensation for the loss of property represented by slaves who fled
north during the war.

This would present a dilemma for the United States. For all the furor over the Emancipation Proclamation, it is often forgotten that the slavery was not abolished in the United States until after the Civil War. In our counterfactual world, it is even less likely that the Union would have managed to complete the work of emancipation begun by Lincoln.[12] Slavery would therefore still be legal in the United States after the war, and under federal law slaves were still property, not people. The fugitive slave laws that had been passed in the 1850s would still be applicable for slave property owned by Union slaveholders. Confederate slaveholders might easily make a case that they should be compensated for their losses through the actions of the Union army. While Union negotiators would surely resist agreeing to such compensatory payments, they would be careful not to press too hard on that point. At the very least, the United States would have to agree to recognize the property rights of Confederate slaveowners who sought the return of slaves who had run away *after* the armistice. This means that the fugitive slave laws that were an object of so much resistance before the war would now be applied to any slave entering the United States from the Confederacy without the consent of his or her master. This would not be a popular decision in the North, and it is likely that the return of runaway slaves would be a persistent irritant between the two countries. The greatest hope for resolution of this problem would be the elimination of slavery in the two countries. That, as we note below, was not beyond the realm of possibilities. In the meantime, the issue of contraband slaves would continue to be a source of constant irritation between the two countries.

The final aspect of the slave question would involve the future of slaves whose owners had stayed within the Union throughout the war. There would still be slaves residing in Missouri, Maryland, and Delaware. Although emancipation was not yet enacted in the United States, the handwriting was clearly on the wall. In fact, having a slave society in the South might considerably expedite emancipation in the North. Most slaveholders in the border states would have Southern sympathies. Moving to the Confederacy before the United States took any action to abolish slavery would be a wise move for these people. The Confederacy might welcome the refugees and their chattel labor after the loss of life during the war.[13]

There would be a host of smaller issues to work out at Toronto, but the major contours of a peaceful agreement between the United States and the Confederate States of America would rest on the three issues discussed above. Slave property rights and territorial expansion had been the issues that had created the greatest crises in the sectional disputes of the antebellum period. There remains of course the possibility that the arrangements worked out at the peace conference would *not* resolve the issues between the two belligerents and that hostilities would break out again in a few years. We disregard this scenario not because it is improbable but because it implies that the "war" was not really over in 1865. If there is to be a Confederate States of America, they must eventually succeed in getting the United States to accept breakup of the Union as a fait accompli. One way in which this might be assured at the conference in Toronto would be the active participation of Britain and France in extending "guarantees" to the Confederacy in the form of treaties that promised assistance in the event of a Union attack. We shall develop this theme more fully in the next chapter.

WITH THE signing of the Treaty of Toronto, we have moved one step farther along in our counterfactual story. The South would have won its independence and would be ready to take its place in the international world. Could the new nation survive? Not everyone thought that it could. Many historians argue that the failure of the Richmond government to prosecute the war successfully is in itself sufficient evidence of the "failure" of Confederate nationalism, created from an ideology based on states' rights.[14] On the other hand, while the problems facing the new nation were substantial, one should not jump to the conclusion that the Confederacy was doomed. There is a tendency for historians to assess the future of the Confederate nation in terms of the Southern defeat in the war.[15] But if the South had not lost the war, then Confederate politics of 1864 and 1865 might have been very different. The embers of nationalism so evident in 1860 might well have been fanned to new heights by the announcement that the United States and the Confederacy had signed the Treaty of Toronto in the spring of 1865.

There were strong parallels between the situation of the counterfactual Confederate nation in 1865 and the experience of the American colonists who had broken away from Britain seventy-five years earlier. The American Revolution, while not nearly so destructive as the Civil War, nonetheless took a heavy toll in both lives and property.[16] After the Treaty of Paris ended the Revolutionary War, political quarrels and economic rivalries among the individual states in 1783 produced so much chaos that the Articles of Confederation had to be scrapped after only seven years. Moreover, although the defeated British had withdrawn, the military threat posed by their presence in North America had hardly disappeared, as the War of 1812 forcefully demonstrated. Finally, the economic outlook for the new nation in 1783 was bleak indeed until war in Europe rescued the American economy from its postrevolution doldrums.[17]

Despite these odds, the American Republic not only survived but flourished. The Confederates had the experience of the American Revolution and the intervening seventy-five years to draw upon in establishing their own country. They used that knowledge to draw up the Constitution of the Confederacy, which was patterned very closely after the U.S. Constitution. One obvious difference, however, was that the Confederate Constitution explicitly protected slave property rights in the new Republic. Recalling the fuss over passage of a Fugitive Slave Law in the United States, Article IV, Section 2.3 of the CSA Constitution states that any slave who "escaped" into another state or territory must be "delivered up on claim of the party to whom such slave belongs." The men writing the CSA Constitution also remembered the difficulties created by the failure of the U.S. Constitution to state clearly the authority of Congress to legislate slave rights in the territories. Article V of the CSA Constitution says: "In all such territory the institution of negro slavery, as it now exists in the Confederate States, shall be recognized and protected by Congress and by the Territorial government." In most other respects, the CSA Constitution mirrors its Northern counterpart.[18]

A Confederate nation that emerged victorious in 1865 would have some very powerful factors working in its favor. The South had abundant raw materials and a plantation system of agriculture that was the most efficient producer of cotton throughout the world. By itself the antebellum economy of the American South ranked among the richest countries in the world in terms of per capita income. In place of the dispirited Confederacy of 1864 that was losing the war, our counterfactual victory would create a sense of political solidarity forged in battle. The settlement at Toronto would provide the impetus for the speedy establishment of international ties throughout the world. In 1865 no Southerner doubted that the South would soon regain its position in the world economy. The new nation would have powerful allies and an army, led by a group of veteran commanders that could be a major military force in the Western Hemisphere.

This is not to ignore the severe effects of a long and bloody war. Heavy loss of life and the destruction and dislocation caused by the fighting would require time to heal. Yet it is doubtful that this would take very long. Despite the casualties incurred in the war, the Confederacy would not have suffered the enormous physical destruction that is so often associated with warfare in the twentieth century. Within a few years the losses from neglect of buildings, fences, and agricultural capital could be replaced.[19] With huge stocks of cotton on hand resulting from the Union blockade, planters would be in a position to take advantage of the extraordinarily high prices of cotton immediately after the war.

This would be complicated by the state of finances in the Confederate economy at the end of our counterfactual war. The antebellum South had relied heavily on Northern and British capital markets for its financial arrangements, and as a result, it was ill prepared to finance the enormous costs of the war. The rather sketchy data on the actual expenditures of the Confederate government suggest that only $258 million—barely 12 percent of the total costs of the war—were raised by taxes or other sources of government income.[20] The result, as we have already noted, was a spiraling inflation that undermined the government's credit both at home and abroad. Figure 4.1 shows the actual increase of prices in the Confederate States of America during the war. Prices rose almost 10,000 percent (100 times) between 1860 and 1865. This erosion of the value of Confederate currency left the Southern economy in chaos in the wake of a Northern victory.

Inflation is basically a monetary phenomenon: too much money chasing too few goods. It can be argued that up to the middle of 1863 the price increases were largely the result of the money printed to finance the war. But as the war raged on, the cause of inflation became more complex; after 1865, prices rose much more rapidly than the supply of money. One explanation is that the military fortunes of the Confederate armies had a pronounced effect on prices as expectations of defeat produced an increasingly pessimistic view of the future. Note the rise in prices in Figure 4.1 after Lee's disastrous defeat at Gettysburg, followed by a period of lower inflation in the spring and summer of 1864, when prices actually fell slightly as Lee seemed to be holding Grant at bay while Sherman was still struggling to take Atlanta. Then the roof caved in; with the fall of Atlanta in September and Lincoln's reelection in November, prices soared out of sight. In our counterfactual war, the government would have still run a sizable budget deficit, and we therefore expect that counterfactual prices would have followed the path of actual prices up to the middle of 1863.

We shall assume that at this point in our counterfactual world, Lee's victory at Gettysburg had a sufficiently positive effect on Confederate

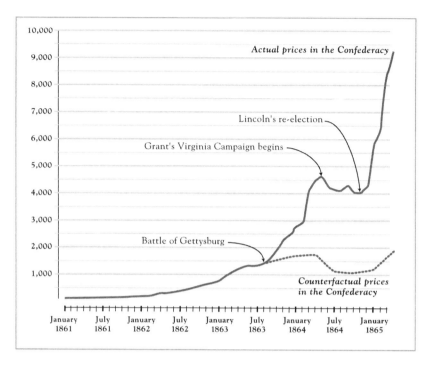

FIGURE 4.1
REAL AND COUNTERFACTUAL PRICES IN THE
CONFEDERACY, 1861–65
(JANUARY 1861=100)

morale that the Richmond government was able to slow the rate of inflation to the counterfactual price line in Figure 4.1. In addition to being buoyed by Lee's successes, prices fell to about ten times the level at the beginning of the war as the result of a drastic reorganization of the currency in the spring of 1864.[21] This would still represent a huge rise in prices, but getting a handle on inflation would represent an enormous plus for a Confederacy struggling to win the war.

Lee's success at Gettysburg and the subsequent campaigns in 1864 would also have a beneficial impact on the financial stability of the Confederacy by boosting the confidence of European investors who were buying Confederate bonds in the expectation that the Rebel government would survive. A financial innovation actually used by the

Richmond government was to secure the CSA bonds sold abroad with cotton (which the Confederacy had a large supply of) instead of gold (which by 1863 was in very short supply in the CSA). These bonds proved to be extremely popular in Europe.[22] In a counterfactual world in which inflation had slowed down perceptibly in 1864 and military prospects were more favorable, the credit of the Richmond government abroad would be greatly strengthened in the final year of fighting.

Stabilizing the currency would be an essential first step toward establishing postwar financial markets. The next step would be reestablishing the cotton trade that had been the bulwark of the South's antebellum economy. Credit relations with the merchants in the United States who had handled much of the cotton crop before the war would be strained by the Southern victory, and in many cases the interruption might become permanent. Nevertheless, there is ample basis for expecting commerce to recover quickly. Southern planters would have accumulated ample stocks of cotton during the war that they could offer as an inducement to reestablish their old ties with factors either in the North or in Britain. Data on the actual behavior of cotton prices in Liverpool suggest that by the end of 1864 British buyers were paying five times the prewar price in real terms. Had the Union blockade persisted until the Toronto Treaty was signed sometime in mid-1865, the price might have gone still higher.[23] High prices would provide a huge economic boost to the Confederate economy as cotton was shipped to eager consumers in Europe and the United States. To be sure, there would be glitches to deal with before life finally settled into a "normal" situation after the war. But it is reasonable to expect that speculators on both sides of the Atlantic, including some in the United States, would begin preparations to resume trade at the earliest possible moment. Once the blockade was lifted, cotton could be shipped to Europe, imported goods would begin to reappear on the wharves of Confederate ports, and the coastal trade among the Confederate ports would resume in our counterfactual world.

All this assumes of course that the planters in the independent Confederacy would be able to return quickly to their prewar levels of production. The other great challenge facing planters would be dealing with the attitude of slaves, many of whom would have tasted a substantial degree of freedom. In the Mississippi Valley, Tennessee, and Kentucky, where Union troops had been stationed for many months, a sizable number of slaves would have sought protection from the occupying troops. As they learned of the impending peace conference, slaves in these areas might well try to move north in the hope that they would escape reenslavement in a victorious Confederacy. The fate of these contraband slaves would be determined by the deliberations at the conference in Toronto.

Even in the heart of the Confederacy, where Union troops did not penetrate during the counterfactual war, slaves would have learned something of the experience of those who had, at least for a time, experienced a glimpse of freedom. Under the harsh hand of slavery African-Americans had managed to offer resistance to the regimen imposed by the planters, and it is reasonable to think that those efforts would be redoubled in the wake of the war. Offsetting this heightened awareness of liberty among the slave population would be the depressing realization that the day of jubilee was not going to arrive soon in the heartland of the Confederate States of America. Once the reality of Northern defeat set in, coercive measures—harsh discipline and the gang system that had worked so well before 1860—would again prevail to force slaves back into the cotton fields.

With some semblance of financial stability restored, and most of the slaves back in the fields, the Confederacy would experience a rapid economic recovery in the late 1860s that would carry over into the 1870s. An important implication of this favorable economic climate is that it would make the political environment far more conducive to the establishment of a peacetime regime. By 1867, when the first peacetime presidential election would be held, the economic situation would no longer be the dominating political issue that it had been during the last years of the war. In this scenario the Confederacy would survive its infancy and grow into adolescence.[24]

LOOKING BACK at the experience of the United States following its victory over the British in 1783, we can see that economic conditions played a significant role in launching the new nation on its path to success. The economic confusion that gripped the American economy after the Revolutionary War was a major factor behind the cries for the Constitutional Convention in 1787 to reorganize the federal government. The change in the economic climate created by the effects of the Napoleonic Wars after 1793 and the growth of the cotton economy of the South contributed substantially to the successful implementation of the Constitution adopted in 1790.[25] While the institutional arrangements of the Confederacy were not as novel as those developed by the Constitutional Convention seventy-five years earlier, the economic prospects facing the South in 1865 would have played an important role in getting the new country off to a solid beginning.

The short-term outlook for our independent Confederacy seemed favorable; what of the longer term? The social and economic foundation of the new Republic would rest upon the same foundations as the slave society that had specialized in producing short-staple cotton for a world market before the war. The antebellum South had experienced five decades of extraordinary prosperity fueled by a huge demand for raw cotton in Europe and the American North. Four years of war would produce major disruptions in the supply of American cotton, disruptions that would drive European cotton prices to record levels and wreak havoc on European textile producers. But the disruptions would be temporary. The question we must answer in assessing our counterfactual future of the South is: What effect would a Southern victory have been on the *long-run* demand for raw cotton in the world?

Two divergent scenarios have emerged in regard to the economic future of an independent Confederacy. The first, which I call the optimistic view, asserts that the factors promoting the antebellum growth of the American South would resume after the war as an economic base for an independent South. In that case the Confederates would be in an excellent position to exploit their monopoly position in the world's market for raw cotton. Throughout the 1850s Southern exports of cotton accounted for between three-quarters to four-fifths of the cotton imported into Europe.[26] This is an incredibly high share of a very large market, more than enough to allow changes in the supply of Confederate cotton to affect the world price of cotton. If Southerners managed to control the world supply for cotton, and if the demand for cotton continued to grow at the rate exhibited for the previous three decades, the long-term economic future of the Confederacy would be assured. That of course is exactly what the Southerners hoped for at the time: a continuation of the antebellum prosperity. Robert Fogel carries the argument one step further by conjecturing that an independent South after the war could not only have attained economic prosperity but also have enjoyed a considerable amount of political leverage in the Atlantic community. "Shrewd manipulation of its monopoly of cotton," Fogel insists, "would have permitted the Confederacy to reward its international friends and punish its enemies."[27] Innovative fiscal policy could have further enhanced the Confederacy's international position. A modest export tax on cotton would be able to generate revenue for the government in Richmond that would, by Fogel's reckoning, amount to "50 percent more than the entire federal budget [of the United States] on the eve of the Civil War."[28]

This optimistic scenario assumes that the world demand for cotton would continue to grow as it did before the war, and it asserts that the antebellum Southern economy could serve as a solid foundation for growth and development of the South as an independent nation after 1865.[29] There is, however, a more pessimistic view of Southern economic prospects in 1865. Proponents of this view state that despite the antebellum South's prosperity, the cotton culture did *not* create the diversified economic activity and investment outside agriculture that was so visible in the North. The pessimists also argue that the international boom in raw cotton was *not* likely to continue, and a Southern victory in the war would not change this situation. Taken together, these points suggest that economic prospects for economic growth of a Confederate society dominated by an agriculture tied to the production of cotton would be severely limited.

We have already touched upon the first of these arguments in chapter 1 when we pointed out that the South had failed to develop several salient characteristics of a diversified market society by the time of the Civil War. The South was a wealthy and rapidly expanding economy on the eve of the Civil War. Indeed, per capita income in the antebellum Southern economy grew at roughly the same rate as the rest of the United States from 1840 to 1860.[30] However, rapid growth of the antebellum South was due to a shift of resources, particularly slaves, from the soil-depleted regions of the Southeast to the richer soils of the Mississippi Valley and the Southwest. In layman terms, this means that Southern economic growth depended on a continual shift of slaves and capital to more fertile land in the West. In the decades leading up to the Civil War, there was an abundance of fertile land in the Black Belt regions of Georgia, Alabama, and Mississippi; in the delta regions of the Mississippi River; and in some areas of Louisiana and Texas. The settlement of these regions, with their high cotton yields, more than offset the declining yields of cotton and other crops grown on the depleted soil in the East.

Southerners clearly recognized this feature of their economy; that is one reason they fought so hard to keep the Western territories open for settlers using slave labor. Even though the cotton culture had not yet reached the point where a scarcity of good land would choke off economic growth at the time of the Civil War, signs of the declining productivity were already evident to perceptive observers. Along the eastern seaboard, constant cotton plantings had already reduced yields to levels at which the only way for planters to break even was to sell slaves as well as cotton. While the income from the "internal slave trade" propped up the dwindling returns from cotton to planters in the eastern half of the South, such activity did not bode well for the economic future of King Cotton. Historians writing in the first half of the twentieth century argued that soil depletion and the closing of land sales on the frontier would create a natural limit to the expansion of cotton cultivation that would eventually stymie Southern economic growth.[31]

The natural limits hypothesis was a bit too simplistic; among other things it ignored the fact that there was still a great deal of land available *within* the South where cotton could be grown, and in fact much of this land was brought into cultivation of cotton after 1865. However, upland cotton required more intensive use of labor and greater use of fertilizer to offset the poorer quality of the soil. Fertilizer costs reduced the farmer's ability to save and invest in more productive capital over time. Moreover, in the long run, increasing use of fertilizer only postponed the inevitable. As time went on, more and more fertilizer would be required just to maintain the level of productivity.[32] There is no reason to expect that the use of slave labor in a free Confederacy would have entailed any lower level of fertilizer use on these lands. If we take the actual experience of Southern cotton farms after the Civil War as a guide, we conclude that the Confederate South would face a steady increase in fertilizer consumption as it strove to maintain the production of cotton.

The second issue raised by the pessimistic view of growth in the South focuses on the limitations facing a one-crop economy hoping to maximize its income through "shrewd manipulation" of the international cotton market. This is an updated and somewhat grander version of the King Cotton diplomacy that failed the Confederacy during the war. Such a policy would be equally unsuccessful after the war. The wartime experience with the embargo and the Northern blockade suggests that the South's "monopoly" of cotton was not nearly as power-

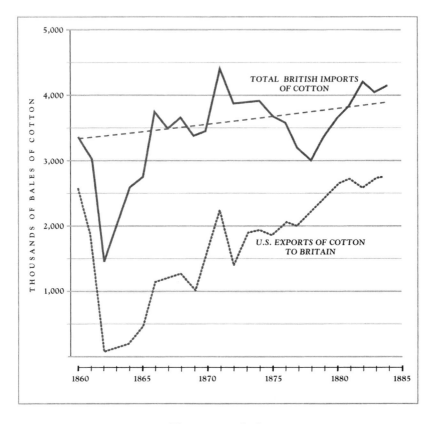

FIGURE 4.2

BRITISH IMPORTS OF RAW COTTON, 1865–84

ful as proponents of cotton diplomacy believed. The simple fact was that even before the outbreak of the Civil War, cotton was no longer king. Figure 4.2 charts the actual imports of cotton into Great Britain between 1860 and 1884. It is immediately apparent why the cotton famine failed to bring Britain to its knees. Within a few years British textile producers had managed to reestablish the prewar level of imports, thanks to substantial increases in cotton imports from India, Egypt, and Brazil. The result was a drastic shift in market shares. In 1866, the first full year after the end of the blockade, the postbellum American South's market share fell from 75 percent before the war to just over 30 percent. Southern producers did eventually recover most of their share of the world market, but it took them fifteen years. The clear implication from the aftermath of the actual Civil War is that while American short-staple cotton was cheaper and of better quality than its rivals, the marginal advantage of the American product was not so great that Southerners could easily manipulate supply to control cotton prices in Europe in our counterfactual world.

An additional difficulty with the optimistic projections that the Confederacy could rely on a postwar cotton boom to support its economy lies with what we know about the world's demand for cotton in the years following the American Civil War. Unfortunately for the South, the extraordinary rates of growth in the demand for cotton typical of the first half of the nineteenth century were not sustained over the last four decades of the century. Figure 4.2 reveals that the overall level of British imports of raw cotton in 1885 was only slightly higher than it had been in 1860.[33] A Southern victory in the war would not change this situation. The experience of the international cotton market both before and after the Civil War suggests that cotton exports alone would not support continued prosperity of a Confederate economy tied to cotton.

Could the Confederacy escape the worst effects of a collapse of demand for cotton by diversifying its agriculture? The opportunity was clearly there. Outside the cotton regions, slave farms had experienced some success with diversified farming, and in some areas, such as the Shenandoah Valley, that success was pronounced. The antebellum South had been self-sufficient in foodstuffs even within the cotton regions because the yeoman farmers of the South followed a safety first strategy of farming that gave first priority to seeing that the food requirements of the farm were met before the farmers turned their attention to cotton. On plantations slave labor could be used to grow food because the slaves could devote time to those crops during the part of the year when the cotton crop did not require attention. But corn and wheat were not the primary interest of cotton planters, and yields of those crops were far below those of the free farms in the West, which supplied the demands of the Eastern and international markets. The yeomen farmers of the South could live comfortably alongside their wealthy plantation neighbors because they complemented each other well. The marketing arrangements for selling cotton created by the plantations allowed family farms or farms with one or two slaves to eke out comfortable livings by selling a bale or two of the cash crop to plantations.[34] Contemporary accounts from Northern travelers and many historical accounts written in the aftermath of the war have given the impression that "free" farms in the antebellum South were poor relative to their Northern counterpart. But as we saw in chapter 1, these impressions were often misleading. The agricultural system of the South had worked well enough before the war for Southern farms to be self-sufficient and have a little bit to spare. The war did not do anything to change that situation fundamentally.

Any move to diversify away from cotton would have flown in the face of the enormous comparative advantage that the slave farms had in the production of cotton. If they had turned to grains and foodstuffs in the international market, Southern producers would have been forced to compete with producers in the United States who had consistently demonstrated their ability to outproduce Southern farms in the market for grains. The demand for cotton might decline, but that crop would still offer better returns and lower risks for most planters than foodstuffs.[35] To create a truly diversified agriculture would mean planters would have to abandon the great advantage of large slave plantations. As long as there was slavery in the South, that was not an option that planters were likely to choose.

IF AGRICULTURAL diversity was unlikely, the other option facing the Confederacy would be to move resources out of agriculture and develop manufacturing. One possibility would be for the Confederacy to concentrate its efforts on the development of a domestic textile industry to provide a market for raw cotton. Here independence offered some promise of actions that might lead to a change in the pattern of economic development. At the very least, an independent South could enact tariffs as a protection for an "infant" textile industry. Other industries might also form the basis for an industrial expansion if they were shielded from outside competition. Observers who portray the antebellum South as purely agricultural overlook the small-scale manufacturing and processing that served its local markets. Southern manufacturing establishments, particularly those in such processing industries as flour milling and cotton ginning, were actually comparable to their counterparts in the Midwest. What differentiated manufacturing in the two regions was not so much a lack of entrepreneurship or the characteristics of slave labor as the size of the Southern market.[36] While the defeated South did not turn out to be a fertile ground for industrial growth, the industrial prospects for an independent Confederacy might be more appealing.

Even with all that economic potential, and with a population energized by the euphoria of escaping from the grasp of the hated Yankees, the situation would still not favor the rapid growth of industry in an independent Confederate States of America. The small size of markets in the South, the absence of a well-developed infrastructure providing finance and transportation, and the challenge of implementing a program of political economy that would encourage industrial development all would work against the emergence of an industrial sector in the CSA. Adding to these difficulties would be the crippling effects of slavery.

The greatest of these obstacles would be the smallness of markets. As our map of urban centers in chapter 1 clearly illustrated, all the major cities were on the periphery of the Confederacy; there were virtually no towns of any consequence in the heart of the Cotton Belt. "Specialization," claimed Adam Smith, "is limited by the extent of the market," and specialization is the key to the growth of a manufacturing and commercial sector. Southern manufacturers could make a modest profit producing goods and services for a local market. But the absence of urban markets meant that producers faced limited opportunities for an expansion of production that would allow them to reach a scale of operation to compete in the international marketplace. That situation would persist in our counterfactual Confederacy.

Protective tariffs might offer firms in an independent Confederacy protection from foreign competition, which included the firms in the United States that had traded freely in the South before the war. But where would the protected firms of the Confederacy find markets that would allow them to grow into "adults"? Tariffs could keep foreign goods out, but tariffs alone could not create domestic markets for Southern producers. Only a tiny fraction of firms in the Confederacy would ever reach a point where they could compete with British or American producers in the international marketplace. The principal effect of Confederate tariffs would be to punish consumers by raising the prices of manufactured goods at home in order to subsidize perpetually inefficient industries producing import "substitutes."

Another possibility is that the mobilization of resources to fight the war for independence might encourage industrial development in the Confederacy. This is an intriguing thought. However, it is hard to see how a Southern victory would invigorate Confederate industrial development. The South did not have a well-developed industrial infrastructure in 1861. Warfare in the middle of the nineteenth century had not yet reached a point where military needs of the armies and navies by themselves would be sufficient to foster a market that would call for a huge military-industrial complex. The Confederate government did make prodigious efforts to develop an industrial capability to provide the weapons and supplies necessary to supply armed forces during the war. This included converting Richmond's Tredegar Iron Works into a cannon factory; developing large new ironworks at Columbus, Georgia, and Selma, Alabama; constructing powder works at Augusta, Georgia, and Columbia, South Carolina; and developing shipyards that constructed more than a hundred vessels.[37] Many of these sites were comparable to the best facilities in Europe or the United States. It is likely that the Richmond government would continue to foster further development of some of the sites used to produce arms during the war. However, the military industries were state-sponsored, did not rely heavily on slave labor, and were primarily focused on producing supplies for the war effort. They might be enough to allow the Confederacy to maintain a respectable military establishment. By themselves, however, the demands of the war would not be enough to constitute the basis for an Industrial Revolution.

We have been considering the possibilities of diversification into industry as if the Confederate lawmakers wanted to encourage industry and trade. But it is not at all clear that voters in the new country would support the sort of political economy we have been discussing. Consider, for example, our comments about the efficacy of a protective tariff. Before the war Southerners had vociferously opposed the efforts of Yankee manufacturers to protect their markets from cheap imports. In 1832 efforts to introduce even a modest increase in the tariff sparked a major political crisis that some have argued spawned the secessionist movement.[38] Protective tariffs were so abhorrent to the men writing the Confederate Constitution that they explicitly forbade "any duties or taxes on importations from foreign countries" that might be levied "to promote or foster any branch of industry."[39] The CSA Constitution also made it difficult to pass an export tax, which required a two-thirds vote of both houses of Congress.[40]

A major argument made by those urging secession in 1860 was the need for the South to escape the corrupting influences of a capitalist North, an example of which was the practice of pork barrel legislation that annually expropriated large sums for various rivers and harbors throughout the United States. Southerners believed that they consistently got the short end of these political deals. Here again, the men writing the Confederate Constitution were determined to leave nothing to chance; they insisted that no clause should "ever be construed to delegate to Congress the power to appropriate money for any internal improvement intended to facilitate commerce."[41] These attitudes might change over time, but they strongly suggest that the initial effects of independence would be to discourage explicitly the development of industry within the Confederacy. This is hardly surprising. For Southerners to embrace industrial expansion in their own country immediately would require an abrupt about-face in their "vision" of an agricultural slave society. Intellectual paradigms are not easily changed, and Southerners, rich and poor, were likely to view their triumph in the war as support for their belief that independence was all it would take for them to continue the prosperity that had elevated the South to become one of the richest nations in the world.

A final obstacle to either agricultural or industrial diversification within the Confederacy was the institution of slave labor. Slavery was a cornerstone of the Confederate economy, and that commitment to chattel labor would not have encouraged industrial development. The problems that stemmed from a system of chattel labor were both subtle and pervasive. One of the reasons that there were so few urban centers in the South was the slave plantation system. Plantations were self-contained economic units that did not require many additional services that might encourage the growth of towns. In fact, plantation owners were more than content to maintain isolated existences that would limit any opportunities for the slave labor to escape. While the absence of towns fitted well with the needs of slaveowners to control their slaves, the rural environment meant that there was no domestic market for local entrepreneurs to exploit.[42] Slavery also contributed indirectly to a shortage of investment capital. Slavery requires a massive investment in the chattel labor that its owners regard as financial assets. Such investment reduced the funds available for investment in real capital. This "burden" of slavery was a significant deterrent to investment in the antebellum slave economy, and it would also be a burden in the slave Confederacy.[43]

The statesmen who founded the Confederacy fervently believed that cotton would be the foundation upon which a prosperous slave economy could thrive. Our counterfactual assessment of the years following independence suggests that cotton would become a millstone around their necks, producing a downward spiral that would leave the new nation falling farther and farther behind the rest of the Atlantic community. There is little reason to expect independence would change this situation. Prospects for imperial expansion into Mexico and Cuba would obviously beckon, as they had before the war. But would a Confederacy struggling to recover from the costs of a prolonged war with the United States be able to sustain territorial acquisitions of this sort? We shall return to this issue in the next chapter.

ALL THIS would be of little importance to the citizens of the Confederacy as they struggled to deal with the challenge of independence in the aftermath of a long and bloody war. Looking at the future of their new nation in 1865, they would see what they had always seen: a plantation economy with a slave labor force concentrating on cash crops together with thousands of family farms producing for their own needs and a modest surplus for the marketplace. The "Revolution of 1861" had succeeded in establishing the Confederate States of America. The South's "peculiar institution" and the way of life that went with it would be preserved.

While economics might ultimately play a major role in determining the long-term prospects for the Confederacy, the more immediate task confronting leaders of the new nation would be to create a smoothly functioning government from the chaos following the war. Much of this would be familiar ground because the Confederacy's founders adopted a constitution that closely paralleled that of the United States. But there were still a good many details that needed to be worked out. One of the initial challenges for the new political system would be the election of its first peacetime president. Jefferson Davis, the man who had led them through the war, was prohibited by the Constitution from seeking a second term as president. This would raise the possibility of a significant shift in policy with the election of a new chief executive. In 1800 the United States had faced a similar challenge when Thomas Jefferson defeated the incumbent president, John Adams. In later years Jefferson termed his victory over Adams a revolution because it represented a transfer of power from the Federalist Party of Adams and Alexander Hamilton, to Jefferson's Republican faction. What made that transfer of authority all the more remarkable was that it was accomplished without major disruption, despite the fact that the popular vote was so close that no candidate received a majority in the electoral college, and the outcome eventually had to be determined by the House of Representatives.

In the fall of 1867 Confederate voters would face a similar test of their system's ability to change leadership. Where would they find a strong leader to take the place of Jefferson Davis? The obvious choice would be the hero of the war for independence, Robert E. Lee. No person in the Confederacy had the stature and enormous political popularity to match Lee's. Like George Washington in 1788, Lee not only was a successful military leader but had shown exceptional shrewdness dealing with the political demands on a commander during the war. However, Lee always professed a profound distaste for politics, and he would likely have no great enthusiasm in running for president. This reluctance could probably have been overcome by appeals to his sense of duty were it not for a more serious problem. The sacrifices of the war had taken their toll on the former commander of the Army of Northern Virginia, and by the fall of 1867 he was not in good health. Despite the pleas of his supporters, the general would surely decline the honor on the ground that his health would not permit him to serve.

Who else might step forward? Two other generals who served with Lee in the Army of Northern Virginia (and who demonstrated some political acumen in the Reconstruction South of the United States) come quickly to mind. First would be James Longstreet, Lee's second-in-command, who would have the advantage of a strong endorsement from his former boss. Although Longstreet became a highly controversial figure in the Reconstruction South, in the event of a Confederate victory he would be in an excellent position to capitalize on his accomplishments while serving in the Army of Northern Virginia.[44] Another officer would be Wade Hampton, the cavalry commander who eventually rose to be governor of the Reconstruction South Carolina and served two terms in the U.S. Senate. Hampton had strong family connections in his home state; his main liability in a Confederate presidential election was his close alliance with the planter elite of the Deep South. A third possibility would be Thomas "Stonewall" Jackson, who was almost as revered as Lee. However, Jackson had none of his chief's talent for politics, and it seems unlikely that the man who was instrumental in shaping many of Lee's victories would be a viable candidate for the highest office in the land.[45]

While either Longstreet or Hampton might be an effective candidate, the person most likely to emerge as the second president of the Confederacy was someone who was a successful general during the war and had enjoyed a distinguished political career before the war. John C. Breckinridge of Kentucky fought in the Army of Tennessee, and briefly served as secretary of war under Davis. Breckenridge had been elected vice president of the United States in 1856, and in 1860 he had run for president of the United States on a ticket favoring secession. Carrying all the states in the Deep South, he finished with the second-highest electoral vote behind Abraham Lincoln. Many of the delegates meeting in Montgomery in 1861 favored Breckinridge for the presidency of the Confederacy. At the time, however, he was actively seeking in the U.S. Senate a compromise that might avoid war. The war greatly enhanced Breckinridge's reputation. Coming from a border state, he would not stir up fears that many of the politicians from the upper South had of the planter elite of the cotton South. His political experience would be invaluable, and he was particularly noteworthy for his efforts at compromise, a talent that would certainly be tested if he became president of the Confederacy.[46] Breckinridge's record in the war and his political experience would propel him to the presidency.

This political unity would be quickly tested in office by the challenge of guiding the Confederacy through a difficult period of adjustment to the postwar world.

Our counterfactual account of the Confederacy after the war has thus far assumed that despite some problems during and immediately after the war, the cotton market would rebound and business would resume "as usual." Southern planters confidently expected that this meant slavery would remain profitable far into the future. But there were clouds on the horizon of this optimistic scenario. The cotton market would bounce back from the interruption of the war; however, the data of Figure 4.2 indicate that British imports of cotton supplied by Southern planters would remain significantly below the prewar level long after the end of the Union blockade. The man who succeeded Breckinridge as president of the CSA in 1874 would take office amid growing concerns about the health of King Cotton. Unfortunately, there was not a great deal that Southerners could do to change a situation that was determined several thousand miles away in Europe. Moreover, the situation would get only worse.

A weakening demand in the international demand for cotton would eventually lead to a decline in the price of slaves. At first, the only noticeable effect would be a realization that the gains from selling slaves were smaller than in the past. But as time went on and slave prices stagnated, planters along the eastern seaboard who counted on the proceeds from slave sales to make ends meet would begin to feel the pinch. Like retirees who become worried when prices of stocks in their investment portfolios fall, slaveholders seeing the price of the human chattel decline would feel the first twinge of concern that their economic future was not as secure as they had strongly believed only a few years earlier.

At the time of the 1874 presidential election the situation was not desperate, since the annual growth in the slave population ensured that seaboard planters would still have slaves to sell to buyers in the West. But as the situation in the cotton market continued to deteriorate, Western planters would become increasingly less eager to buy slaves. The result would be that slave prices throughout the Confederacy would eventually start to decline. Exactly when this might happen is difficult to predict, but it is possible that by the mid-1870s the value of slaves would have slipped well below the peak reached in 1860.[47] Declining slave prices, especially a *persistent decline* in slave values, would threaten the economic security of *all* slaveholders. What we described as the pessimistic assessment of the postwar cotton market could cause Southerners to rethink their commitment not only to cotton but to slavery as well.

AT FIRST, one might think that Southerners would be loath to abandon an institution that had served them well for three hundred years and in which they had invested billions of dollars. On the other hand, the prospect of losing that huge investment is exactly why slaveowners *would* consider a scheme of compensated emancipation that might forestall any further capital losses. The final obstacle to passage of any emancipation scheme by the government in Richmond would be political, not economic. While they were still in the American Union, Southerners had fiercely resisted any attempt by Northern antislavery groups to interfere with their peculiar institution. Whether or not they owned slaves, whites living in the antebellum South feared that efforts to free the slaves would lead to serious interference by Northern abolitionists with regard to the status of freed African-Americans living in the South. Independence would mean that whites in the Confederacy could enact whatever measures were necessary to keep African-Americans subservient.

The growing economic pressures within the Confederacy to do away with slave assets would be strongly reinforced by political pressures from the international community for the Southerners to abandon slavery. The British had freed the slaves in their West Indian colonies in the 1830s, by 1880 the remaining slaves left in the United

States would surely have been freed, and Brazil, the last major slave society in the Americas, was moving toward emancipation of its slaves by the mid-1880s. The Confederacy had already agreed to prohibit the import of slaves into the South. With the economic significance of slavery declining, at least some of the political leaders and planter elite in the Confederacy might be receptive to a scheme that would free them from the problems of maintaining an economic system that was now a millstone around their neck.

Given the political obstacles to emancipation, it would be an uphill fight. But we know that with sufficiently powerful incentives, the resistance to freeing slaves could be overcome. Looking defeat in the eye at the end of 1865, the Confederate Congress had reluctantly agreed to arm blacks and offer them freedom if they served the Confederate army. This proved to be a case of too little too late. But it illustrates the possibility that Southerners were willing to entertain the thought of emancipation when the situation became sufficiently dire. The economic situation in the 1870s hardly qualifies as a crisis equal to that facing a defeated South in 1865, but it would have been sufficiently serious that proposals to ease the pressure on planters through government purchase of slaves would surely have surfaced in the Confederate Congress. It is even plausible to argue that debates on the issue of emancipation for blacks had become sufficiently divisive that the electorate was divided into political factions.

By the 1880 presidential election the question of what to do about slavery would be the single most important issue facing Confederate voters. By then the boom of the cotton market of the 1850s would be nothing more than a distant memory. The cumulative effect of declining prices would confront every slaveholder with the risk of financial ruin. At some point a significant number of the planter elite would finally become convinced that their future depended on getting rid of their slave assets before their value fell still lower.[48] For these men, it was not a question of ideology; it was a question of financial survival. When it became apparent that no one else was interested in purchasing their chattel labor, proposals to have the government buy slaves would look very appealing.

Even with the support of the slaveowners, the cause of emancipation would face an uphill battle in 1880. As groups coalesced into rival factions, we can speculate what the political parties in the presidential election of 1880 would look like as they debated the issue of how to deal with the slave problem.

The party favoring emancipation—most likely an invigorated version of the antebellum Whig Party—would be formed from a coalition comprised of:

Cotton planters who were suffering substantial losses as slave prices fell each year. Once the strongest supporters of the slave system, these people now hoped to convince the government to replace their slave assets with government bonds.

Farmers who owned only a few slaves. More than half of all slaveholders owned five or fewer slaves. Many of these farmers depended on slave capital as collateral for loans to finance their annual crops. As the prices of both slaves and cotton declined, these farmers would see their collateral melting away with no prospect of relief. The immediate advantages of owning government bonds rather than slaves would appeal to this group even more than to the wealthier planters.

Entrepreneurs, businessmen, and financiers who had always believed that the presence of slave labor stifled economic growth. As a group they stood to gain from the infusion of government bonds that could provide a valuable source of capital for investment outside agriculture.

Agriculturalists who believed that overproduction of cotton was the root of the country's agricultural problem and that slavery was the reason for planters' commitment to cotton. This group hoped that getting rid of slavery would open the door for a more diversified agriculture in the Confederacy.

Abolitionists who regarded the slave system as a moral abomination. Pilloried by virtually everyone in the South before the war, this group had always found its moral arguments overcome by the enormous economic profits from slavery. With those profits dwindling, the moralists might finally be heard. Their cause would find supporters abroad, particularly from British and Northern abolitionists eager to see the largest system of slavery in the Western world dismantled.

The economic rationality and moral arguments of the proabolition group would not go unchallenged. There would be opposition to any proposal of emancipation by a powerful coalition of old-line Democrats. They would include:

Planters who stood to lose from government purchase of their slaves. Not every planter would be losing money producing cotton, and those who were prospering would guess correctly that the government was not likely to offer them top dollar for their slave assets. Many planters would fear that emancipation would spell the demise of the gang system of labor and a huge loss of efficiency. This view rested on the deep-seated conviction of planters that free blacks would not work without compulsion.

Yeomen farmers who owned no slaves. This group would object to the cost of an emancipation scheme that it viewed as nothing more than a subsidy for rich planters. These farmers also feared that the wage labor of freed slaves in the labor markets would undermine the prosperity of farms using free labor.

Proslavery advocates who viewed slavery as the essential foundation to racial and class divisions in Confederate society. Spokesmen for this group, which would include people from all walks of life, would vigorously oppose giving African-Americans *any* form of economic, political, or social freedom. For these people, abolition was not a matter of economics; it was a question of defending the principles on which the Confederacy was founded.

Would the proemancipation coalition be able to convince enough of the electorate to abandon its commitment to slave ideology so easily? It would certainly require some bold leadership. Here the political power of the Confederate president could be the difference between success and failure. In its effort to curtail the powers of Congress to intervene in a wide range of matters, and motivated by a distrust of political parties, the Confederate Constitution created a broad range of powers for the president. It thus seems likely that by the second decade of its existence, the presidency would have emerged as a pivotal center of political power. Economic factors would make the question of falling slave values a major political issue in every election after 1873. By that time the presidential election would amount to nothing less than a referendum on slavery and emancipation. If the proemancipation group could gain the presidency, its hopes of getting a constitutional amendment freeing the slaves would be greatly enhanced.[49]

The key to the eventual victory by proemancipation forces would be to gather the support of a substantial number of slaveholders. History is filled with examples of economic and political elites going down with the ship rather than addressing a crisis in their midst. Yet it is hardly beyond the realm of possibilities that Southern planters—particularly the wealthiest—would choose to cut their losses by letting the government buy their slaves. They faced a difficult choice: Either stand pat defending the ideology of their fathers and watch the value of their slave investments erode away, or take an active position to stem the downward spiral of slave prices and create a huge pool of agricultural labor that they could still manipulate through their control of land and credit in the South. As the financial picture continued to worsen, the pressures to abandon ideology would increase accordingly. We shall assume that by the 1885 presidential election, emancipation would be a foregone conclusion.

What would emerge from the political debates and legislative maneuvering would be a program of compensated emancipation in which all slaves were set free. A feasible scheme of emancipation that could be enacted in the mid-1880s is presented in Appendix 2. According to our plan, each slaveowner would receive an emancipation allowance based on the number of adult slaves he or she owned. A child under fourteen would not be eligible for any compensation allowance; he or she would, however, be apprenticed to the person who owned his or her mother until the child reached eighteen. An element of this plan is that *all* slaves would remain apprenticed to their former masters for three years from the time of emancipation. Our counterfactual plan calculates that the government in Richmond would have to issue between $25 and $30 billion in bonds to pay the emancipation allowance owed to slaveholders in 1880. The annual interest costs would be between $10 and $12.5 million per year.[50]

In assessing the magnitude of these "costs," one must realize that the interest payments on this debt would be distributed to bondholders, all of whom would initially live in the CSA. The emancipation debt would represent a huge shot in the arm to the Confederate economy because the bonds would provide slaveholders with negotiable financial assets in place of their illiquid slave assets. How much of this financial equity would be transformed into productive investment in agriculture or in other areas of economic activity is hard to guess. But even if most slaveholders held on to their bonds and simply collected the interest, the economy would receive a boost.[51] The significant difference between the Confederacy's emancipation scheme in 1880 and the forced emancipation that accompanied a Union victory in the spring of 1865 is that the CSA scheme would not have wiped out 50 percent of the slaveholders' assets. The financial assets created by the emancipation allowance would provide the capital needed to move from slave to free labor.

This is a significant point. Planters in the defeated postbellum American South had no capital from the loss of slave assets, and they had no time to work out arrangements for labor with the freedmen. The result, as countless historians have documented, was the emergence of flawed economic institutions that hindered economic progress in the South for a century.[52] In the Confederacy, of course, there would have been no transformation to free labor at the end of the war, and the structure of agriculture in the Confederate economy of 1880 would look very much like that of the antebellum South in 1860, with a preponderance of the slaves working on large plantations.[53]

How would the labor arrangements between planters and their former slaves work out in the Confederacy? We have at least a glimpse of what to expect from the experience in the postbellum American South, where state governments during presidential Reconstruction enacted a series of black codes that spelled out what Southerners thought would be appropriate rights for freedmen in the "New South." The codes provide clear evidence that planters would limit the options of black laborers so that employers would be assured a servile labor force. The three-year indenture system that accompanied the emancipation scheme we have outlined for the Confederacy would limit the ability of blacks to negotiate fair labor contracts, and it would give the ruling white classes time to refine the limitations on blacks' freedom to choose in the market for "free" labor. With a government more than willing to enforce regulations for a controlled labor market of "freed" slaves, the continued use of a gang system of labor using wage payments would have been feasible in many areas where cotton production on a large scale was still profitable. What is important to note here is that even on smaller farms that used slaves, wage labor using the freed blacks would have been feasible. The record of cotton production in the postwar American South leaves no doubt that farms of varying size could still compete in the world market for cotton. In our counter-factual world the transition to wage labor would have been far smoother than the experience of the Reconstruction American South.

The Confederate emancipation scheme of the 1880s would be designed to ensure that whites would retain the benefits of economic exploitation from the slave system—albeit in diminished amounts. Steps would be taken to ease the transition into a free labor market. The influx of cash and bonds would temporarily relieve the economic pressures of the declining cotton market. But as time went on, planters would still face hard choices if they were to prosper. The more difficult counterfactual question is whether emancipation would prompt the planter class to consider a more diversified approach to its economic situation. We have already noted the substantial obstacles to diversification in the Confederacy. Switching to a free labor system would offer flexibility and, perhaps, add investment capital to build a more diversified economy. But the process would be slow. Reorganizing the labor system would not immediately transform a system of plantations that were designed for producing a single cash crop into efficient farms for the production of foodstuffs. Even more important is the fact that conversion from slave to free labor would not do anything in the short run to create home markets that might stimulate industry.

Emancipation would almost surely improve the situation of whites, particularly those who had owned slaves. The planters who had dominated the Confederacy since antebellum times would still control most of the wealth and much of the best land in the South. Those who had owned farms with one or two slaves at the time of emancipation would gain—if they had managed to hang on to their slave capital through the hard times of the 1870s. For these people, the emancipation bonds would be a significant economic boost. For some, the windfall would give them enough of an economic stake to emulate the family farms of the North and combine family and wage labor in pursuing more diversified farming. Much would depend on the extent to which they had managed to stay out of debt during the years after the war. It is likely that many farm owners had to mortgage their slave assets to finance their cotton crops. If so, the emancipation allowance would at least allow them to get out of debt. Farmers who did not own slaves would see very little immediate impact from the abolition of slavery. For most of these people, any benefits would have to be in the form of a trickle-down effect.

To capitalize truly on the opportunities offered by the abolition of slavery, the people who controlled the land and capital in the Confederacy would have to alter significantly their vision of a slave South embodied in the revolution that established the CSA in 1865. Intellectual paradigms pose the greatest obstacle to institutional change. People who for generations have pursued the same way of life and demonstrated a willingness to fight to preserve those values tend to be reluctant to change their mind-sets simply because things are not going well at the moment. By itself the economic boost from emancipation would not be enough to transform the intellectual milieu of the Confederacy from an agricultural slave society to an industrial society. Generations of historians have insisted that planters had an anticapitalist mind-set that would always block the emergence of an industrial sector in the American South.[54] That mind-set would not easily be changed.

There is one other way in which freeing the slaves might help. If emancipation did produce a higher rate of investment in the Confederacy, it is possible that these new investments could attract attention in the international investment market. The last part of the nineteenth century witnessed a substantial export of capital from Great Britain to its worldwide dominions. One of the probable consequences of a Confederate victory would be closer political and economic ties to the United Kingdom and Europe. A spurt of domestic investment, most likely focused on transportation improvements, might send a message to foreign investors that the South was finally moving in a new direction. This could mean that the CSA might be added to the list of favored spots for British investors. While foreign investment could provide an economic boost to the Confederate economy, there could also be a downside to funds coming from abroad. The Confederacy, with its small industrial sector and an agricultural sector still heavily dependent on cotton, could become increasingly dependent on the British economy in a way not unlike the way the postbellum American South became dependent upon Northern industry after the war.[55]

Emancipation would almost certainly mean a brighter economic future for the Confederacy than the pessimistic view we painted at the outset of this chapter. However, almost all these gains would have gone to the white population. The group that clearly would gain the least from emancipation in purely economic terms would be the "freed" African-Americans. Released from the fetters of slavery, blacks would remain a subservient class of laborers without property, bound to landowners who effectively could deny them freedom of choice regarding where they might work or live. Racial segregation that severely limited the rights of blacks would be rigidly enforced throughout the Confederacy, and the possibilities of attaining even a modicum of economic or social status would be effectively denied. It is worth noting that the segregated society in the Confederacy would be far more repressive than that which emerged in the postbellum American South at the end of the nineteenth century. Even though they were largely ignored by white Southerners for the better part of a century, the civil liberties embedded in the Thirteenth, Fourteenth, and Fifteenth Amendments to the U.S. Constitution formed a legal foundation that eventually provided the basis for the advancement of black freedom in the United States during the last half of the twentieth century. Moreover, the principal means by which free blacks in the American South eventually improved their economic position was through migration to other parts of the United States. Had the Confederacy succeeded in forming a separate nation, this option would not have existed for the slaves freed by a Confederate emancipation in 1880. It is difficult to imagine that a counterfactual United States of America with a small black population in 1880 would have welcomed a stream of black refugees from the Confederacy—even if the Confederate landlords had been willing to part with their servile labor force. Under the best of scenarios, blacks in the Confederacy would be denied citizenship; they would remain trapped in a caste system based on race with no hope of escape.

Our emphasis on the obstacles to long-term progress for free African-Americans in the Confederacy should not blind us to the fact that emancipation by itself would have been a huge benefit to the enslaved population. However grim their future might be in economic terms, liberation from a system of chattel labor that treated people as property rather than individuals would still be seen as a day of jubilee in the black communities of the Confederacy.

OUR COUNTERFACTUAL history of the Confederate States of America has taken us nearly to the end of the nineteenth century. What do we find when we look over those last four decades? If the United States and the Confederacy managed to hammer out the details of a meaningful peace treaty in 1865, there is good reason to expect that the Confederacy would be able to establish itself as an independent player in the North Atlantic Community. Once it was so established, three scenarios could emerge:

The *optimistic scenario* predicted a nation that parlayed its economic advantage in the international cotton market into a place where it prospered in both economic and political terms and became a major player in the international scene. This would be the world that the Confederate founding fathers envisioned when they started a war to break free from the United States. King Cotton would reign supreme, and the slave republic would prosper. Unfortunately, such a scenario is extremely unlikely. It would not only require that the cotton boom of the 1850s extend indefinitely into the future but also require economic policies and political diplomacy that fly in the face of everything we know about the political and economic leadership of the South before and after 1860. Imagining the Confederate States of America becoming an economic and political force of this magnitude requires a leap of faith in the power of King Cotton that exceeds any reasonable assessment of the situation.

At the other extreme was the *pessimistic scenario* of a country faced with an abrupt end to the cotton boom, a growing level of international competition for the cotton market, and a slave system that becomes an economic anchor holding back any long-term growth and development. This Confederacy was in most respects worse off than the postbellum American South that had lost the war. It would be an economy struggling with the aftermath of the war, beset with a host of economic problems that would almost surely lead to corresponding political unrest. Whites might take some comfort from the fact that they had preserved their antebellum slave society, but even that would come under pressure from groups both inside and outside the Confederacy.

Between these extremes we found a third possibility that might be termed the *emancipation scenario*. In this world the Confederates simply elect to abolish slavery—possibly as early as the 1880s. Like our first option, this requires something of a leap of faith. But it may not be as improbable as it seems at first glance. One of the ironies of a civil war that is won by the South is that with the question of how to deal with the emancipated slaves left in their own hands, Southerners might have realized that they could have their cake and eat it too. Slavery always served two roles in Southern society: a means of race control and a form of economic organization that was hugely profitable. With the collapse of the cotton market, the slaves would become an economic liability. Emancipation would offer a way to eliminate the economic liability so long as some form of control was instituted to keep African-Americans "in their place." By the 1880s this could have been worked out. Emancipation would remove some of the obstacles of growth that stymied development up to that point, and as a result, the Confederate economy would probably be considerably better off in 1900 than in our pessimistic scenario.

Our counterfactual scenarios share a feature with the actual experience of the American South that lost the Civil War. They all were dependent on the export of a single crop, cotton. Our argument has been that the outcome of the American Civil War was *not* likely to change the forces at work in the international market for cotton. Unless the Confederates could find some way to break free of the grasp of King Cotton, the economic future of their new nation was probably just as bleak as that of the American South after the Civil War. Our exploration of counterfactual possibilities suggests that it is unlikely that the CSA would be any more successful in diversifying its economy than its counterparts in the real world of the postbellum South. The economic scenarios of the two historical possibilities would be quite similar—with one notable difference. Whites in the victorious Confederacy would almost certainly be better off than was the case in postbellum American South, and African-Americans would surely be much worse off. It is also well to remember that even in the most pessimistic scenario the Confederacy would be an economy that was well off by the standards of the late nineteenth century.

The major differences between a world with a victorious Confederacy and the world where the Rebels were defeated would be political, not economic. Up to this point we have concentrated our attention on the internal situation of the Confederate States of America. Our conclusion was that the Confederacy could survive and within limits grow into an economy that would place it among the wealthier nations of the world. As we look at the rest of the world up to 1900, we shall assume that the emancipation scenario is the one that prevails in our counterfactual world. Slavery would be abolished following the elections of 1880, and by the end of the century the Confederacy would have managed to make some strides in its effort to diversify its economy through domestic investment from the proceeds of emancipation bonds and the establishment of close ties to the European—particularly the British—markets. By itself, this development would have profound effects on the political situation not only in North America but in the world as a whole. It is to those issues that we now turn.

Chapter Five

. . . .

WHAT MIGHT HAVE BEEN: THE CIVIL WAR AND THE "WHOLE FAMILY OF MAN"

> [T]his issue embraces more than the fate of these United States. It presents to the whole family of man the question whether a Constitutional Republic or Democracy—a government of the people by the people [—] can or cannot maintain its territorial integrity against its own domestic foes. It presents the question whether discontented individuals . . . [can] break up their government, and thus practically put an end to free government upon the earth. It forces us to ask: "Is there, in all republics this inherent and fatal weakness?" "Must a government of necessity be too strong for the liberties of its own people, or too weak to maintain its own existence?"
>
> —Abraham Lincoln (July 4, 1861)

JUST A FEW WEEKS before the first major engagement of the war took place, Abraham Lincoln addressed Congress to apprise it of the current crisis. The struggle with the Rebel Confederate states, he argued, was a "people's contest," whose outcome would affect the "whole family of man." The president's assertion that the meaning of the American Civil War went far beyond the boundaries of the United States has been largely ignored on both sides of the Atlantic. In the United States the war is usually seen as an essentially American struggle that decided if our form of government could survive in the face of sectional differences that were peculiar to the United States. In Europe, where the effects of the Union's triumph were overshadowed by the Prussian victory over the French in 1871 and the formation of the German Empire, the war is seen in essentially the same light. Not until American economic and military might became the decisive factor enabling the Allies to win the First World War did the presence of a strong American state in the Western Hemisphere become an integral part of European history.

Lincoln's concern over whether or not there was an "inherent and fatal weakness" in the American system of government came at a time when the fortunes of liberalism throughout the world were at a low ebb. In the middle of the nineteenth century the ruling classes of Europe regarded the United States of America as an experiment in republican government that had already endured longer than most would have expected a half century earlier. This was a time when European liberalism was struggling just to survive in the face of stiff opposition. In 1848-49 a burst of revolutionary fervor swept across Europe. Liberal revolutionaries demanded constitutional reforms and greater representation in the governments of France, Prussia, Russia, and the Austro-Hungarian Empire. These movements were eventually crushed, and conservative regimes remained in power after granting only minor concessions to the rebels. To the dispirited liberals of Europe—more than a few of whom had migrated to America following the revolutions of 1848–49—the United States had become a beacon of light in an otherwise dark world. Though they were seldom in a position to be heard in their own country, liberal parties all around the world took notice of what was going on in the United States. One of the longest-lasting experiments in liberal government was being tested in the crucible of war. The outcome would have momentous consequences for the "whole family of man."[1]

Up to now we have centered our counterfactual analysis of the effects of the war on the future of the Confederate States of America. As we turn to the question of how a Confederate victory would affect the rest of the world—and particularly the United States—our task becomes much more speculative. Data from the real experience of a victorious Union will be of limited help in constructing the historical mold for a counterfactual story of the defeated United States. Our recipe will therefore call for larger doses of imagination and common sense, and our historical mold will be less likely to confine the results of that mixture.

FROM THE outset of the rebellion, Lincoln steadfastly insisted that the primary purpose of the war was preservation of the Union, not a crusade to abolish slavery. In August 1862 he sent an open letter to Horace Greeley, the founder and editor of the *New York Tribune*. "If I could save the Union without freeing any slave," Lincoln wrote, "I would do it, and if I could save it by freeing all the slaves, I would do it—and if I could save it by freeing some and leaving others alone, I would do that also."[2] While many regarded Lincoln's views on the question of emancipation and the war as the height of cynicism, the survival of the Union—with or without slavery—*was* what the war was all about in the eyes of many Americans. One of their greatest fears was that if the South succeeded in destroying the constitutional arrangements that held the states together in 1861, the United States would disintegrate into a mélange of petty states jockeying for power on the North American continent. As an example of that view, consider the words of Governor Oliver P. Morton of Indiana in a speech dedicating a monument at the Gettysburg battlefield in 1869. Looking back on the implications of the recent war, Morton claimed that "if the Rebellion had triumphed [and] the bond of union been broken, the various parts would have crumbled to pieces. We should have a slave-holding confederacy in the South; a republic on the Pacific; another in the Northwest, and another in the East. With the example of one successful secession, dismemberment of the balance would have speedily followed; and our country, once the hope of the world, the pride of our hearts, broken into hostile fragments, would have been blotted from the map, and become a byword among nations."[3] Morton's emotional scenario, delivered when the memories of the war were still fresh in everyone's mind, may have been a bit apocalyptic. But he was not alone in believing that the weakening of central authority that would inevitably follow in the wake of a successful rebellion by the Southern states would allow regional divisiveness to pull apart the government of the United States.

These fears were not without some foundation. For most of its relatively brief experience, the United States had been buffeted by bitter sectional divisions. By the time of Lincoln's election in 1860 the powers of the federal government had become so crippled by sectional strife that it could barely respond to the secession crisis.[4] The situation is best summed up by the dilemma articulated by President James Buchanan, who thought that secession was clearly illegal but at the same time maintained that he did not have the power to do anything about it. So the Buchanan administration stood idly by in the months following the election while Lincoln fumed on the sidelines and watched the authority of the federal government in the Southern states steadily diminish. Upon taking the reins of government in March 1861, Lincoln made it clear that he was determined to prevent a further erosion of federal authority in the South. The new president hoped to hold the Union together without war; however, he was willing to risk war even with a weak central government if that was what it took. His gamble when he accepted war as an option was not only the possibility that the United States might lose the war but also the risk that if his government failed to keep the South from seceding, it might not be strong enough to prevent further defections from the Union.

At first glance the defeated Union would indeed look fragile. However, closer consideration of the situation facing the United States in 1866 suggests that the bonds holding the Union together might have been stronger than Governor Morton suspected. Secession required the formation of a very strong consensus among those in the South wishing to leave. The leading Southern secessionists were a cohesive group that had a clear vision of what they hoped to gain: the preservation of their slave society. Nor was this an action taken in response to a sudden development; Southern politicians had talked about secession for more than two decades before they finally took the plunge in 1861. Which of the remaining states in the Union would have reason enough to strike out suddenly on their own in the years immediately following 1865?

No region outside the South had exhibited anything like the sense of cohesion that induced the secessionist movement in 1861. Governor Morton may have been basing his pessimistic conjectures on the situation in his own state of Indiana, where there had been a great deal of dissatisfaction with the government's conduct of the war. But these protests over the war would not be easily translated into the formation of a political coalition that would advocate leaving what was left of the Union. It would be incumbent upon those favoring secession to show that there would be some sort of advantage to following the South's strategy of setting up an independent republic.

The South's successful rebellion would pose a serious challenge to the economic stability of the Old Northwest. At a time when the only economically feasible route to outside markets for many Midwesterners was the Mississippi River, the prospect of having an independent Confederacy controlling that waterway would be unnerving, to say the least. Without that access to the Atlantic, Midwestern producers would have to depend on the rail and canal interests of the eastern seaboard for their access to outside markets. As one commentator noted, this would mean that Westerners would eventually become little more than the "slaves and serfs of New England."[5]

Offsetting the threat of economic control of transportation would be the enormous gains waiting to be harvested by Western producers shipping to the markets of the Eastern United States and the rest of the world. Despite the strain of wartime shortages and scarce labor, most farms in the Midwest prospered during the conflict. The peace following the Treaty of Toronto would not change that. Producers selling in the markets of the Eastern United States and abroad would find ready buyers, and even those who depended on the antebellum Southern market would be able to reestablish ties with customers in the Confederacy. Midwesterners might chafe at the threat of economic dominance by the Eastern bankers and railroad interests, but they could not ignore the fact that Western farmers needed those banking and transportation services. Breaking political bonds with the East would isolate the Western states politically and economically without offering any obvious advantages. The Midwestern states were not likely to leave the Union.

Next to the slave states the region with the greatest economic, political, and social cohesion in the antebellum United States was New England. This was the heartland of the antislavery movement, and voters would continue to offer strong support for the Republican program of political economy. With a population that was no longer expanding rapidly, many New Englanders might fear that the growing economic and demographic power of the mid-Atlantic states and the Old Northwest would eventually eclipse that of the New England states. Such a shift in political power might interfere with the efforts of New Englanders to infuse the country with an ideology of laissez-faire capitalism that was the intellectual underpinning of the Republican legislation passed during the war. Amid the crisis of the Republican Party following the election losses of 1864, party elders might even recall the Hartford Convention of 1814, when there was considerable pressure for

New England to pull out of the Federal Union.[6] But that was a long time ago; it is unlikely that a generation of New Englanders who had just been through a terrible war would find secession attractive in 1866.

There was, moreover, an additional obstacle to any serious thoughts of secession on the part of the New England states: They were simply too small. Only about 3.25 million people lived in the six New England states in 1870. The manufacturing and commercial interests in the region depended heavily on markets outside the region, and political isolation could easily lead to economic isolation. The New Englanders might flex their economic muscle from time to time, but they would almost surely opt to stay within the American Union.

The final region mentioned by Governor Morton was the Pacific coast. California, Oregon, and the territory of Washington would be isolated from the rest of the country, and California would still be struggling with the aftermath of the gold rush and its annexation from Mexico. Not surprisingly, the political situation in this region would be very volatile. Republican majorities in the coastal counties around San Francisco had been the key to Lincoln's success in carrying California in 1860, while the areas around Portland and the upper Willamette Valley had done the same for Oregon. But large areas in these states had also gone for either Breckinridge or Douglas. The idea of forming a Pacific Union stretching from Puget Sound to southern California might seem appealing to various groups in the region but it is unlikely that the territories east of the Rocky Mountain states would be eager to join such a move toward secession. As with New England, the most obvious constraint on the creation of an independent Pacific republic would be the sparse population. There were barely half a million people living in the three Pacific coast states at the end of the Civil War, hardly enough people to form a viable nation.

The presence of predatory neighbors that might hope to gain territory at the expense of the United States would be a final deterrent to any hasty action on the question of secession by the Pacific states: The British still coveted their claim to the Oregon Territory, which they had relinquished in the settlement of 1846, and the Confederates might have ambitions to establish a presence on the Pacific coast that could easily encourage them to seize Southern California. These are both plausible scenarios of territorial realignment in the Far West following our counterfactual Civil War; however, we shall assume for the moment that the Pacific states elect to stay with the United States and that the other powers are not willing to risk further conflict by trying to annex portions of them.

These considerations suggest that at least for the period immediately after the war, the political boundaries of the United States and the Confederacy after the Civil War would be those displayed in Map 4.1.

Governor Morton's fears that the United States might fall apart into three or four federations were unduly pessimistic. But the tensions that caused him to worry about such a possibility were very real, and defeat in the war would surely weaken the federal government's ability to deal with them. The Republican Party had propelled itself into a dominant position in Northern politics before the war with an aggressive platform that attacked the slave power and offered voters a program of political economy designed to appeal to those who took part in the market revolution in the North. But the failure to put down the rebellion of slave states created a new set of problems for politicians in the United States smarting from the recent defeat in the war.

EACH OF the two political parties that had dominated the scene before the war would face serious challenges in the counterfactual postwar environment. At first glance it would appear that the Republicans had the most to lose from the defeat in the war since they were the group that had championed the cause of the war, ineptly carried out the strategy and conduct of the war, and resisted the peace of 1865. We argued in chapter 3 that these actions would have cost them the presidency and control of Congress in 1864, and in the turmoil immediately following the war it is unlikely that they would have recouped many of their lost seats by the presidential election in 1868. Nevertheless, as things finally settled down, Republicans would have two important constituencies that would become the foundation of their party after the war.

Having secured a major portion of their legislative program in the early years of the war, the Republicans would center the cornerstone of their platform after 1865 on the same issues that formed their political economy before the war: protective tariffs, reorganization of the banking system, support for internal improvements, and cheap land.[7] Large numbers of voters in New England and on the Atlantic seacoast would continue to support this program, and there would also be strong support in the Western areas adjacent to the Great Lakes.[8] The other group of voters likely to strongly favor Republicans would be the 1.85 million veterans who had fought in the war.[9] Though individual politicians might suffer from their association with the Lincoln administration during the war, it would be the Democratic Party and the administration of Horatio Seymour that would be burdened with the onus of actually accepting the peace treaty that gave the Confederates their independence. By continuing to champion the cause of the war, by blaming the defeat on the Democrats, and by supporting federal government pensions and payments to disabled men, the Republicans could fashion strong support from veterans' groups after the war.

Elsewhere in the country the Republican program would surely meet serious resistance. Democrats would try to place the stigma of defeat in the recent war on the Republicans. Initially this would provide them with valuable political capital. We shall assume that Seymour's victory in the 1864 presidential election would be followed by a second term based on the efforts of his administration to get the country back to a stable peacetime footing. However, as things settled down, the Democrats would encounter increasing difficulty trying to use the war as an issue to their advantage. Not wishing to promote further hostilities, President Seymour would have to find some means of accommodation when dealing with the CSA. Any program that involved reconciliation with the South would not be popular with large blocs of voters in the North.

Democrats in our counterfactual scenario would have maintained or even increased their political advantage right after the war if they could have offered voters a cohesive program to counter the Republican political proposals enacted soon after the outset of the war. But the Democrats would not have a coherent program. In fact, with the slaveholders gone, Democratic Party leaders would find themselves trying to hold together a loose coalition of groups—nativists, tradesmen, wage earners, and tenant farmers—whose only common cause was blockage of various aspects of the Republican program. Eventually the inability of urban wage earners and tradesmen on the one hand, and rural farmers on the other, to agree on an agenda would fragment the Democratic Party into competing groups. Each group would feel pressured by the effects of the economic expansion of markets and industry. However, their difficulties stemmed from seemingly different sources. Wage earners would be primarily concerned with the need to deal with problems in urban labor markets, where wages could fluctuate widely in a short period of time and long-term employment was seldom guaranteed. Tradesmen would be concerned over the rise of factories and sweatshops that were steadily eroding the position of self-employed artisan establishments. The problem for the tradesmen and wage earners was to gain some degree of economic security for themselves and their families.[10] On the other hand, farmers faced a different set of problems from the challenges of commercial farming that accompanied the worldwide boom in foodstuffs of the 1870s and 1880s.[11] Their complaints focused on the monopoly power of such middlemen as banks, merchants, and railroads.

In the defeated United States both groups would have good reason to resist major elements of the Republican agenda, and many of the individuals in the groups would also resent the influx of foreigners who flocked to the United States after the peace. Their frustration with both the Democrats and the Republicans might easily result in a movement to form the Populist Party of the United States, a group of disaffected voters determined to resist the growing economic power of those who controlled the capitalist-industrial system of the United States. Catering primarily to the less affluent members of the agricultural sector, the Populists would probably never seriously be in contention for the presidency of the United States, but they would become a major force in elections throughout the West and in the border states, where they might win a number of statehouses in the 1880s and 1890s. More significant in the long run, the Populists would not simply disappear; they would remain a strong enough political bloc to provide the swing vote that was necessary for either of the two major parties to enact a legislative program.[12]

WE BEGAN this chapter by asking if the United States could hold itself together in the face of wartime failure. Our answer is that it would survive, though there would be three major political parties—Republicans, Democrats, and Populists—contesting elections rather than the two-party system that dominated the United States before the war. This proliferation of parties would do more than simply stymie one another's competing agendas. It would mean that to win the presidency, any party would have to have a moderate candidate who could appeal beyond his own party. On the basis of the unstable political situation in the North during the 1850s, we can speculate that the fragmenting of political parties would seriously weaken the influence of the federal government, which was already weak at the outbreak of the Civil War. We turn now to the question of how this political uncertainty would affect the economic and political future of the United States after 1865.

The most obvious effect of political and economic uncertainty in a defeated America would be to weaken the program of reform that the Republicans introduced after their victory in 1860. Parts of that agenda would escape unscathed. The wartime tariff would not be popular, but in the context of massive postwar debt and pension costs, cutting the only reliable source of government revenues would not be a feasible option for either party. With the South out of the picture, it is likely that cheap Western land, efforts to encourage internal improvements, and the creation of land grant colleges would also gain fairly strong support. However, efforts to centralize the banking system through the expansion of the national banking system created during the war would meet stiff resistance from Democrats and Populists alike.

The most vocal disputes between Republicans and their opponents would probably center on the United States' role in the evolution of the gold standard. The emergence of the gold standard in the last quarter of the nineteenth century is another one of those historical forces that would not be greatly affected by the outcome of the Civil War. Much has been made in previous chapters about the importance of world markets in shaping economic prospects for both the United States and the Confederacy. Both countries would continue to be active in the international marketplace, and both would therefore be drawn into the debates and changes that accompanied the rise of a worldwide standard of exchange. It will be useful, therefore, to look briefly at how the gold standard became the focus of a heated political debate and how the division of the Union would affect that debate.

As international trade expanded in the middle of the nineteenth century, the challenge of "paying" for imports and exports received growing attention. To deal with this problem, Great Britain adopted a policy of always being willing to exchange British currency for gold at a fixed rate in the mid-1820s.[13] In the years just after the American Civil War, most of the nations trading with Britain had followed its lead by pegging their currencies to the price of gold. The advantage of a currency fixed in value was not only that it facilitated payments for contracts for commodity trading but also that international investors need not worry about fluctuations in currency values when they assessed the risk of their investments. Since the United States was a major trading partner with most of these countries, the question of whether or not Americans would join those tying their currencies to gold became an issue that carried both domestic and international implications.[14]

While the gold standard facilitated international payments, a commitment to exchange openly dollars for gold or silver carried with it rather stringent monetary constraints on the actions of the U.S. Treasury. During the Civil War the price level in the United States doubled. This meant that the "value" of a dollar in terms of gold at the end of the war had fallen to one-half its prewar level. This posed a problem to the postwar Republican administrations of Grant and Rutherford B. Hayes. The Republicans were committed to a policy of resumption, but they were reluctant to change the value of a "gold" dollar. By following a policy of debt retirement, which included the retirement of greenbacks issued during the war, the Treasury managed to create a situation in which the money supply remained almost constant and prices fell by one-third over the course of the 1870s. This allowed the United States to resume convertibility by 1879. Democrats decried this policy of deflation and called for an expansion of the monetary base through the Treasury's purchase of silver as well as gold.[15] Two decades later emotions were still running high. Accepting the presidential nomination of the Democratic National Convention in 1896, William Jennings Bryan told the delegates: "[W]e will answer their demand for a gold standard by saying to them: You shall not press down upon the brow of labor this crown of thorns, you shall not crucify mankind upon a cross of gold." Despite his flamboyant rhetoric, Bryan lost that election, and Congress passed the Gold Standard Act four years later, finally putting to rest a bitter debate that had lasted more than three decades.

The splitting up of the American economy in our counterfactual world would have produced an element of added uncertainty to monetary systems throughout the world. The program of debt retirement and monetary stringency that characterized the Reconstruction United States would be far more difficult to enact in our counterfactual world following a Confederate victory. President Seymour and the Democrats would not see resumption of the currency by the end of the 1870s as a likely goal. Under Democratic administrations in the seventies, the Treasury would announce a one-time reduction in the value of the dollar immediately after the war and subsequently follow it by a mildly expansionist monetary policy that sought to combat the effects of a continued decline in prices. The United States therefore would have been on a bimetallic standard following the Southern victory.[16]

Would all this turmoil make a great deal of difference to the economic development of the United States in our counterfactual world? At a time when the United States was still importing large sums of capital from abroad, it would certainly make it more risky to engage in international transactions involving dollar payments. The likely solution to this problem would be to maintain the gold premium that existed on all international payments during the Civil War and into the Reconstruction years. The need to track gold and dollar values might have a discernible negative effect on the willingness of foreign investors to put their money in a United States economy struggling to overcome the impact of defeat in the Civil War. It is difficult to put a magnitude on such an effect, but we can be certain that it is a negative effect.

Another area where the political uncertainty following a defeat in the war would affect economic development was corporation law. The corporation was just emerging as a viable form of economic organization for business firms at the outbreak of the Civil War. Questions regarding the legal status of a corporation abounded. A major issue involved the question of whether the states or the federal government had the primary responsibility for chartering and regulating corporations. At an even more basic level was the question of whether or not corporations had legal rights similar to those of individuals. In the period immediately after the Northern victory, these issues were quietly addressed with a clause guaranteeing every "person" equal protection and due process under the law that was inserted into the Fourteenth Amendment to the Constitution. Ostensibly written to protect the rights of freedmen in the Reconstruction South, the clause was subsequently interpreted by the courts to mean that corporations also had a right to due process. This meant that the protection of the rights of a corporation shifted away from state or local courts toward the jurisdiction of the federal judiciary. The due process clause represented a major shift in the legal interpretation of the corporation.[17]

In the United States after a Confederate victory there would be no need for an amendment to protect the rights of freedmen in the South. Without that umbrella to cloak the intent of the corporate interests, would there be enough support for a constitutional amendment to strengthen the legal status of corporations? Probably not. That status would therefore remain largely under the aegis of state rather than federal courts. This would not end the rise of corporations, but it does suggest that the evolution of a corporate structure would be slowed by the need to wrestle with additional layers of possible legal entanglements caused by each state creating its own corporate laws. For those who argue that the emergence of the corporation after the war was a major factor in the rapid industrialization of the United States, the weakening of legal protection for corporate rights would, at the very least, have slowed the rate of growth of the American economy.[18]

One final area in which the effects of the war could have had a negative impact on American society would be on the willingness of Europeans to emigrate to the United States. Immigration has always been regarded by native-born Americans as a two-edged sword. On the one hand, the flow of people alleviated the chronic shortage of labor in the United States and provided an important impetus to aggregate demand in the economy. The immigrants tended to be young people who were highly motivated and included large numbers of innovative entrepreneurs who brought their skills and ideas across the Atlantic. Yet at the same time that it promoted economic and territorial expansion, immigration created major social and political challenges. The native-born population resented the intrusion of people with different languages, religious beliefs, and customs who arrived from other countries seeking jobs.

In a counterfactual United States, the fragmentation of political parties would provide ways for voters to give vent to their frustrations through political activism supporting limits on the entry of immigrants. It is quite likely that in the event of an independent Confederacy along the southern border of the United States, the Northern government would try to limit the entry of African-Americans seeking to move to the United States from the CSA. It seems equally likely that nativist voices in the Democratic and Populist parties would push an anti-immigration agenda with measures targeting specific ethnic groups as early as the 1880s. If they succeeded, one of the major forces promoting growth of the American economy would be muted.

Before we become overwhelmed by the problems associated with political and economic confusion in the wake of a Confederate victory, we should remind ourselves that some significant factors would ensure that the economic picture in 1865 was not entirely bleak for the Union. On the eve of the Civil War the United States was rapidly becoming the richest and most industrial economy of the world. It also enjoyed the most productive agriculture in the world. Despite the loss of nearly one-third of its territory, the country still had an abundance of resources and raw materials to fuel the expansion of both industry and agriculture. The U.S. economy had witnessed extraordinary economic expansion in the face of Southern obstructionism in Congress before the war. With the Southerners no longer around to block legislation, why wouldn't there be a quick resumption of the antebellum pattern of growth?

The answer is that while there would be a resumption of growth in the North, it would not either match the rapid rate of growth in the antebellum period or reach the explosive level of industrial expansion that followed the North's victory in the war. Virtually every study of the industrial expansion of the United States after 1865 identifies the formation of *national* markets as one of the keys to the extraordinary economic expansion after the defeat of the South. The formation of a stronger central state that emerged victorious in the war was an important factor promoting the extension of transportation and communication links, the encouragement of corporate business organizations that were able to take advantage of the economies of scale in marketing and production possible in large markets, and the expansion of a national capital market.[19]

The secession of eleven states not only meant a perceptible reduction in markets for Northern manufacturers and farmers but also meant that the central government, which was weak when the war began, would be weak when our counterfactual war ended. No single party would emerge powerful enough after the defeat to create a strong central authority. In this sort of political environment it seems likely that our counterfactual United States would continue to expand after losing the War of Southern Rebellion at a steady, but not spectacular, rate of growth. By the end of the century the United States would have evolved into a major economic and military power, certainly the largest nation in the Western Hemisphere. But like it or not, there was another kid on the block.

TO THIS point our discussion of both the victorious Confederacy and the defeated Union has been carried on as if they were separated from each other physically as well as politically and economically. In fact, the two nations would share more than three thousand miles of border and would be in continual contact with each other. Not all this interaction would be friendly, and as Lincoln astutely noted at the outset of the war, the political separation would make it more difficult to resolve differences. There would be strong economic incentives that would encourage the two countries to reestablish their antebellum pattern of economic cooperation and trade, but there would also be areas of economic rivalry. Anxious to capitalize on their advantage in the production of raw cotton, Southerners might impose export taxes on their staple crops. The North had few options with which to retaliate in this economic "warfare." It might try to place restrictions on the flow of investment capital to the Confederacy and perhaps restrict the trading of some commodities. Neither country would be anxious to encourage the movement of people across their borders. To the extent that either country allowed economic "nationalism" to override the gains and incentives for international trade, both would lose. Nevertheless, the history of international trade provides numerous examples in which perceived national interests overrode rational economic policy.[20]

Even more pronounced than the economic rivalry would be the political rivalry that would quickly surface as each country sought to exert its influence throughout the Western Hemisphere, often at the expense of the other. A major problem for the Confederacy in its international relations with the United States would be coping with the disparate size of the two countries. The rapid increase in both economic and demographic power of the Northern states before 1860 had been one of the major threats that Southerners had hoped to escape through their decision to secede. By the end of the 1850s the political clout of Southerners in the national government had shrunk to the point where a Northern majority could prevail on any given issue. Rather than see that situation persist, secessionists advocated that the South leave the Union.

Unfortunately for the South, breaking the political bonds with the North would not eliminate either the economic or military threat posed by the Northern colossus; it would merely change an internal problem into one of international affairs. When war broke out in 1861, the United States had twice as many people as the Confederacy, and this demographic advantage would continue to expand somewhat after the war. By the end of the century it is probable that the population of our counterfactual United States would be something on the order of fifty to fifty-five million people, two and a half times the number of people living in the Confederacy.[21] Our discussion of the relative performance of the two postwar economies suggests that the United States would also continue to build up a preponderance of economic power as the South struggled to free itself from the grips of the cotton economy. Southerners could see all too clearly that they still lived in the shadow of their former countrymen, and that shadow would grow larger as time went on. The Confederates had overcome long odds to win a war of independence, but how secure would their freedom be in the face of an antagonistic neighbor to the North that was several times as large as the Confederacy? In the immediate aftermath of the war the South would be obliged to seek help by forming a long-term alliance with Britain and France, the two countries that would have championed their cause at the end of the War of Southern Independence.

Though the United States had a huge resource base and an economy that ranked among the most developed in the world, it would also have concerns in the period after our counterfactual war. As a glance at Map 5.1 clearly shows, the geographical and political implications of secession would be profound. Before secession the Atlantic coast of the United States would have stretched from Maine to the southern tip of Texas. Access to the Atlantic Ocean and the Gulf of Mexico (including access using the Mississippi River system) posed no problem to Northern producers. After secession the East Coast would stretch only from Maine to Baltimore, and the southern half of the Mississippi would be controlled by the Confederacy. The postwar United States would be effectively "boxed in" by the presence of British Canada to the north and the Confederate States of America to the south. Particularly galling to the Americans would be the fact that the landmass of the Confederacy effectively cut the United States off from the states in the central and southern part of the hemisphere.

What would this imply for the development of the region bordering the Gulf of Mexico and the islands in the Caribbean? Throughout the antebellum period the United States had fiercely resisted any intrusions by European powers into the affairs of countries in the Western Hemisphere. In 1825 President James Monroe boldly announced that

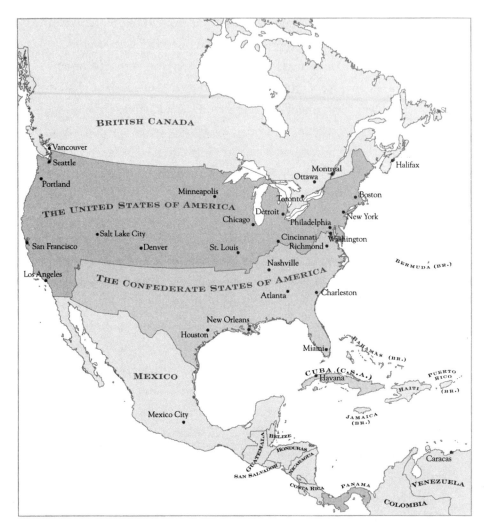

MAP 5.1

A COUNTERFACTUAL NORTH AMERICA IN 1900

the United States would "view any interposition for the purpose of oppressing" states in this hemisphere as "manifestation of an unfriendly disposition toward the United States." Though it was largely empty rhetoric at the time of his speech, the Monroe Doctrine eventually became an integral part of an American foreign policy that had effectively discouraged European involvement in the affairs of the Western Hemisphere.[22] With the creation of the Confederacy, the ability of the United States to enforce the Monroe Doctrine would be seriously compromised.

In fact, the Monroe Doctrine had been seriously compromised even before the American Civil War ended. In the spring of 1861 Mexican President Benito Juárez issued a decree suspending payment on all foreign loans issued by previous Mexican governments. In response to this action, a joint force of French, British, and Spanish troops landed at Veracruz, Mexico, ostensibly for the purpose of protecting foreign investments in a country that had been torn by years of civil strife. The British and Spanish quickly reached an agreement with the Mexican government and withdrew their troops. The French emperor Louis Napoleon had more ambitious plans. Rather than go back to France, French troops, intent on the overthrow of the Juárez regime, headed toward Mexico City. After a serious setback at Puebla in May 1862, the French contingent was reinforced, and the troops eventually occupied Mexico City. At this point the French proclaimed the Austrian archduke Maximilian to be emperor of Mexico. Juárez continued his resistance; however, by 1865 only five states in Mexico were controlled by the Juárez government. It appeared that Maximilian was on the verge of success. As it turned out, events in Europe and the North's triumph in the American Civil War induced the French to withdraw their troops, and without the support of the foreign contingent, Maximilian's forces were eventually defeated.[23]

France's intrusion into Mexico was a clear challenge to one of the cornerstones of American foreign policy. As it turned out, the Northern victory in the American Civil War and problems at home for the French forestalled that event. But what if it was the Confederacy rather than the United States who were the neighbors to the north of Mexico? Eager to accommodate their new allies, and perhaps hoping to gain a foothold in the formation of a friendly state just to the south of their own borders, Confederate leaders might be quite comfortable with the establishment of a Hapsburg monarch in Mexico. Nevertheless, it is doubtful that the French intervention would have produced a European monarchy in Mexico even in our counterfactual world. A Confederacy just emerging from a devastating war would not want to commit troops to ensure that Maximilian could stay in office, and events in Europe alone would still have forced the French to pull out of their Mexican adventure.

Nevertheless, France's attempt to create a client state in North America would send a clear signal that European powers were ready to challenge the ability of a weakened United States to enforce its Monroe Doctrine. The appearance of an independent Confederacy interposed between the United States and Mexico would mean that the Confederacy, not the United States, was now the northern neighbor of Mexico. In return for their guarantees of support in the event it was attacked by the United States, the Confederacy would be willing to invite its European allies to further expand their long-standing colonial interests in the Western Hemisphere. If nothing else, countries in Central America would have to realize that they now had to contend with the possibility of outside intervention not only from the United States but from the Confederacy and European nations as well.

OUR COUNTERFACTUAL possibilities have expanded to the point where it is increasingly difficult to attempt to deal with all the possible paths that history might take. Therefore, we shall adopt the counterfactual narrative employed in chapter 3 to describe a war that was won by the South. The counterfactual narrative of this section traces one possible outcome of the international rivalry that would have emerged following a Confederate victory. As with the case of the counterfactual war in chapter 3, this is only one of many possible scenarios; it is easy to imagine many others. We present it as if it actually took place, with notes to point out the divergence of this counterfactual scenario from reality.

Though they might fume over the collapse of the Monroe Doctrine, Americans trying to reorganize their foreign policy in the wake of the Southern victory in 1865 soon realized that there was not much they could do about their lack of influence in the Caribbean. One result of this closing off of the southern part of the Western Hemisphere was a renewed interest in developing the Far Western areas of the United States. In the years just prior to the Civil War, wrangling between Southern and Northern interests in Congress had blocked the passage of the Pacific Railway Act. With the Southerners gone, support for several transcontinental rail routes quickly materialized into multiple proposals to build rail connections to the Pacific coast. The first project was completed to San Francisco in 1869; within another decade railroads connected Portland, Seattle, and Los Angeles to the Eastern rail network. The hinterlands of these cities got huge economic boosts; by the mid-1890s the fertile lands of northern California and the Pacific Northwest were shipping huge amounts of grain and wide ranges of fruits and vegetables to markets throughout the world. Two important side effects of this development of the Pacific region had surfaced by the end of the century. One was the persistent pressures to build a water route across Central America that would link the Pacific Ocean with the Caribbean and drastically reduce the cost of shipment from the West Coast of the United States. The other was an expanded interest in Asia on the part of the United States. Seemingly cut off from the possibility of imperial ventures in Latin America, the United States was determined to push westward across the Pacific.

With the Monroe Doctrine pushed aside, the United States, the Confederacy, and the French and the British all were eager to capitalize on the growing chaos in Spain's American colonies. In the twenty years after the end of the American Civil War there was growing political unrest in Cuba, Haiti, and Puerto Rico. All the major powers were concerned that something be done to restore stability; however, any unilateral action taken by one country ran the risk of provoking serious objections from one of the other powers. This gridlock was finally broken in the fall of 1889, when the president of the Confederacy pro-posed a conference including the Confederate States, the United States, France, Britain, and Spain to discuss the deteriorating political situation in the Spanish colonies of Cuba and Puerto Rico and the problems on the island of Haiti. The French, disillusioned by their Mexican venture twenty years earlier and embroiled in their own political problems at home, declined the invitation, though they did send an observer to the conference. Representatives from the other four countries met in Richmond in March 1890 and drew up a docu-ment, which became known as the Richmond Agreement, designed to mitigate conflicting interests of the major powers in the Gulf of Mexico and the Caribbean.

Confronted with what amounted to an ultimatum from the signato-ries of the Richmond Agreement, Spain caved in. To make that deci-sion easier for the Spanish, the countries meeting in Richmond agreed to provide Spain with a sizable indemnity for the loss of its colonies. The Confederates got Cuba, a prize Southerners had coveted since before the Civil War. The British were able to consolidate their hold-ings in the Bahamas and Antilles by taking over Puerto Rico. The United States received "custody" of the island of Guam and of the Philippines. In return for agreeing to the loss of their colonies, the Spanish received fifteen million dollars from the Confederacy, ten million from the British, and fifteen million from the United States.[24]

The Richmond Agreement addressed another source of potential friction in the region, the construction of a canal across the Isthmus of Panama. In the 1880s a French company had attempted to dig such a canal, but the project failed amid problems of corruption, insufficient financing, and the challenges of tropical illnesses. Adding to all the other problems facing such a project was the rivalry of the three major powers over which would have sovereignty over the canal if one were built. The signatories of the Richmond Agreement pledged to cooper-ate in the construction of a canal and agreed that any canal that linked the two oceans must be open to the ships of all nations on an equal basis. A consortium of firms from the United States had already been working on a proposed canal at the time of the conference, and in the summer of 1892 the United States and Britain agreed that the United States should be given a free hand in building and operating the canal. A final problem, obtaining the right-of-way for the canal, was conveniently solved by a revolution in Colombia (instigated by the United States) that established the "independent" country of Panama in July 1896. The United States promptly negotiated a treaty creating a "zone" under American control in which the canal could be constructed. The project was completed in 1910.[25] This was a major breakthrough for the United States, which now at least had a limited entry into the Caribbean and controlled a vital transportation link between the Pacific and Atlantic oceans. The completion of the Panama Canal also meant that the United States could now quickly move forces from the western coast of North and Central America to the Caribbean.

By the end of the century some sense of order had been restored to the Caribbean, but it was Britain and the Confederacy, not the United States, that were the principal players in the region. The biggest gains from all this fell to the British, who now had naval installations at Halifax, Bermuda, and Jamaica and a joint facility with the Confederacy at Havana. This dramatic shift in naval power would not be lost on the governments of smaller states in Central America. Though nominally independent, such states as Mexico, Venezuela, and Colombia would have to worry about the possibility of unwanted interference from either the CSA or Britain.

With the acquisition of the Philippines under the terms of the Richmond Agreement and the annexation of Hawaii, the major imperial interests of the United States would be focused in the Pacific. While Britain and the Confederacy were busily gobbling up Spanish possessions in the Caribbean, the Americans established themselves as a major power in the Pacific, and together with other Western nations they began to cast a covetous eye on the disintegrating Chinese Empire. Imperialist successes in the Pacific would alleviate some of the frustration from events closer to home. But the growing dominance of Britain and the Confederacy in the Caribbean would still be a hard pill for Americans to swallow. They were not used to being a second-rate major power in their own neighborhood. The Republicans had been courting the votes of disgruntled veterans ever since the end of the Civil War, constantly reminding voters that it was the Democrats that had signed the peace and created the problem of a resurgent Confederacy and the intrusion of John Bull into the Americas. In the late 1880s the Republicans began advocating a tougher stance in foreign affairs dealing with the Confederates and their allies in the Western Hemisphere. This bellicose stance found instant appeal to a large group of voters whose chauvinistic instincts called for an expansion of America's role in Central America. The cornerstone of the policy was a significant expansion of the U.S. Navy, a program that not only promised to restore some measure of prestige to the depleted military fortunes of the United States but also provided much-needed jobs for workers in the Northeast.

The United States felt the pressure of being surrounded on three sides by potentially hostile states, but it was still confident that it was the strongest military and economic power in the Western Hemisphere. As the twentieth century wound down, an uneasy standoff would exist between the three powers controlling North and Central America: the United States, the Confederate States of America, and Great Britain. The determined success of the Republicans in escalating the military preparedness of the United States produced an arms race to maintain military and economic parity between the two sides. Here again, the Confederacy would need outside assistance to maintain their armaments, providing one more way in which the creation of an independent country to rival the United States inexorably drew European nations into the affairs of the Western Hemisphere.

WHILE ALL this was going on in the Western Hemisphere, events in Europe were moving forward at a rapid pace. The most significant development was the rise of the German Empire as the dominant political, economic, and military force on the European scene. Following the defeat of France in the Franco-Prussian War of 1870–71, King Wilhelm I of Prussia was crowned kaiser of the German Empire. Over the next twenty years, Chancellor Otto von Bismarck, who had been the architect of German unification, orchestrated the creation of a network of treaties designed to protect German interests throughout Central Europe and the Balkans. Bismarck's strategy was to guarantee peace by ensuring a network of defensive coalitions that would discourage any single power from disrupting the status quo. The German chancellor followed a simple rule: Germany should always be allied with at least two other major European powers. To this end in 1873 he successfully negotiated the Three Emperors' League, an agreement that bound the German Empire, the Austro-Hungarian Empire, and the Russian Empire together into a mutual defense pact. When the Russians became estranged from Austria over issues in the Balkans in 1879 and pulled out of the Three Emperors' League, Bismarck negotiated a new alliance with Austria and sought ways to forestall any alliances among Russia, France, and Britain.[26]

When Wilhelm I died in 1890, his son, Wilhelm II, quarreled with Bismarck and summarily dismissed him. Without the "Iron Chancellor" the complex system of alliances that Bismarck had so carefully designed to protect Germany gradually came apart, and by the mid-1890s France had seized the diplomatic initiative by forging a three-way alliance with Britain and Russia. These efforts were eventually rewarded in 1907 with the formation of the Triple Entente. This new alliance meant that Bismarck's worst nightmare had finally materialized. Germany faced not only the prospect of a two-front war in the event of a crisis involving either Russia or France but also the power of the British Navy in the event of war with the entente powers. The German military command, led by General Alfred von Schlieffen, responded to this threat by developing a plan that assumed France and Russia would be simultaneously at war with Germany. What became known as the Schlieffen Plan called for the German armies to defeat the French before the British could intervene and then turn their attention to the Russians.[27]

The Germans were not the only nation with a plan for war. All the European countries had developed detailed plans to mobilize their forces in the event of a crisis. There were several problems with this situation. The plans were not flexible, and once the process of mobilization was begun, it was virtually impossible to stop or change the process. Moreover, the plans were drawn up on a set of circumstances that might or might not actually prevail at the time of mobilization. The Schlieffen Plan, for example, assumed a war against *both* Russia and France, whichever country actually posed a threat at the time of mobilization.

Realizing the threat posed by encirclement, the Germans sought ways to neutralize the economic and military power of the entente. One key to the entente's power was the enormous resource base represented by the British Empire and its American ally, the Confederate States of America. In exchange for British support in protecting their interests in the Western Hemisphere, the Confederates had promised to aid the British if they were attacked. That left only one major power, the United States, with no major treaty commitments. While the United States had little desire to be drawn into European conflicts, it found itself in a similar position to Germany's: boxed in on two sides by potentially antagonistic countries. As early as the late 1870s Bismarck had noted the growing annoyance of the United States with the emerging alliances among the Confederates, the British, and the French. When former President Horatio Seymour visited Germany in the fall of 1878, Bismarck went out of his way to meet him and comment on the mutual interests of Germany and the United States. Over the next thirty years the two countries maintained increasingly cordial relations. Spurred on by the formation of the entente and its treaty with the Confederates, Germany and the United States signed a Neutrality Agreement in 1909 that stipulated that either country would remain neutral in the event the other was attacked. Though it was not a binding agreement that committed either country to provide military assistance to the other in case of attack, it was clearly understood that in any conflict involving either country, the other country would regard a violation of neutrality as a casus belli.

The Neutrality Agreement of 1909 was a huge diplomatic victory for Germany, for it virtually guaranteed that if either country went to war, the other would be sure to follow sooner or later. One of the issues that had created enormous frictions throughout the nineteenth century between Britain and the United States was the difficulty posed by neutral countries in the event of a naval blockade. During the Napoleonic Wars the British had imposed a blockade against Napoleon's empire in Europe. The United States objected to the blockade, and the refusal of the British to honor the neutrality of American vessels had been a major factor leading to the War of 1812. Fifty years later the roles had been reversed when the United States imposed a blockade on the Confederacy during the American Civil War. This time it had been the British who argued that their rights as a neutral nation were being violated. By the end of the century it was clear that if there were a conflict between Britain and Germany, the British would impose a blockade of German ports on the North Sea. This would presumably be a casus belli for the United States in the event that the Royal Navy intercepted American ships. And what would the entente's response be to the prospect of American or German ships' intercepting a "neutral" Confederate ship on its way to either France or Britain?

All this diplomatic maneuvering was played out in the context of the most massive buildup of arms the world had ever seen. Technology had dramatically changed the nature of war. On the ground there were repeating rifles and machine guns and artillery weapons that ranged from rapid-fire low-caliber field pieces to huge howitzers capable of throwing hundreds of pounds of high explosives in a single round. At sea there was a whole new class of warships called dreadnaughts that could travel at speeds of up to thirty knots and carry fifteen-inch guns, as well as submarines capable of launching torpedoes that could sink ships with or without warning. Finally, the Industrial Revolution meant that even the most backward major power had the productive capacity to arm and supply millions rather than thousands of infantrymen. By the end of the first decade of the twentieth century every major power in Europe and America had assembled a massive arsenal with which to wage war.[28]

The world was a powder keg ready to explode. All that was needed was for someone to light a match.

WE HAVE pushed our counterfactual recipe as far as it can go; the historical mold has become so speculative that it can no longer handle our counterfactual pudding. No matter what mix of ingredients we come up with, the result will be too heavily weighted with imagination. The counterfactual world we have constructed for 1914 is in some ways similar to that which one reads about in the standard sources on the beginning of the twentieth century. This, as we noted at the beginning of chapter 3, results from a deliberate attempt on our part to keep the story sufficiently close to reality that the modern reader can still relate to the historical setting.

Yet upon inspection, it is clear that things *have* changed. In place of the monolithic United States of America of Teddy Roosevelt and Woodrow Wilson, we find a North American continent that is split into two antagonistic states engaged in what today we would call a cold war of acrimony and the buildup of armaments. The economic welfare of people in both the United States and the Confederacy, particularly if one includes the situation of freed African-Americans in the South, would be significantly lower in our counterfactual world, and to make matters worse, the world in which they lived would be far less secure. Adding to the frictions and disputes between the two American states would be the involvement of European states in North American politics. In the actual world of 1914 there was every reason to believe that if a war did break out in Europe, the United States could remain out of it.

Not so in our counterfactual world. What we have described is a situation rife with possibilities for crises that could provide the spark that could explode into a major war. If that conflict broke out, it was almost certain that the two American states would be drawn into the fray rather soon after it began—on opposing sides. And when the battles were finally over, the "cost" in terms of money and men to Americans would be horrendous.

IN 1861 Abraham Lincoln argued that the struggle to preserve the American Union was a struggle "not altogether for today" but "for a vast future" as well. Lincoln of course did not know what that future might be. Combining the ingredients provided by hindsight and imagination, we have tried to trace out in some detail the course of events in a world where the Union was not preserved. Perhaps the clearest conclusion to emerge from those efforts is that Lincoln was right.

The future of not only America but of the "whole family of man" rested on the outcome of the war to preserve the American Union.

THE END OF
THE BEGINNING

ON A COLD, BLUSTERY day in April 1918, Theodore Roosevelt sat in the Oval Office of the White House. A large crowd of invited officials, people from the press, and curious onlookers had gathered in the Red Room and were eagerly waiting for the president to appear and make a statement regarding the recent rumors of a resolution passed by the Congress in closed session dealing with the settlement of the war with the Confederate States of America.

The president was content to let them wait a few more minutes. The strain of seeing the country through the worst war in its history had taken its toll on his health. It had all begun in early 1915, when a joint force of British and Confederate naval units attacked the American naval base in the Panama Canal Zone. The attack was only the latest in a series of incidents between the naval forces of the United States and of Britain and the Confederacy. The Roosevelt administration had managed to ignore them up to that point, but an outright attack on a U.S. naval base was too much. On February 13, 1915, the president addressed the U.S. Congress and asked for a declaration of war against the entente powers and the Confederate States of America. By the time the fighting was over three years later, more than three million Americans—North and South—had died. One of them was the president's son Quentin, who died fighting on the Virginia front in 1917.

Taking a deep breath, Roosevelt looked at the piece of paper on his desk one more time. It was titled A Resolution to Reestablish the United States of America, and it spelled out the terms for peace that had been agreed upon the previous morning by a joint session of Congress. Briefly summarized, the document said that:

> First, all organized resistance against the United States in the Confederate States must cease immediately, and the Confederate government must surrender its authority to the government of the United States of America;
>
> Second, territory constituting the Confederate States of America, including possessions overseas, will be placed under the martial law of the U.S. military until such time as the president, in consultation with a joint committee of Congress, determines that order has been sufficiently restored and that free elections can be held for the establishment of a new state government;
>
> Third, during this period of martial law, all law-abiding citizens who have taken an oath of allegiance to the United States of America will have the full rights and privileges due a citizen of the United States;
>
> Fourth, after duly certified elections have been held, any state government of the former Confederacy may reapply to the U.S. Congress for admission as a state of the Union.

Not until Douglas MacArthur, the brash young brigadier who was one of Roosevelt's personal favorites, came in to see if the "chief" was all right, did the president fold the paper, put it in his pocket, and slowly descend the stairs to address the waiting crowd.

His speech was brief and to the point. Noting that it had been several weeks since Confederate President Woodrow Wilson had asked for an armistice, Roosevelt announced that he and members of the U.S. Congress had been working on a plan for "reunion" to present to the Confederate government. After summarizing the plan and commenting that some details "had yet to be worked out," the president concluded his remarks:

I learned this morning from President Wilson that his government is prepared provisionally to accept these terms. I had hoped that he would be able to join us today for the formal announcement of the peace, but unfortunately his health does not allow him to make the trip. In his place is the former chief of staff of the Confederate Army, General J. E. B. Stuart III. We thank General Stuart for being in attendance for this joint announcement.

With the authority vested in me by this congressional resolution I hereby announce that we shall begin at once the process of having United States officers assume responsibility for government in the territories formerly controlled by the Confederate States of America.

It is my fervent hope that we shall be able to work with Mr. Wilson and his aides to reunite our people into a single nation that is once again "indivisible with liberty and justice for all." This is a task that will be neither quick nor easy. But we shall do it. We must do it. If we succeed, decades from now, people will look back at this moment in our history and say, "That was the end of the beginning."

Following the president's remarks, there was a brief statement from General Stuart acknowledging his government's provisional acceptance of these terms.

At the end of the ceremony, as the president turned to go back upstairs, the band again started playing "Hail to the Chief." Roosevelt paused for a moment and held up his hand for quiet. He whispered something to an aide, who hurried over to the bandstand and exchanged a word with John Philip Sousa.

As Roosevelt began trudging up the stairs, the White House band played "Dixie." For the first time in more than a week the president smiled.

Appendix 1

. . . .

MEASURING
CASUALTIES
IN THE CIVIL WAR

IT IS COMMONPLACE FOR historians writing of battles to refer to the number of casualties suffered by each side. Quantitative historians often use these data to assess the degree of damage to either side and to assess who "won" the battle. At several points in chapter 2 we have succumbed to this tendency and made reference to the number of men engaged and casualties suffered by each side in key battles of the Civil War. This appendix presents a brief discussion of the reliability of those data and comments on the problems and limitation of using engagement and casualty statistics for the Civil War.

For most of the battles discussed in the text, we used the estimates constructed by Thomas Livermore in his *Numbers and Losses for the Civil War in America*.[1]

Livermore presents detailed data for "total effectives" present at the time of the battle and for the number of men "killed, wounded, and missing" in selected battles of the war. These data, first published in 1901, are widely accepted as the most reliable estimates available, and it is significant to note that most of the efforts to improve upon them using other methods or sources have produced results that were not

markedly different from the earlier figures.[2] While Livermore's estimates have held up remarkably well over the years, the fact remains
that in many instances they are hardly more than an educated guess on
the actual number of combatants and casualties in a particular battle.

The most obvious problem facing anyone trying to estimate the
number of men engaged and lost in a battle stems from the quality of
the data available from records at the time. Livermore's basic source for
casualty and engagement figures are the reports of field commanders
published after the war in *The War of the Rebellion: A Compilation of the
Official Records of the Union and Confederate Armies*. These reports were
typically made by officers weeks or even months after the engagement.
Not only were they based on recollections after the fact, but the person making the report sometimes had strong incentives to be less than
candid in providing information on casualties to his superior. Statements to the effect that the unit had lost "about" or "around" so many
men killed, wounded, or missing are common, suggesting that the figures submitted are at best approximations of what happened. Where
the official reports were lacking or unreliable, Livermore collected
data from such sources as personal memoirs of combatants or observers.
Another valuable source of information for the size of engagement and
number of losses was the rolls of individual units, to ascertain their
strengths shortly before and after a battle. If you know the number of
men at any one moment, it may be possible to extrapolate forward to
get the number of men in various units right before the battle. A comparison of men present before and after the battle can reveal the losses
from a fight. While this system can be extremely useful, it is important
to note that you lose a degree of freedom compared with direct estimates of men engaged or lost, since your estimate of one of the two
variables in making the extrapolation depends on the accuracy of the
other. By their nature, estimations of losses or numbers engaged using
extrapolations of unit sizes over time are aggregative in nature, and it
may be difficult to account for all the reasons for a change in size, some
of which may not be associated with the battle itself. The examination

of regimental rolls has also proved to be a valuable source of data for estimating "numbers and losses" in the war.[3]

As the numerous detailed footnotes to Livermore's tables make clear, even after a concerted effort has been made to locate data that directly pertain to a particular battle, significant gaps may remain. To fill in these gaps, and at times to check the accuracy of data in the official reports, Livermore developed "ratios" of loss figures from data that were available from other reasonably comparable situations. For example, the ratio of the number killed and wounded to the number of men engaged in certain units can be used to estimate casualties in other units engaged in the same battle. Needless to say, the numbers derived from such calculations move us even further into conjecture and uncertainty. A major problem with the use of ratios to estimate casualties by unit is that the casualty rates among units can vary widely in a battle depending on the area of fighting where they were engaged. Units involved in charging an enemy dug into a defensive position might easily suffer casualty rates of 50 percent or more, while only a short distance away a unit that was not called upon to take such offensive action might lose less than 10 percent of its strength. Accounting for such variances between units is one of the great advantages of the unit by unit approach to estimating casualties if the data are available. Finally, there are some battles for which there are no reliable estimates of losses from any of the contemporary sources or any proxies to use as an indirect means of estimating losses. At this point, Livermore simply threw in the towel and stated that no information was available.[4]

One might wonder at this point how much confidence should be placed in a statement that "Confederate losses at the battle of Gettysburg totaled 22,874." In fact, as we shall presently point out, estimates of Confederate losses for that battle range as high as more than twenty-eight thousand men. Both results suggest that the battle was terribly bloody, with casualty rates between one-third and one-quarter of the men engaged. But why is there such a variance in the estimates? Part of the discrepancy involves the use of different sources used to gather

the data. There may also be significant differences in what the historian means by "losses" in a battle. Military historians commonly identify three categories of battlefield statistics: the number of men killed,
the number of men wounded, and the number of men missing. While
these measures might seem at first glance to be mutually exclusive, the
fact is, serious overlaps between the categories arise in the process of
estimation.

Soldiers reported as "killed" refer to "battlefield deaths" at the time
of the struggle. There is a grim sense of finality about these numbers;
they represent the best estimates of how many men were left on the
field after the armies retired. For those men who were known to have
died in action, the war was over. But the "body count" from the field
was an incomplete measure of men who were killed in this battle. In
every case of a battle, there will be some fraction of men reported as
"wounded" who will die of their wounds in a relatively short time. We
might reasonably suspect that some of the men who were reported as
"missing" were killed, but their bodies never found. This is particularly
true in the case of a defeated army that leaves the field before burying
its dead.

There are additional issues raised by the situation of men who were
reported "wounded" and survived the battle. Some of them were sent
to the rear permanently crippled, and for them the war was over just
as surely as it was for their comrades who died on the field of battle.
But a significant fraction of those reported wounded recovered enough
to return and fight again. Unlike men killed or crippled from their
wounds, these men were not permanently "lost" to their army. If the
historian adds the total number of wounded men to those killed as a
measure of men "lost," that number will be a reasonable estimate of the
immediate impact of the battle on an army's manpower, but it may
overstate the long-term implications of the battle's outcome on the
manpower available in the future. This problem is compounded if he
includes the total losses for several battles in a single campaign. Unfortunately, there is no way to untangle the degree of injury among the

"wounded" category, so we are left with a statistic—which typically amounts to well over half of all the men reported "lost" in a battle—that is an uncertain guess of an inherently ambiguous measure.

Men reported "missing in action" represent the most ambiguous category of casualties. As we noted above, some portion of these men were probably killed in battle but never found. At the other extreme were those who were missing because they deserted. Experience reveals that many of these deserters were absent without leave—AWOL—and returned to the army in the near future. They were not really casualties at all except in the very short term. The remainder of the "missing in action" category would have been soldiers who were captured by the enemy, in many cases because they had been wounded. Most writers treat prisoners the same as all other casualties—that is, they were permanently lost to the army. But for how long? During the period that is the focus of our study in this chapter there were prisoner exchanges that restored many men to their army. In cases where there were very large numbers of prisoners, the victors sometimes paroled the captives and allowed them to return to their homes. Though these soldiers were not supposed to fight again, they often did return to the army, and even if they stayed home, their labor contributed to the war effort. Unfortunately, there is usually no way to disentangle soldiers in these last categories of "missing in action" without specific data on deserters or the number of prisoners taken by the other side.

If casualty statistics must be regarded with skepticism, the estimates for the number of soldiers "engaged" in a battle are equally problematic. In situations where records were available, Livermore noted that they give the numbers in the various campaigns and battles variously as "present for duty," "present for duty equipped," or "effective."[5] Even if these numbers were accurate, they provided only an approximation of the number of men actually available to fight. None of the measures accounted for stragglers and noncombatants who would not be in action. Because he had no way of accurately measuring these missing persons, Livermore "computed the number of effectives in the infantry and artillery at 93 per cent., and in the cavalry at 85 per cent., of the number present for duty" to get an estimate of those actually available for action.[6] For situations where the number present at the time of the battle were not reported, he estimated the men engaged either by extrapolating backward from reports—often broken down to a regimental level of disaggregation—that enumerated the number present at some point *after* the battle, less the estimated number of men lost in the battle, or by taking a similar inventory of men present sometime *before* the battle and deducting the losses between that time and the beginning of the battle under consideration.

A further problem arises in estimating the number of men engaged for campaigns or battles that stretched over more than one day. Typically, the number of men engaged in the fighting changed as units arrived on the scene, and the number of effectives also changed as a result of casualties over the course of the battle. Significant examples of this sort of situation would be the battles of Shiloh, Antietam, and Gettysburg. At Shiloh Buell's twenty thousand troops did not arrive until the evening of the first day of battle. Their arrival to augment Grant's initial force of forty-two thousand turned a situation in which the Union army was outnumbered into one in which it significantly outnumbered the Confederates and could launch a counterattack the following day. At Antietam, Lee started with only about forty thousand men, and it was the timely arrival of A. P. Hill's ten thousand troops late in the afternoon that helped the Army of Northern Virginia stave off disaster. At Gettysburg a significant number of units on both sides did not arrive on the scene of battle until the second day. Though the estimates for the aggregate numbers for soldiers engaged at Gettysburg show a numerical superiority favoring the Union side, the Confederates actually had a significant numerical advantage on the first day and well into the second day of battle.

All this is not to say that the estimates of casualties and men engaged in battles are useless. Despite all the shortcomings detailed above, the estimates of Livermore and successive generations of historians who have toiled over statistics of battle reports, memoirs, and regimental rosters provide a good approximation of the scale of battles and the number of men lost in action during the war. Our point in discussing the estimation problems is to underscore the need for care in using these data—particularly with regard to comparisons between battles of the war. For the discussion of casualties in chapter 2 we elected to use the estimate for the *total number of men lost* in each battle as the most useful measure of the battle's impact. In part this reflects the problems of estimation and the inherent difficulty of separating out the various components of casualties that create different biases in different battles. In part it reflects the intent of our analysis, which emphasizes the longer-term impact of casualties and stresses how deadly *all* Civil War battles were.

Table A.1 presents a summary of estimates of killed, wounded, and missing soldiers for the battles discussed that were employed in chapter 2 and elsewhere in this book. For the most part, we stayed with Livermore's original figures for the men engaged and lost in the battles listed. A number of authors have developed estimates that more accurately reflect the number of men engaged or lost in a specific battle. Where this is the case, and where the number differs significantly from Livermore's estimates, we have substituted the newer estimate in Table A.1. The source notes explain the reasons for adjusting the original estimates. We suspect that at least for the battles in this table our estimate of losses is an upper limit on the actual depletion of each side's manpower pool. To the best of our ability, we have sought to eliminate any marked bias that would favor one side or another in a particular battle. For those interested in comparing our results with those using the more restrictive statistic "killed and wounded," those data are also presented in this table.

Table A.1 provides the raw data for the estimates of losses and casualty rates presented in Table 2.1 of the chapter. The casualty rates presented in Table 2.1 are computed as the number of men lost to the number engaged, and the table also presents the ratio of Confederate

TABLE A.1
NUMBER OF KILLED, WOUNDED, AND MISSING SOLDIERS, SELECTED BATTLES OF THE CIVIL WAR, 1862–63

Battle	Union Armies				Confederate Armies			
	Men Engaged	Killed and Wounded	Missing in Action	Total Losses	Men Engaged	Killed and Wounded	Missing in Action	Total Losses
Virginia								
Peninsula campaign[a]	173,734	16,046	7,073	25,370	169,120	27,038	1,413	30,450
Williamsburg	40,768	1,866	373	2,239	31,823	1,570	133	1,703
Fair Oaks	41,797	4,384	647	5,031	41,816	5,729	405	6,134
Seven Days	91,169	9,796	6,053	15,849	95,481	19,739	875	20,614
Second Manassas[b]	62,000	10,096	5,958	16,054	48,527	9,108	89	9,197
Antietam	75,316	11,657	753	12,410	51,844	11,724	2,000	13,724
Fredericksburg	100,007	10,884	1,769	12,653	72,497	4,656	653	5,309
Chancellorsville[c]	97,382	11,116	5,676	17,300	57,352	10,746	2,018	13,460
Gettysburg[d]	85,683	17,684	5,365	22,813	75,188	22,638	5,425	28,063
Other Virginia battles	106,153	4,759	1,060	5,819	82,970	3,903	865	4,768
Cedar Mountain	8,030	1,759	594	2,353	16,686	1,338	-	1,338
South Mountain	28,480	1,728	85	1,813	17,852	1,885	800	2,685
Mine Run	69,643	1,272	381	1,653	48,432	680	65	745
Total	700,275	82,242	27,654	112,419	557,498	89,813	12,463	104,971

	Union Armies				Confederate Armies			
Battle	Men Engaged	Killed and Wounded	Missing in Action	Total Losses	Men Engaged	Killed and Wounded	Missing in Action	Total Losses
Kentucky/Tennessee:								
Richmond, Ky.	6,500	1,050	4,303	5,353	6,850	450	1	451
Perryville[e]	23,000	3,696	515	4,211	15,000	3,145	251	3,396
Murfreesboro	41,400	9,220	3,686	12,906	34,732	9,239	2,500	11,739
Chickamauga	58,222	11,413	4,757	16,170	66,326	16,986	1,468	18,454
Chattanooga	56,359	5,475	349	5,824	46,165	2,521	4,146	6,667
Total	185,481	30,854	13,610	44,464	169,073	32,341	8,366	40,707
Mississippi Valley								
Shiloh	62,682	10,162	2,885	13,047	40,335	9,735	959	10,694
River campaigns	172,796	14,842	1,790	16,632	143,265	9,470	47,463	56,933
Donelson[f]	27,000	2,608	224	2,832	21,000	2,000	14,623	16,623
Corinth/Iuka[g]	21,147	2,196	324	3,300	22,000	2,470	1,763	5,700
Chicsaw Bayou	30,720	1,290	563	1,853	13,792	197	10	207
Champion's Hill	29,373	2,254	187	2,441	20,000	2,181	1,670	3,851
Vicksburg Assault[h]	45,556	3,052	147	3,199	31,737	2,340	29,397	31,737
Port Hudson	19,000	3,442	345	3,787	7,679	282	-	282
Total[i]	235,478	25,004	4,675	29,679	156,543	19,205	48,422	67,627
Total all campaigns	1,121,234	138,100	45,939	186,562	883,114	141,359	69,251	213,305

(continued)

losses to Union losses. One major adjustment to the data of Table A.1 was necessary for our analysis. More than forty thousand Confederate troops surrendered at Fort Donelson and Vicksburg. This is more than all other Confederate losses for the battles in the Mississippi theater. By most accounts, a substantial fraction of these men were immediately released on parole or eventually exchanged so that they could return to action. Including such a large number of paroled prisoners in the data for Confederate casualties seriously distorts the nature of losses in the Mississippi theater and indeed in the data for the Confederacy as a whole.[7]

There is one final caveat that must be considered in assessing the costs of battles and campaigns. The men who died or were wounded in battle represented only a fraction of all those who died or were crippled by the war. Nearly twice as many men died of disease during the war as

---

Notes to Table A.1

a. Total losses are estimated by Sears for the entire Peninsula campaign "from Yorktown to Seven Days" (5:355).

b. The estimate for men engaged in the battle for the Army of the Potomac is from McPherson (4:281).

c. Total losses are estimated by Sears (6:493, 501).

d. There is considerable disparity among historians regarding the number of men engaged and casualties at Gettysburg. For the number of men engaged, we have taken the estimates by Bowden and Ward, which appear to be the most detailed effort to ascertain the number of men present (1:551, 582). Noah Trudeau offers the most recent attempt at recomputing the losses for each side. While his estimate for the Union losses seems reasonable, his estimate of 22,813 for Confederate losses is substantially below the estimates of others (7:529). McPherson claims that the Confederates lost "at least 24,000 men" at the battle and that "after accounting for stragglers," Lee's army had "42,000 effectives before crossing the Potomac" (4:358). If that was the case, Livermore's estimate of just over 28,000 in total losses is perhaps not far off the mark. We have therefore elected to accept Livermore's number as a reasonable estimate of total Confederate losses for the entire Gettysburg campaign.

e. Number of men engaged is from McPherson (4:313).

f. Livermore's estimate of the number of men missing in action includes prisoners who surrendered at the end of the battle. Cooling puts this figure at 12,000 to 14,000 (2:215).

g. Total losses for both sides is from McPherson (4:315).

h. The nature of the siege of Vicksburg, which lasted for more than two months, makes it difficult to construct numbers that are comparable to those for other battles in the table. Livermore lists 22,301 Confederates as "effective" for the assault by the Union army on May 22, 1863, and notes that the Rebels lost 2,340 men "prior to June 23 and June 25." However, he notes that 29,396 men surrendered to Grant at the end of the from battle-related injuries. The disease-related deaths were probably positively correlated with the demands of campaigning. One of the best accounts by a historian summing up all the factors we have discussed above—those who were killed, wounded, missing, or died of disease—is provided by Stephen Sears in his description of the carnage wrought on the men who fought in the Peninsula campaign early in the war:

> In pitched battles and skirmishes, from Yorktown to Malvern Hill, some 25,370 Federals and 30,450 Confederates were killed, wounded, or missing. Of that total of 55,820 for the two armies, at least 8,670 died in battle. Perhaps another 5,000 died of disease in these months, raising the death toll to an estimated 13,670. Even that total is no doubt an undercount, for statistics on disease on the Peninsula were

---

siege, and these men are included in the "missing" category. We have added the men lost prior to surrender to those who surrendered as the number of Confederates "engaged" and left the prisoners listed as missing. The Union casualties are apparently for the assault on May 22.

i. It appears that Livermore's methodology in this case tends to exaggerate Confederate losses while minimizing Union losses. As explained in the text, this produces a seriously distorted picture of Confederate losses when compared with other battles. For this reason, the total missing for the river campaigns in Table 2.1 of the text has been reduced by 32,800 men to account for the prisoners taken in these battles.

References

(1) Bowden, Scott, and Bill Ward. *Last Chance for Victory: Robert E. Lee and the Gettysburg Campaign*. Cambridge, Mass.: DaCapo, 2001.

(2) Cooling, Benjamin Franklin. *Forts Henry and Donelson: Key to the Confederate Heartland*. Knoxville: University of Tennessee Press, 1987.

(3) Livermore, Thomas L. *Numbers and Losses in the Civil War in America 1861–1865*. Boston and New York, 1901.

(4) McPherson, James M. *Ordeal by Fire: The Civil War and Reconstruction*, 3rd ed. Vol. 2. New York: McGraw-Hill, 2001.

(5) Sears, Stephen W. *To the Gates of Richmond: The Peninsula Campaign*. New York: Ticknor and Fields, 1992.

(6) Sears, Stephen W. *Chancellorsville*. New York: Houghton Mifflin, 1996.

(7) Trudeau, Noah Andre. *Gettysburg: A Testing of Courage*. New York: HarperCollins, 2002.

Source: See text. Except where noted, the figures are from Livermore (3), pp. 78–108. Numbers in italics are from references indicated in the notes above. See text for a discussion of column definitions and how the figures are computed.

incomplete, and many men reported as missing were surely dead. Better than 24 percent—almost one in four—of the quarter-million men who took part in the Peninsula campaign were counted wounded or missing or dead of battle or disease.[8]

We may never know the precise numbers of men "lost" in Civil War battles. What the estimates tell us is that by any standard of modern warfare, the toll was horrendous.

. . . .

THE COSTS OF EMANCIPATION IN 1880

IN CHAPTER 4 WE present a scenario in which the Confederacy introduced a program of compensated emancipation around 1880. The scheme discussed in the text was based on experience with emancipation schemes that were proposed and enacted in the United States and elsewhere in the world in the middle of the nineteenth century.

Even when the solution to a problem seems obvious, political and economic factors can make it difficult to implement a policy that will deal with the problem. Virtually any examination of the costs of the American Civil War shows that it would have been far cheaper for the U.S. government simply to purchase the slaves from slaveholders than to fight a costly war. Yet there were several reasons why compensated emancipation was not feasible in the context of the antebellum United States. First, the costs of such a program were magnified by the effects of a cotton boom that had caused the value of the slave stock to almost triple over the past decade (see Figure 1.1). The rising value of slaves not only increased the current costs of any compensated emancipation scheme but made most slaveowners sanguine enough about the future to demand a premium for selling their property. Notwithstanding the loud cries of abolitionists in New England seeking the end of slavery, the rank and file of voters in the Northern and Western states had little interest in paying higher taxes to free African-American slaves. To propose an emancipation scheme that included taxes to compensate Southern slaveholders in payment for freeing their slaves would be political suicide. In addition to strong objections over the exorbitant costs of such a buyout, most people in the North would think that a proposal that paid the slaveholders the market price to free their slaves was immoral. Why reward the very people who had profited from this evil system for more than two centuries?

Finally, there was the question of what would be done with the blacks once they were free. Southerners objected to the idea of a scheme that would emancipate African-Americans and leave them free citizens in the South. Northerners were hardly enthusiastic about large numbers of free blacks coming north after emancipation. Slavery was not only a profitable economic system but a very effective form of racial control—for white people in the North as well as in the South. Not surprisingly, no comprehensive emancipation scheme that proposed paying slaveowners a substantial allowance for their slaves ever got off the ground in the U.S. Congress.

There were, however, a number of cases in which states in the North enacted statutes that freed slaves.[1] Vermont and Massachusetts abolished slavery in the 1770s; Pennsylvania, New York, and New Jersey, the Northern states with the largest number of slaves, followed suit. All these states instituted gradual schemes that involved little or no cost to the taxpayers. The basic provision of the emancipation laws was that any child born to a slave after a certain date would be free; all children who were currently slaves would be bound to the masters of their mothers until some specified age. In effect, a master and his slaves would swallow the cost of emancipation over a period of years. Two things should be pointed out with regard to these schemes. First, by the time of the Constitution very few slaves lived in these states so both the cost of financing the scheme and the number of people involved were relatively small. Second, a slaveholder who saw legislation to free slaves being considered by their state government could either sell his slaves to buyers who lived in a slave state or migrate to the South with his slaves rather than wait for the emancipation to take effect. Consequently, the acts of abolition did not raise a hue and cry from the body politic when they were passed. This would hardly be the case in the CSA of the 1880s. If emancipation were to work in the context of our counterfactual world, the Confederates would have to eschew efforts at gradual emancipation and have the government in Richmond exercise its right of eminent domain to purchase all the slaves.

The estimates of costs associated with emancipation in the Confederacy presented in chapter 4 are conjectures based on what we know about slave prices and demography in 1860. We know from the 1860 census that there were roughly 3.75 million slaves living in the twelve states that formed our counterfactual Confederacy in 1865. We also know that the rate of growth of slaves in the United States between 1840 and 1860 was just over 2 percent per annum. If we assume that the population of slaves in the CSA grew at a rate of 2 percent each year, there would be 5.5 million slaves living in the country by 1880, with almost equal numbers of males and females.

Estimating the emancipation allowance for slave property is highly speculative because it involves both economic and social changes of some significance. Some consideration would have to be made for age, particularly for young children. Most emancipation proposals provided only minimal reimbursement for slave children aged ten to fourteen, since at those ages their present value was very low. Most children under ten had a negative present value, and an owner would be due no emancipation allowance. However, there was a potential problem here. Because they would represent a cost to maintain, young children might be abandoned by their former owners and become orphans. To discourage this, our emancipation scheme would have to mandate that children under a certain age would be apprenticed to the masters for some period after emancipation. During this period of apprenticeship children would receive room and board and some modest allowance for their efforts.[2] Consideration would also have to be given to women of childbearing age. The "emancipation" allowance for these women would be less than the market price of a female slave because the discounted value of children would no longer be relevant. Finally, our counterfactual Confederate emancipation plan would follow the British example in the West Indies and have all adult slaves "apprenticed" to their former masters for three years. This would not only lessen the emancipation allowance paid to the slaveholders but also allow for a period of adjustment while planters worked out labor arrangements that would be in place when the slaves actually became free.

What might constitute a reasonable emancipation allowance in 1880? First of all, we know that the average price of a healthy adult field hand in the New Orleans slave market in 1860 was just over fifteen hundred dollars; a "prime" field hand could bring twice that amount. In computing the costs for 1880, we must take into account the inflation of prices that took place during the war. We assumed that the Confederate government got control of inflation when the price level was ten to fifteen times higher than at the beginning of the war. It seems likely that the government, having checked the *increase* in prices, would be content to see that they did not get any higher. A deflation that returned prices to their 1860 level would be a debilitating economic policy. We shall therefore assume for purposes of our calculations in this appendix that the prices of 1880 are ten times those of 1860. While that represents a startling departure from price trends in the nineteenth century, modern experience shows that it is hardly beyond the ability of markets to adjust. If the prices of slaves had returned to their "1860 level" by 1880, the cost of an adult male slave would be about fifteen thousand dollars.

The Confederate government would choose an emancipation allowance substantially less than this for several reasons. First of all, 1860 was the peak of slave prices during the antebellum period, and

TABLE A.2

ESTIMATES OF THE COST OF

EMANCIPATION IN 1880

(IN 1880 DOLLARS)

		Maximum Estimate		Minimum Estimate	
	Number of Slaves [Thousands]	Value per Slave [Dollars]	Cost of Emancipation [$ Millions]	Value per Slave [Dollars]	Cost of Emancipation [$ Millions]
Adult males	1,521	12,000	18,240	10,000	15,200
Adult females	1,517	9,000	13,640	7,500	11,370
Children < 14	2,436	0	0	0	0
Total	5,500	5,800	31,900	4,830	26,580

our counterfactual scenario argues that slave prices would have declined substantially from the prewar peak by the 1880s. A more reasonable estimate of prices in 1880 would be the average of New Orleans prices through the 1850s, which was $1,175, or just under $12,000 in 1880 prices. An estimate based on the New Orleans price would exaggerate prices throughout the South since that market reflected the value of male slaves in one of the most productive regions of the South. The emancipation allowance must be reduced to reflect the fact that slaveowners would get labor services below market wages for the three-year apprenticeship of slaves at the outset of emancipation. Therefore, we have set a range of $10,000 to $12,000 as the emancipation allowance for adult male slaves in 1880. The data show that the value of female slaves was comparable to that of a male slave before the war. However, this price included the value of any children the slave might have, who would belong to the owner. With emancipation, the value of the woman would reflect only the value of her labor. A rule of thumb in antebellum times was that a female slave rented out for between two-thirds and three-fourths of a male field hand. We therefore have estimated the emancipation allowance of female slaves to be 75 percent of the allowance for a male slave. Table A.2 presents minimum and maximum estimates of the cost to the government of the emancipation scheme outline in chapter 4.

The emancipation bonds would be issued in perpetuity and given to the owners at the time of emancipation. They would carry an interest rate of 4 percent per annum and would be negotiable instruments whose price would vary with the rate of interest in the economy. The total interest cost to the Confederate government would be between $10.6 million and $12.7 million each year, or less than eighty cents per head for the population of the Confederacy—including the freed slaves.[3]

While this may seem to be an extremely large debt, it would be an internal debt paid by the CSA government to its own citizens. The interest payments therefore would be transfer payments from one group to another. The overall fiscal effect of these transfer payments depends on who pays the taxes and who winds up with the bonds and receives the interest payments. The scheme that would produce the lowest burden on Confederate citizens would be one in which the interest on the emancipation bonds was financed with a flat tax on cotton exports. A portion of the tax would then fall on *buyers* of cotton, most of whom would live outside the CSA. If that were the case, the Confederacy could actually succeed in making foreigners pay for part of the emancipation. Since the interest payments on the emancipation bonds would go to Confederate citizens who had owned slaves, there would initially be a redistribution of resources toward wealthy planters. If however, planters sold their bonds to investors, then subsequent interest payments would go to the new bond owner. As we note in the text, this could provide a source of investment outside the agricultural sector.

THE CONSTITUTION OF
THE CONFEDERATE
STATES OF AMERICA

Preamble

We, the people of the Confederate States, each State acting in its sovereign and independent character, in order to form a permanent federal government, establish justice, insure domestic tranquillity, and secure the blessings of liberty to ourselves and our posterity—invoking the favor and guidance of Almighty God—do ordain and establish this Constitution for the Confederate States of America.

Article I.—The Legislative Branch

Section 1—The Legislature

1. All legislative powers herein delegated shall be vested in a Congress of the Confederate States, which shall consist of a Senate and House of Representatives.

Section 2—The House

1. The House of Representatives shall be composed of members chosen every second year by the people of the several States; and the

electors in each State shall be citizens of the Confederate States, and have the qualifications requisite for electors of the most numerous branch of the State Legislature; but no person of foreign birth, not a citizen of the Confederate States, shall be allowed to vote for any officer, civil or political, State or Federal.

2. No person shall be a Representative who shall not have attained the age of twenty-five years, and be a citizen of the Confederate States, and who shall not when elected, be an inhabitant of that State in which he shall be chosen.

3. Representatives and direct taxes shall be apportioned among the several States, which may be included within this Confederacy, according to their respective numbers, which shall be determined by adding to the whole number of free persons, including those bound to service for a term of years, and excluding Indians not taxed, three-fifths of all slaves. The actual enumeration shall be made within three years after the first meeting of the Congress of the Confederate States, and within every subsequent term of ten years, in such manner as they shall by law direct. The number of Representatives shall not exceed one for every fifty thousand, but each State shall have at least one Representative; and until such enumeration shall be made, the State of South Carolina shall be entitled to choose six; the State of Georgia ten; the State of Alabama nine; the State of Florida two; the State of Mississippi seven; the State of Louisiana six; and the State of Texas six.

4. When vacancies happen in the representation from any State the executive authority thereof shall issue writs of election to fill such vacancies.

5. The House of Representatives shall choose their Speaker and other officers; and shall have the sole power of impeachment; except that any judicial or other Federal officer, resident and acting solely within the limits of any State, may be impeached by a vote of two-thirds of both branches of the Legislature thereof.

Section 3—The Senate

1. The Senate of the Confederate States shall be composed of two Senators from each State, chosen for six years by the Legislature thereof, at the regular session next immediately preceding the commencement of the term of service; and each Senator shall have one vote.

2. Immediately after they shall be assembled, in consequence of the first election, they shall be divided as equally as may be into three classes. The seats of the Senators of the first class shall be vacated at the expiration of the second year; of the second class at the expiration of the fourth year; and of the third class at the expiration of the sixth year; so that one-third may be chosen every second year; and if vacancies happen by resignation, or other wise, during the recess of the Legislature of any State, the Executive thereof may make temporary appointments until the next meeting of the Legislature, which shall then fill such vacancies.

3. No person shall be a Senator who shall not have attained the age of thirty years, and be a citizen of the Confederate States; and who shall not, then elected, be an inhabitant of the State for which he shall be chosen.

4. The Vice President of the Confederate States shall be president of the Senate, but shall have no vote unless they be equally divided.

5. The Senate shall choose their other officers; and also a president pro tempore in the absence of the Vice President, or when he shall exercise the office of President of the Confederate States.

6. The Senate shall have the sole power to try all impeachments. When sitting for that purpose, they shall be on oath or affirmation. When the President of the Confederate States is tried, the Chief Justice shall preside; and no person shall be convicted without the concurrence of two-thirds of the members present.

7. Judgment in cases of impeachment shall not extend further than to removal from office, and disqualification to hold any office of honor, trust, or profit under the Confederate States; but the party

convicted shall, nevertheless, be liable and subject to indictment, trial, judgment, and punishment according to law.

Section 4—Elections, Meetings

1. The times, places, and manner of holding elections for Senators and Representatives shall be prescribed in each State by the Legislature thereof, subject to the provisions of this Constitution; but the Congress may, at any time, by law, make or alter such regulations, except as to the times and places of choosing Senators.

2. The Congress shall assemble at least once in every year; and such meeting shall be on the first Monday in December, unless they shall, by law, appoint a different day.

Section 5—Membership, Rules, Journals, Adjournment

1. Each House shall be the judge of the elections, returns, and qualifications of its own members, and a majority of each shall constitute a quorum to do business; but a smaller number may adjourn from day to day, and may be authorized to compel the attendance of absent members, in such manner and under such penalties as each House may provide.

2. Each House may determine the rules of its proceedings, punish its members for disorderly behavior, and, with the concurrence of two-thirds of the whole number, expel a member.

3. Each House shall keep a journal of its proceedings, and from time to time publish the same, excepting such parts as may in their judgment require secrecy; and the yeas and nays of the members of either House, on any question, shall, at the desire of one-fifth of those present, be entered on the journal.

4. Neither House, during the session of Congress, shall, without the consent of the other, adjourn for more than three days, nor to any other place than that in which the two Houses shall be sitting.

Section 6—Compensation

1. The Senators and Representatives shall receive a compensation for their services, to be ascertained by law, and paid out of the Treasury of the Confederate States. They shall, in all cases, except treason, felony, and breach of the peace, be privileged from arrest during their attendance at the session of their respective Houses, and in going to and returning from the same; and for any speech or debate in either House, they shall not be questioned in any other place. No Senator or Representative shall, during the time for which he was elected, be appointed to any civil office under the authority of the Confederate States, which shall have been created, or the emoluments whereof shall have been increased during such time; and no person holding any office under the Confederate States shall be a member of either House during his continuance in office. But Congress may, by law, grant to the principal officer in each of the Executive Departments a seat upon the floor of either House, with the privilege of discussing any measures appertaining to his department.

Section 7—Revenue Bills, Legislative Process, Presidential Veto

1. All bills for raising revenue shall originate in the House of Representatives; but the Senate may propose or concur with amendments, as on other bills.

2. Every bill which shall have passed both Houses, shall, before it becomes a law, be presented to the President of the Confederate States; if he approve, he shall sign it; but if not, he shall return it, with his objections, to that House in which it shall have originated, who shall enter the objections at large on their journal, and proceed to reconsider it. If, after such reconsideration, two-thirds of that House shall agree to pass the bill, it shall be sent, together with the objections, to the other House, by which it shall likewise be reconsidered, and if approved by two-thirds of that House, it shall become a law. But in all such cases, the votes of both Houses

shall be determined by yeas and nays, and the names of the persons voting for and against the bill shall be entered on the journal of each House respectively. If any bill shall not be returned by the President within ten days (Sundays excepted) after it shall have been presented to him, the same shall be a law, in like manner as if he had signed it, unless the Congress, by their adjournment, prevent its return; in which case it shall not be a law. The President may approve any appropriation and disapprove any other appropriation in the same bill. In such case he shall, in signing the bill, designate the appropriations disapproved; and shall return a copy of such appropriations, with his objections, to the House in which the bill shall have originated; and the same proceedings shall then be had as in case of other bills disapproved by the President.

3. Every order, resolution, or vote, to which the concurrence of both Houses may be necessary (except on a question of adjournment) shall be presented to the President of the Confederate States; and before the same shall take effect, shall be approved by him; or, being disapproved by him, shall be repassed by two-thirds of both Houses, according to the rules and limitations prescribed in case of a bill.

Section 8—Powers of Congress

The Congress shall have power—

1. To lay and collect taxes, duties, imposts, and excises for revenue, necessary to pay the debts, provide for the common defense, and carry on the Government of the Confederate States; but no bounties shall be granted from the Treasury; nor shall any duties or taxes on importations from foreign nations be laid to promote or foster any branch of industry; and all duties, imposts, and excises shall be uniform throughout the Confederate States.

2. To borrow money on the credit of the Confederate States.

3. To regulate commerce with foreign nations, and among the several

States, and with the Indian tribes; but neither this, nor any other clause contained in the Constitution, shall ever be construed to delegate the power to Congress to appropriate money for any internal improvement intended to facilitate commerce; except for the purpose of furnishing lights, beacons, and buoys, and other aids to navigation upon the coasts, and the improvement of harbors and the removing of obstructions in river navigation; in all which cases such duties shall be laid on the navigation facilitated thereby as may be necessary to pay the costs and expenses thereof.

4. To establish uniform laws of naturalization, and uniform laws on the subject of bankruptcies, throughout the Confederate States; but no law of Congress shall discharge any debt contracted before the passage of the same.

5. To coin money, regulate the value thereof, and of foreign coin, and fix the standard of weights and measures.

6. To provide for the punishment of counterfeiting the securities and current coin of the Confederate States.

7. To establish post offices and post routes; but the expenses of the Post Office Department, after the 1st day of March in the year of our Lord eighteen hundred and sixty-three, shall be paid out of its own revenues.

8. To promote the progress of science and useful arts, by securing for limited times to authors and inventors the exclusive right to their respective writings and discoveries.

9. To constitute tribunals inferior to the Supreme Court.

10. To define and punish piracies and felonies committed on the high seas, and offenses against the law of nations.

11. To declare war, grant letters of marque and reprisal, and make rules concerning captures on land and water.

12. To raise and support armies; but no appropriation of money to that use shall be for a longer term than two years.

13. To provide and maintain a navy.

14. To make rules for the government and regulation of the land and naval forces.

15. To provide for calling forth the militia to execute the laws of the Confederate States, suppress insurrections, and repel invasions.

16. To provide for organizing, arming, and disciplining the militia, and for governing such part of them as may be employed in the service of the Confederate States; reserving to the States, respectively, the appointment of the officers, and the authority of training the militia according to the discipline prescribed by Congress.

17. To exercise exclusive legislation, in all cases whatsoever, over such district (not exceeding ten miles square) as may, by cession of one or more States and the acceptance of Congress, become the seat of the Government of the Confederate States; and to exercise like authority over all places purchased by the consent of the Legislature of the State in which the same shall be, for the erection of forts, magazines, arsenals, dockyards, and other needful buildings; and

18. To make all laws which shall be necessary and proper for carrying into execution the foregoing powers, and all other powers vested by this Constitution in the Government of the Confederate States, or in any department or officer thereof.

Section 9—Limits on Congress, Bill of Rights

1. The importation of negroes of the African race from any foreign country other than the slaveholding States or Territories of the United States of America, is hereby forbidden; and Congress is required to pass such laws as shall effectually prevent the same.

2. Congress shall also have power to prohibit the introduction of slaves from any State not a member of, or Territory not belonging to, this Confederacy.

3. The privilege of the writ of habeas corpus shall not be suspended, unless when in cases of rebellion or invasion the public safety may require it.

4. No bill of attainder, ex post facto law, or law denying or impairing the right of property in negro slaves shall be passed.

5. No capitation or other direct tax shall be laid, unless in proportion to the census or enumeration hereinbefore directed to be taken.

6. No tax or duty shall be laid on articles exported from any State, except by a vote of two-thirds of both Houses.

7. No preference shall be given by any regulation of commerce or revenue to the ports of one State over those of another.

8. No money shall be drawn from the Treasury, but in consequence of appropriations made by law; and a regular statement and account of the receipts and expenditures of all public money shall be published from time to time.

9. Congress shall appropriate no money from the Treasury except by a vote of two-thirds of both Houses, taken by yeas and nays, unless it be asked and estimated for by some one of the heads of departments and submitted to Congress by the President; or for the purpose of paying its own expenses and contingencies; or for the payment of claims against the Confederate States, the justice of which shall have been judicially declared by a tribunal for the investigation of claims against the Government, which it is hereby made the duty of Congress to establish.

10. All bills appropriating money shall specify in Federal currency the exact amount of each appropriation and the purposes for which it is made; and Congress shall grant no extra compensation to any public contractor, officer, agent, or servant, after such contract shall have been made or such service rendered.

11. No title of nobility shall be granted by the Confederate States; and no person holding any office of profit or trust under them shall, without the consent of the Congress, accept of any present, emolument, office, or title of any kind whatever, from any king, prince, or foreign state.

12. Congress shall make no law respecting an establishment of religion, or prohibiting the free exercise thereof; or abridging the

freedom of speech, or of the press; or the right of the people peaceably to assemble and petition the Government for a redress of grievances.

13. A well-regulated militia being necessary to the security of a free State, the right of the people to keep and bear arms shall not be infringed.

14. No soldier shall, in time of peace, be quartered in any house without the consent of the owner; nor in time of war, but in a manner to be prescribed by law.

15. The right of the people to be secure in their persons, houses, papers, and effects, against unreasonable searches and seizures, shall not be violated; and no warrants shall issue but upon probable cause, supported by oath or affirmation, and particularly describing the place to be searched and the persons or things to be seized.

16. No person shall be held to answer for a capital or otherwise infamous crime, unless on a presentment or indictment of a grand jury, except in cases arising in the land or naval forces, or in the militia, when in actual service in time of war or public danger; nor shall any person be subject for the same offense to be twice put in jeopardy of life or limb; nor be compelled, in any criminal case, to be a witness against himself; nor be deprived of life, liberty, or property without due process of law; nor shall private property be taken for public use, without just compensation.

17. In all criminal prosecutions the accused shall enjoy the right to a speedy and public trial, by an impartial jury of the State and district wherein the crime shall have been committed, which district shall have been previously ascertained by law, and to be informed of the nature and cause of the accusation; to be confronted with the witnesses against him; to have compulsory process for obtaining witnesses in his favor; and to have the assistance of counsel for his defense.

18. In suits at common law, where the value in controversy shall

exceed twenty dollars, the right of trial by jury shall be preserved; and no fact so tried by a jury shall be otherwise reexamined in any court of the Confederacy, than according to the rules of common law.

19. Excessive bail shall not be required, nor excessive fines imposed, nor cruel and unusual punishments inflicted.

20. Every law, or resolution having the force of law, shall relate to but one subject, and that shall be expressed in the title.

Section 10—Powers Prohibited of States

1. No State shall enter into any treaty, alliance, or confederation; grant letters of marque and reprisal; coin money; make anything but gold and silver coin a tender in payment of debts; pass any bill of attainder, or ex post facto law, or law impairing the obligation of contracts; or grant any title of nobility.

2. No State shall, without the consent of the Congress, lay any imposts or duties on imports or exports, except what may be absolutely necessary for executing its inspection laws; and the net produce of all duties and imposts, laid by any State on imports, or exports, shall be for the use of the Treasury of the Confederate States; and all such laws shall be subject to the revision and control of Congress.

3. No State shall, without the consent of Congress, lay any duty on tonnage, except on seagoing vessels, for the improvement of its rivers and harbors navigated by the said vessels; but such duties shall not conflict with any treaties of the Confederate States with foreign nations; and any surplus revenue thus derived shall, after making such improvement, be paid into the common treasury. Nor shall any State keep troops or ships of war in time of peace, enter into any agreement or compact with another State, or with a foreign power, or engage in war, unless actually invaded, or in such imminent danger as will not admit of delay. But when any river

divides or flows through two or more States they may enter into compacts with each other to improve the navigation thereof.

Article II.—The Executive Branch

Section 1—The President

1. The executive power shall be vested in a President of the Confederate States of America. He and the Vice President shall hold their offices for the term of six years; but the President shall not be reeligible. The President and Vice President shall be elected as follows:

2. Each State shall appoint, in such manner as the Legislature thereof may direct, a number of electors equal to the whole number of Senators and Representatives to which the State may be entitled in the Congress; but no Senator or Representative or person holding an office of trust or profit under the Confederate States shall be appointed an elector.

3. The electors shall meet in their respective States and vote by ballot for President and Vice President, one of whom, at least, shall not be an inhabitant of the same State with themselves; they shall name in their ballots the person voted for as President, and in distinct ballots the person voted for as Vice President, and they shall make distinct lists of all persons voted for as President, and of all persons voted for as Vice President, and of the number of votes for each, which lists they shall sign and certify, and transmit, sealed, to the seat of the Government of the Confederate States, directed to the President of the Senate; the President of the Senate shall, in the presence of the Senate and House of Representatives, open all the certificates, and the votes shall then be counted; the person having the greatest number of votes for President shall be the President, if such number be a majority of the whole number of electors appointed; and if no person have such majority, then from the persons having the highest numbers, not exceeding three, on the list of those voted for as President, the House of Representatives

shall choose immediately, by ballot, the President. But in choosing the President the votes shall be taken by States ~ the representation from each State having one vote; a quorum for this purpose shall consist of a member or members from two-thirds of the States, and a majority of all the States shall be necessary to a choice. And if the House of Representatives shall not choose a President, whenever the right of choice shall devolve upon them, before the 4th day of March next following, then the Vice President shall act as President, as in case of the death, or other constitutional disability of the President.

4. The person having the greatest number of votes as Vice President shall be the Vice President, if such number be a majority of the whole number of electors appointed; and if no person have a majority, then, from the two highest numbers on the list, the Senate shall choose the Vice President; a quorum for the purpose shall consist of two-thirds of the whole number of Senators, and a majority of the whole number shall be necessary to a choice.

5. But no person constitutionally ineligible to the office of President shall be eligible to that of Vice President of the Confederate States.

6. The Congress may determine the time of choosing the electors, and the day on which they shall give their votes; which day shall be the same throughout the Confederate States.

7. No person except a natural-born citizen of the Confederate States, or a citizen thereof at the time of the adoption of this Constitution, or a citizen thereof born in the United States prior to the 20th of December, 1860, shall be eligible to the office of President; neither shall any person be eligible to that office who shall not have attained the age of thirty-five years, and been fourteen years a resident within the limits of the Confederate States, as they may exist at the time of his election.

8. In case of the removal of the President from office, or of his death, resignation, or inability to discharge the powers and duties of said

office, the same shall devolve on the Vice President; and the Congress may, by law, provide for the case of removal, death, resignation, or inability, both of the President and Vice President, declaring what officer shall then act as President; and such officer shall act accordingly until the disability be removed or a President shall be elected.

9. The President shall, at stated times, receive for his services a compensation, which shall neither be increased nor diminished during the period for which he shall have been elected; and he shall not receive within that period any other emolument from the Confederate States, or any of them.

10. Before he enters on the execution of his office he shall take the following oath or affirmation: "I do solemnly swear (or affirm) that I will faithfully execute the office of President of the Confederate States, and will, to the best of my ability, preserve, protect, and defend the Constitution thereof."

Section 2—Civilian Power over Military, Cabinet, Pardon Power, Appointments

1. The President shall be Commander-in-Chief of the Army and Navy of the Confederate States, and of the militia of the several States, when called into the actual service of the Confederate States; he may require the opinion, in writing, of the principal officer in each of the Executive Departments, upon any subject relating to the duties of their respective offices; and he shall have power to grant reprieves and pardons for offenses against the Confederate States, except in cases of impeachment.

2. He shall have power, by and with the advice and consent of the Senate, to make treaties; provided two-thirds of the Senators present concur; and he shall nominate, and by and with the advice and consent of the Senate shall appoint, ambassadors, other public ministers and consuls, judges of the Supreme Court, and all other officers of the Confederate States whose appointments are not

herein otherwise provided for, and which shall be established by law; but the Congress may, by law, vest the appointment of such inferior officers, as they think proper, in the President alone, in the courts of law, or in the heads of departments.

3. The principal officer in each of the Executive Departments, and all persons connected with the diplomatic service, may be removed from office at the pleasure of the President. All other civil officers of the Executive Departments may be removed at any time by the President, or other appointing power, when their services are unnecessary, or for dishonesty, incapacity, inefficiency, misconduct, or neglect of duty; and when so removed, the removal shall be reported to the Senate, together with the reasons therefor.

4. The President shall have power to fill all vacancies that may happen during the recess of the Senate, by granting commissions which shall expire at the end of their next session; but no person rejected by the Senate shall be reappointed to the same office during their ensuing recess.

Section 3—State of the Union, Convening Congress

1. The President shall, from time to time, give to the Congress information of the state of the Confederacy, and recommend to their consideration such measures as he shall judge necessary and expedient; he may, on extraordinary occasions, convene both Houses, or either of them; and in case of disagreement between them, with respect to the time of adjournment, he may adjourn them to such time as he shall think proper; he shall receive ambassadors and other public ministers; he shall take care that the laws be faithfully executed, and shall commission all the officers of the Confederate States.

Section 4—Disqualification

1. The President, Vice President, and all civil officers of the Confederate States, shall be removed from office on impeachment for and

conviction of treason, bribery, or other high crimes and misdemeanors.

Article III.—The Judicial Branch

Section 1—Judicial Powers

1. The judicial power of the Confederate States shall be vested in one Supreme Court, and in such inferior courts as the Congress may, from time to time, ordain and establish. The judges, both of the Supreme and inferior courts, shall hold their offices during good behavior, and shall, at stated times, receive for their services a compensation which shall not be diminished during their continuance in office.

Section 2—Trial by Jury, Original Jurisdiction, Jury Trials

1. The judicial power shall extend to all cases arising under this Constitution, the laws of the Confederate States, and treaties made, or which shall be made, under their authority; to all cases affecting ambassadors, other public ministers and consuls; to all cases of admiralty and maritime jurisdiction; to controversies to which the Confederate States shall be a party; to controversies between two or more States; between a State and citizens of another State, where the State is plaintiff; between citizens claiming lands under grants of different States; and between a State or the citizens thereof, and foreign states, citizens, or subjects; but no State shall be sued by a citizen or subject of any foreign state.

2. In all cases affecting ambassadors, other public ministers and consuls, and those in which a State shall be a party, the Supreme Court shall have original jurisdiction. In all the other cases before mentioned, the Supreme Court shall have appellate jurisdiction both as to law and fact, with such exceptions and under such regulations as the Congress shall make.

3. The trial of all crimes, except in cases of impeachment, shall be by

jury, and such trial shall be held in the State where the said crimes shall have been committed; but when not committed within any State, the trial shall be at such place or places as the Congress may by law have directed.

Section 3—Treason
1. Treason against the Confederate States shall consist only in levying war against them, or in adhering to their enemies, giving them aid and comfort. No person shall be convicted of treason unless on the testimony of two witnesses to the same overt act, or on confession in open court.
2. The Congress shall have power to declare the punishment of treason; but no attainder of treason shall work corruption of blood, or forfeiture, except during the life of the person attainted.

Article IV.—The States

Section 1—Each State to Honor All Others
1. Full faith and credit shall be given in each State to the public acts, records, and judicial proceedings of every other State; and the Congress may, by general laws, prescribe the manner in which such acts, records, and proceedings shall be proved, and the effect thereof.

Section 2—State Citizens, Extradition
1. The citizens of each State shall be entitled to all the privileges and immunities of citizens in the several States; and shall have the right of transit and sojourn in any State of this Confederacy, with their slaves and other property; and the right of property in said slaves shall not be thereby impaired.
2. A person charged in any State with treason, felony, or other crime against the laws of such State, who shall flee from justice, and be found in another State, shall, on demand of the executive author-

ity of the State from which he fled, be delivered up, to be removed to the State having jurisdiction of the crime.

3. No slave or other person held to service or labor in any State or Territory of the Confederate States, under the laws thereof, escaping or lawfully carried into another, shall, in consequence of any law or regulation therein, be discharged from such service or labor; but shall be delivered up on claim of the party to whom such slave belongs; or to whom such service or labor may be due.

Section 3—New States

1. Other States may be admitted into this Confederacy by a vote of two-thirds of the whole House of Representatives and two-thirds of the Senate, the Senate voting by States; but no new State shall be formed or erected within the jurisdiction of any other State, nor any State be formed by the junction of two or more States, or parts of States, without the consent of the Legislatures of the States concerned, as well as of the Congress.

2. The Congress shall have power to dispose of and make all needful rules and regulations concerning the property of the Confederate States, including the lands thereof.

3. The Confederate States may acquire new territory; and Congress shall have power to legislate and provide governments for the inhabitants of all territory belonging to the Confederate States, lying without the limits of the several States; and may permit them, at such times, and in such manner as it may by law provide, to form States to be admitted into the Confederacy. In all such territory the institution of negro slavery, as it now exists in the Confederate States, shall be recognized and protected by Congress and by the Territorial government; and the inhabitants of the several Confederate States and Territories shall have the right to take to such Territory any slaves lawfully held by them in any of the States or Territories of the Confederate States.

4. The Confederate States shall guarantee to every State that now is,

or hereafter may become, a member of this Confederacy, a republican form of government; and shall protect each of them against invasion; and on application of the Legislature or of the Executive (when the Legislature is not in session) against domestic violence.

Article V.—Amendment

1. Upon the demand of any three States, legally assembled in their several conventions, the Congress shall summon a convention of all the States, to take into consideration such amendments to the Constitution as the said States shall concur in suggesting at the time when the said demand is made; and should any of the proposed amendments to the Constitution be agreed on by the said convention ~ voting by States ~ and the same be ratified by the Legislatures of two-thirds of the several States, or by conventions in two-thirds thereof ~ as the one or the other mode of ratification may be proposed by the general convention ~ they shall thenceforward form a part of this Constitution. But no State shall, without its consent, be deprived of its equal representation in the Senate.

Article VI.—The Confederacy

Section 1—Transition from the Provisional Government
1. The Government established by this Constitution is the successor of the Provisional Government of the Confederate States of America, and all the laws passed by the latter shall continue in force until the same shall be repealed or modified; and all the officers appointed by the same shall remain in office until their successors are appointed and qualified, or the offices abolished.

Section 2—Debts of the Provisional Government
2. All debts contracted and engagements entered into before the adoption of this Constitution shall be as valid against the Confed-

erate States under this Constitution, as under the Provisional Government.

Section 3—Supremacy of the Constitution

3. This Constitution, and the laws of the Confederate States made in pursuance thereof, and all treaties made, or which shall be made, under the authority of the Confederate States, shall be the supreme law of the land; and the judges in every State shall be bound thereby, anything in the constitution or laws of any State to the contrary notwithstanding.

Section 4—Oaths of Office

4. The Senators and Representatives before mentioned, and the members of the several State Legislatures, and all executive and judicial officers, both of the Confederate States and of the several States, shall be bound by oath or affirmation to support this Constitution; but no religious test shall ever be required as a qualification to any office or public trust under the Confederate States.

Section 5—Reservation of Unenumerated Rights

5. The enumeration, in the Constitution, of certain rights shall not be construed to deny or disparage others retained by the people of the several States.

Section 6—State Powers

6. The powers not delegated to the Confederate States by the Constitution, nor prohibited by it to the States, are reserved to the States, respectively, or to the people thereof.

Article VII.—Ratification

1. The ratification of the conventions of five States shall be sufficient for the establishment of this Constitution between the States so ratifying the same.

2. When five States shall have ratified this Constitution, in the manner before specified, the Congress under the Provisional Constitution shall prescribe the time for holding the election of President and Vice President; and for the meeting of the Electoral College; and for counting the votes, and inaugurating the President. They shall, also, prescribe the time for holding the first election of members of Congress under this Constitution, and the time for assembling the same. Until the assembling of such Congress, the Congress under the Provisional Constitution shall continue to exercise the legislative powers granted them; not extending beyond the time limited by the Constitution of the Provisional Government.

Adopted unanimously by the Congress of the Confederate States of South Carolina, Georgia, Florida, Alabama, Mississippi, Louisiana, and Texas, sitting in Convention at the capitol, in the city of Montgomery, Alabama, on the Eleventh day of March, in the year Eighteen Hundred and Sixty-One.

HOWELL COBB,
President of the Congress.

1. South Carolina: R. Barnwell Rhett, C. G. Memminger, Wm. Porcher Miles, James Chesnut, Jr., R. W. Barnwell, William W. Boyce, Lawrence M. Keitt, T. J. Withers.
2. Georgia: Francis S. Bartow, Martin J. Crawford, Benjamin H. Hill, Thos. R. R. Cobb.
3. Florida: Jackson Morton, J. Patton Anderson, Jas. B. Owens.
4. Alabama: Richard W. Walker, Robt. H. Smith, Colin J. McRae, William P. Chilton, Stephen F. Hale, David P. Lewis, Tho. Fearn, Jno. Gill Shorter, J. L. M. Curry.
5. Mississippi: Alex. M. Clayton, James T. Harrison, William S. Barry, W. S. Wilson, Walker Brooke, W. P. Harris, J. A. P. Campbell.

6. Louisiana: Alex. de Clouet, C. M. Conrad, Duncan F. Kenner, Henry Marshall.

7. Texas: John Hemphill, Thomas N. Waul, John H. Reagan, Williamson S. Oldham, Louis T. Wigfall, John Gregg, William Beck Ochiltree.

NOTES

Preface

1. Ward Moore, *Bring the Jubilee Again* (New York: Farrar, Straus and Young, 1952).

2. Ward Moore, "Bring the Jubilee," *The Fantastic Civil War*, ed. Frank McSherry, Charles G. Waugh, and Martin Harry Greenberg (New York: Bren Books, 1952): 18–19.

3. Ibid.: 130–31.

4. Roger L. Ransom and Richard Sutch, *One Kind of Freedom: The Economic Consequences of Emancipation*, 2nd ed. (New York: Cambridge University Press, 2001); Roger L. Ransom and Richard Sutch, "Conflicting Visions: The American Civil War as a Revolutionary Conflict," *Research in Economic History* 20 (2001); Roger L. Ransom and Richard Sutch, "Capitalists without Capital: The Burden of Slavery and the Impact of Emancipation," *Agricultural History* (Fall 1988); and Roger L. Ransom and Richard Sutch, "Growth and Welfare in the American South in the Nineteenth Century," *Explorations in Economic History* 16 (April 1979).

Prologue. What If?: The Historian's Favorite Secret Question

1. Geoffrey Hawthorn, *Plausible Worlds: Possibility and Understanding in History and the Social Sciences* (New York: Cambridge University Press, 1991): 4.

2. Edward Hallett Carr, *What Is History? The George Macaulay Trevelyan Lectures* (New York: Alfred A. Knopf, 1961): 167.

3. Ibid.: 127–28.

4. Hugh Trevor-Roper, "History and Imagination," *History and Imagination: Essays in Honour of H. R. Trevor-Roper*, ed. Hugh Lloyd-Jones, Valerie Pearl, and Blair Worden (London: Gerald Duckworth, 1981): 363.

5. Robert Cowley, ed., *What If ?: The World's Foremost Military Historians Imagine What Might Have Been* (New York: G. P. Putnam's Sons, 1998): ix–x.

6. Carl von Clausewitz, *On War*, trans. Michael Howard and Peter Paret (Princeton: Princeton University Press, 1976).

7. Ibid.: 86.

8. A number of such asides can be found in the collection of essays edited by Robert Cowley, who was the founding editor of *MJQ: The Quarterly Journal of Military History*. In 1996 Cowley asked a group of eminent historians: "What do you consider the most important might-have-been in military history?" The answers ranged over nearly three millennia; from a Persian victory at Salamis in 701 B.C. through the cold war toward the end of the twentieth century. Yet despite the cleverness and insightful ideas presented by Cowley's authors, most historians would still regard these essays as little more than "parlor games," and they are probably justified in that assessment. It is apparent that for most of the authors Cowley queried, writing counterfactual history still represented an "aside," a sort of off-the-cuff speculation on what might have been.

9. Peter Tsouras, *Gettysburg: An Alternate History* (London: Greenhill Books, 1997): 9.

10. Jonathan North, ed., *The Napoleon Options: Alternate Decisions of the Napoleonic Wars* (London: Greenhill Books, 2000): 10.

11. David Downing, *The Moscow Option: An Alternative Second World War* (London: Greenhill Books, 2001): 11. Downing explains: "For those interested in sorting out the fiction from the fact, there is a Notes and References section at end of the book, in which references are given for genuine quotations and the minor fictional characters are listed. All the central characters are or were real people; they act as I believe it is reasonable to assume they would have acted in the fictional situations created."

12. Ibid.: 11.

13. Geoffrey Parker, "The Repulse of the English Fire Ships," *What If?*, loc. cit.: 151–52.

14. Downing, *Moscow Option*: 207.

15. Wade G. Dudley, "Be Careful What You Wish For: The Plan Orange Disaster," *Rising Sun Victorious*, ed. Peter Tsouras (London: Greenhill Books, 2001): 58. According to Dudley, "Even Yamamoto, [Japan's] premier naval strategist, knew that the industrial might of the United States must prevail in the long run. And Pearl Harbor was little more than a bee sting on the foot of a sleeping giant, awakening both an industrial power and personal commitments among

Americans that eventually doomed Japan while allowing the United States to support their allies in the destruction of European fascism" (58–59).

16. Downing, *Moscow Option*: 207.

17. The term "cliometrics," which was formed by combining "Clio," the muse of history, with "metrics," the science of quantitative measurement, first became fashionable in the 1970s. It was coined by a group of scholars who met annually at Purdue University in the early 1960s. By the 1970s the annual Cliometrics Conference, funded by the National Science Foundation, had become one of the most influential intellectual forums for researchers in quantitative economic history.

18. The Beards first articulated the argument in Charles Beard and Mary Beard, *The Rise of American Civilization*, 2 vols., vol. 1 (New York: Macmillan, 1927). The argument was subsequently elaborated more fully by Louis Hacker (*The Triumph of American Capitalism: The Development of Forces in American History to the End of the Nineteenth Century* [New York: Columbia University Press, 1940]) into what became known as the Beard-Hacker thesis.

19. Thomas C. Cochran, "Did the Civil War Retard Industrialization?," *Mississippi Valley Historical Review* 48 (September 1961).

20. We shall return to this debate more fully in chapter 1. For a discussion of the debates mentioned in the text, see Roger L. Ransom, "Fact and Counterfact: The 'Second American Revolution' Revisited," *Civil War History* 45 (March 1999).

21. Alfred H. Conrad and John R. Meyer, "The Economics of Slavery in the Ante Bellum South," *Journal of Political Economy* 66 (April 1958). The key insight in the Conrad-Meyer model was that because slaves were economic assets, the value of slave children should be included in the computation of the return to slaveholders. This produced a much higher rate of return than the computations that had relied solely on the economic output of slaves working in the fields.

22. Ibid.: 360.

23. The research on the economics of slavery has been a highly contentious field of inquiry. In 1974 Robert Fogel and Stanley Engerman published a two-volume study that went far beyond Conrad and Meyer's argument in an effort to show that slavery was not only "profitable" for slaveowners but, in fact, an economically efficient system of labor and capital that was the foundation of the antebellum Southern economy. Robert W. Fogel and Stanley L. Engerman, *Time on the Cross: The Economics of American Negro Slavery*, 2 vols. (New York: Little, Brown, 1974). Not all historians or cliometricians were prepared to carry the argument to the point that Fogel and Engerman pushed it; however, in the debates that followed, nearly everyone conceded that the slave system in the Southern United States was "profitable." We shall explore the implications of

this conclusion more fully in chapter 1. For a review of the debates on slavery, see Gavin Wright, "New and Old Views on the Economics of Slavery," *Journal of Economic History* 33 (June 1973); Roger L. Ransom, *Conflict and Compromise: The Political Economy of Slavery, Emancipation, and the American Civil War* (New York: Cambridge University Press, 1989): ch. 3; and Robert W. Fogel, *Without Consent or Contract: The Rise and Fall of American Slavery* (New York: W. W. Norton, 1989).

24. Turtledove's books dealing with the world following a Southern victory include: Harry Turtledove, *How Few Remain: A Novel of the Second War between the States* (New York: Ballantine Books, 1997) and a trilogy of books, Harry Turtledove, *The Great War: American Front* (New York: Ballantine Books, 1998); *The Great War: Walk in Hell* (New York: Ballantine Books, 1999); *The Great War: Breakthrough* (New York: Ballantine Books, 2000).

25. Occasionally alternative historical fiction and counterfactual history merge. One of the few examples of a counterfactual narrative of the Civil War constructed by a respected historian is MacKinlay Kantor's book *If the South Had Won the Civil War* (New York: Bantam Books, 1961). Kantor wrote his book when Americans were celebrating the centennial commemoration of their Civil War. Though he presents some useful insights into how the South won the war, he devotes only a quarter of his book (twenty-seven pages) to events after 1865. The underlying theme in the book, one that was very much in vogue at the time it was written, was that the essential unity in American culture made any long-term breakup of the Union improbable. Thus Kantor's scenario—in sharp contrast with Turtledove's pessimistic view of a United States and Confederate States at each other's throats—has the two countries (led by Teddy Roosevelt and Woodrow Wilson) entering World War I together on the side of the Allies against Germany. Later the American states again collaborate on the side of the Allies in World War II, and by 1960 the United States and the Confederate States have reconciled their differences sufficiently that the two nations are about to convene a conference to seek a new American Union. Kantor devotes very little attention to any of the serious counterfactual issues that would be raised by a Southern victory, and like his counterparts who write alternative historical fiction, Kantor relies on real personages (or their progeny) to play out the counterfactual narrative of his book. This is parlor table history on a very grand scale.

26. Niall Ferguson, "Virtual History: Towards a 'Chaotic' Theory of the Past," *Virtual History: Alternatives and Counterfactuals*, ed. Niall Ferguson (London: Macmillan, 1997): 18.

27. See in particular the discussion of Ferguson, "Alternatives and Counterfactuals" ibid.: 84; italics in original.

28. David Potter, *The Impending Crisis: 1848–1861* (New York: Harper Torchbooks, 1976): 95.

29. Hawthorn, *Plausible Worlds*: 186.

Chapter 1. Conflicting Visions: Was the Civil War Inevitable?

1. Charles Beard and Mary Beard, *The Rise of American Civilization*, 2 vols., vol. 1 (New York: Macmillan, 1927): 51.

2. Ibid.: 3.

3. For a discussion of the economic challenges facing the new nation, see Douglass C. North, *The Economic Growth of the United States, 1790–1860* (Englewood Cliffs, N.J.: Prentice Hall, 1961) and *Growth and Welfare in the American Past: A New Economic History* (Englewood Cliffs, N.J.: Prentice Hall, 1966).

4. Cited in Winthrop Jordan, *White over Black: American Attitudes toward the Negro: 1550–1812* (Chapel Hill: University of North Carolina Press, 1968): 324.

5. The average value of a slave varied from region to region, and the per capita estimate quoted in the text includes slave children. This figure will understate the value of an adult slave by roughly one-half. See the discussion in Roger L. Ransom and Richard Sutch, "Capitalists without Capital: The Burden of Slavery and the Impact of Emancipation," *Agricultural History* (Fall 1988): Table A.1, pp. 150–51.

6. A considerable controversy has always surrounded the question of whether or not planters "bred" slaves with the expectation of selling them. At the time planters vehemently denied such crass motives. One of the implications of the cliometric research is that whether or not they intended to breed slaves, as a group planters in the Southeast consistently sent a "surplus" of slaves to markets in the Western states. Without the returns from those sales, most planters along the eastern seaboard would not have been able to sustain their plantations.

7. Gerald Gunderson, "The Origin of the American Civil War," *Journal of Economic History* 34 (December 1974): 922.

8. Roger L. Ransom and Richard Sutch, "Conflicting Visions: The American Civil War as a Revolutionary Conflict," *Research in Economic History* 20 (2001): 254.

9. Allan Nevins, the doyen of Civil War historians in the years immediately following World War II, was unable to find any rationale for the war. "It was not," he wrote, "primarily a conflict over State Rights" or "born of economic

grievances." Nor was it "primarily a war about slavery alone—though that institution seemed to many the grand cause." Nevins concluded that the war could—indeed should—have been avoided, and the ultimate blame must therefore rest with the politicians who failed to prevent it. "Much of what happens in human affairs is accidental," he observed. "When a country is guided by true statesmen the role of accident is minimized; when it is not unforeseen occurrences are numerous and dangerous." Allan Nevins, *The Emergence of Lincoln: Prologue to Civil War, 1859–1861*, vol. 4, *Ordeal of the Union* (New York: Charles Scribner's Sons, 1950): 470.

10. There is a large literature on the political crisis of the 1850s. My favorite is still David Potter, *The Impending Crisis: 1848–1861* (New York: Harper Torchbooks, 1976). However, as his title suggests, Potter's take leans distinctly toward the view that the war was inevitable. Michael Holt provides the most recent account of the period in his monumental study of the Whig Party: *The Rise and Fall of the American Whig Party: Jacksonian Politics and the Onset of the Civil War* (New York: Oxford University Press, 1999); also see his earlier work, *The Political Crisis of the 1850's* (New York: W. W. Norton, 1978).

11. It is worth emphasizing that the "compromise" of 1850 was made up of several laws that had to be approved independently of one another because it was impossible to get a majority in either the House or the Senate to approve the set of bills in their entirety. In order to get acceptance of the more controversial sections of the compromise—the Fugitive Slave Act and the admission of California—it was necessary to convince a number of representatives and senators to abstain on these issues rather than cast negative votes. As a result, the Fugitive Slave Act passed the House with a plurality but not a majority. For a discussion of the difficulties in crafting an acceptable compromise, see Roger L. Ransom, *Conflict and Compromise: The Political Economy of Slavery, Emancipation, and the American Civil War* (New York: Cambridge University Press, 1989): 109–20, and Holman Hamilton, *Prologue to Conflict: The Crisis and Compromise of 1850* (New York: W. W. Norton, 1964).

12. Potter, *Impending Crisis*: 85.

13. "The Nashville project," writes historian David Potter, "enjoyed enough public support in the South, especially among Democrats to make it formidable and to indicate that if Congress adopted a free-soil policy [advocated by Northern Whigs], a severe crisis would follow." Potter, *Impending Crisis*: 95; for a more complete treatment of the Calhoun's efforts and the impact of the Nashville Convention, see ibid.: ch. 4 and 5, and Allan Nevins, *The Fruits of Manifest Destiny, 1847–1852*, vol. 1, *Ordeal of the Union*, (New York: Charles Scribner's Sons, 1947): chs. 9 and 10.

14. Speech by David Wilmot in the House of Representatives, February 8,

1847; reprinted in Joel Silbey, ed., *The Transformation of American Politics, 1840–1860* (Englewood Cliffs, N.J.: Prentice Hall, 1967): 72–73.

15. Potter, *Impending Crisis*: 95.

16. Ibid.: 119–20.

17. Ibid.: 120.

18. The international comparison is from Robert W. Fogel, *Without Consent or Contract: The Rise and Fall of American Slavery* (New York: W. W. Norton, 1989). The estimate for per capita income in the United States for 1840 and 1860 is from Stanley L. Engerman, "The Economic Impact of the Civil War," *Explorations in Entrepreneurial History* 2nd Series 3 (Spring 1966).

19. We have already alluded to the enormous concentration of wealth in the slave areas of the South (see Map 1.3). To illustrate just how concentrated the distribution of slaves was, consider that three-quarters of all slaves in the United States in 1860 lived in slaveholdings of ten or more slaves. To put it another way, the seventy-nine thousand slaves who lived in families owning only one slave represented about 20 percent of the slaveholdings but only 2 percent of all slaves.

20. Sugar and rice enter the composition of Southern staple crops on the margin. The most favorable view of the economic situation of the slave South on the eve of the Civil War is that of Robert Fogel and Stanley Engerman, "The Economics of Slavery," *The Reinterpretation of American Economic History*, ed. Robert Fogel and Stanley Engerman (New York: Harper & Row, 1971): Fogel and Engerman, *Time on the Cross: The Economics of American Negro Slavery*, new ed. (New York: W. W. Norton, 1989) and Fogel, *Without Consent or Contract* . It is interesting to note, however, that this view of the South in the first half of the nineteenth century as a developed agricultural economy is widely held by Southern historians. See, for example, the comments in William J. Cooper, Jr., and Thomas E. Terrill, *The American South: A History*, 2nd ed. (New York: McGraw-Hill, 1996): 323–34.

21. Quoted in Eric Foner, *Free Soil, Free Men and Free Labor: The Ideology of the Republican Party before the Civil War* (New York: Oxford University Press, 1970): 41.

22. The comparisons are taken from Ransom, *Conflict and Compromise*: 60–68, 81. The data are based on a sample of farms collected by Ransom and Sutch that is described in Ransom and Sutch, *One Kind of Freedom: The Economic Consequences of Emancipation*, 2nd ed. (New York: Cambridge University Press, 2001): Appendix G.

23. The text describes the process of growing and marketing cotton; the use of slave gangs for tobacco and rice was essentially the same. While the production of sugar differed in that the processing of sugar was a much more intensive

process that required specialized slave labor in a setting that approached that of a factory, the financial arrangements using a factor to market the crop were similar to other areas of the South.

24. There is a considerable literature on the question of whether or not slave plantations were truly efficient in terms of what the economists call economies of scale. The leading proponent of the view that they were economically efficient is Robert Fogel, who claims that the organization of the slave in gangs was the key to its efficiency. See the arguments in Fogel and Engerman, "Economics of Slavery"; Fogel, *Without Consent or Contract*; and Fogel and Engerman, *Time on the Cross*. Richard Sutch and I have taken issue with this position, arguing that the efficiency measured by Fogel is biased upward because of the coercion inherent in the gang system of slave labor. Slaves produced more, in other words, because they were forced to work harder than free labor. See the discussion in Ransom and Sutch, *One Kind of Freedom*: 73–78.

25. The outlying areas of southwestern Texas, which had a high fraction of immigrants, were very sparsely settled in 1860.

26. Looking at the most recently settled areas in 1860, the census reported that just over 50 percent of the native-born population of the West South Central region was born outside the region, but only 7 percent came from outside the South. In the West North Central region, 45 percent of the native-born population was outside the region, with 35 percent coming from other areas of the North and 20 percent from areas of the South. Ransom, *Conflict and Compromise*: 141. As Map 1.4 shows, the free regions of the West had a far higher level of immigrant population than the Southwest.

27. United States Bureau of the Census, *Historical Statistics of the United States, Colonial Times to 1970*, 2 vols. (Washington, D.C.: U.S. Government Printing Office, 1975): Series Y220-71.

28. For an excellent discussion of this revolution and its effects, see Charles Sellers, *The Market Revolution: Jacksonian America, 1815–1846* (New York: Oxford University Press, 1991).

29. For discussions of how the markets of the Midwest developed linkages with commercial centers in the East, see Douglass C. North, "Location Theory and Regional Economic Growth," *Journal of Political Economy* 63 (June 1955); North, *Economic Growth*; and William Cronon, *Nature's Metropolis: Chicago and the Great West* (New York: W. W. Norton, 1991).

30. The only cities of forty thousand or more in the Deep South were New Orleans and Charleston. There were cities along the northern edge of the slave economy, in Missouri, Kentucky, Maryland, and Delaware; however, the economic activities of urban centers, such as St. Louis and Louisville in the West and Baltimore and Wilmington in the East, were tied much more closely to the Northern economy than to the South.

31. See Susan Carter, Roger Ransom, and Richard Sutch, "The Decline in Fertility and the Life Cycle Transition in the Antebellum United States," *History Matters: Economic Growth, Technology, and Population*, ed. Timothy W. Guinnane, William A. Sundstrom, and Warren Whatley (Palo Alto, Calif.: Stanford University Press, 2002) and Ransom and Sutch, "Conflicting Visions."

32. My own analysis of the political turmoil of this period can be found in Ransom, *Conflict and Compromise*: chs. 4 and 5. Writers offering insightful analyses on this topic include: Eric Foner, *Politics and Ideology in the Age of the Civil War* (New York: Oxford University Press, 1980), Foner, *Free Soil, Free Men and Free Labor*, and Foner, "Politics, Ideology and the Origins of the American Civil War," *A Nation Divided*, ed. George Fredrickson (New York: Oxford University Press, 1975); William Gienapp, ed., *Essays on American Antebellum Politics, 1840–1860* (Arlington: Texas A & M University Press, 1982), Gienapp, *The Origins of the Republican Party, 1852–1856* (New York: Oxford University Press, 1987), and Holt, *Political Crisis of the 1850's* and *Rise and Fall of the Whig Party*.

33. Foner, *Free Soil, Free Men and Free Labor*: 11. Robert Fogel also places considerable weight on the negative effects of Northern views of the South. Fogel accepts Foner's description of how Northerners viewed the slave, but he argues at length that this view of the South was colored by a racist perception of African-American slaves that caused Northern observers to view the economic system of the South as being inefficient and a millstone around the neck of the rest of the economy. See Fogel, *Without Consent or Contract*.

34. Lincoln could point to Douglas's speech at Freeport, which reaffirmed the senator's commitment to a policy of choice over slavery in the territories. Douglas was able to capitalize on his opponent's "House Divided" speech, in which Lincoln argued that the policy of popular sovereignty had failed and asserted that the nation could not long endure "half slave and half free," a situation that Douglas and his supporters took as support for emancipation.

35. Historian Kenneth Stampp is hardly alone in his assessment that the "characteristic posture of the conservative northeastern business community was far from anti-Southern. Most merchants, bankers, and manufacturers were outspoken in their hostility to antislavery agitation and eager for sectional compromise in order to maintain their profitable business connections with the South." Kenneth M. Stampp, *The Imperiled Union: Essays on the Background of the Civil War* (New York: Oxford University Press, 1980): 198.

36. James L. Huston, "Property Rights in Slavery and the Coming of the Civil War," *Journal of Southern History* 65 (May 1999): 261. Huston expands on this point in his book, *Calculating the Cost of Union: Slavery, Property Rights, and Economic Origins of the Civil War* (Chapel Hill: University of North Carolina Press, 2004).

37. Much has been written about the Kansas-Nebraska Act and the events in

"Bloody Kansas." The most complete account is that of James A. Rawley, *Race and Politics: "Bleeding" Kansas and the Coming of Civil War* (Philadelphia: J. B. Lippincott Company, 1969). The discussion of the text also draws heavily from Potter, *Impending Crisis*; Allan Nevins, *The Emergence of Lincoln: Douglas, Buchanan, and Party Chaos, 1857–1859*, vol. 3, *Ordeal of the Union* (New York: Charles Scribner's Sons, 1950); Holt, *Political Crisis of the 1850's* and *Rise and Fall of the Whig Party*; and Gienapp, *Origins of the Republican Party*.

38. Speech by Charles Sumner, May 19 and 20, 1856; reproduced in Silbey, ed., *Transformation of American Politics*.

39. Quoted by Nevins, *Douglas, Buchanan, and Party Chaos*: 284–85.

40. Quoted in Nevins, *Prologue to Civil War*: 194.

41. David M. Potter, "Why the Republicans Rejected Compromise and Secession," *The Crisis of the Union*, ed. George H. Knoles (Baton Rouge: Louisiana State University Press, 1965): 105–06.

42. James M. McPherson, "Antebellum Southern Exceptionalism: A New Look at an Old Question," *Civil War History* 29 (September 1983): 243.

43. Abraham Lincoln, First Inaugural Address, March 4, 1861; in Edward McPherson, *The Political History of the United States of America during the Great Rebellion* (Washington, D.C.: Philp and Solomons, 1864): 106.

44. Ibid.: 107.

Chapter 2. The Southern Gamble: Could the South Have Won?

1. Jubal A. Early, "The Campaigns of Robert E. Lee," *Lee the Soldier*, ed. Gary W. Gallagher (Lincoln: University of Nebraska Press, 1996): 66–67.

2. Ibid.: 71.

3. The criticism of Lee stirred up a storm of controversy that persists to the present day. The first significant criticism of Lee was offered by the British military historian J. F. C. Fuller in his 1933 book comparing Lee and Grant: *Grant and Lee: A Study in Personality and Generalship* (London: Eyre and Spotswood, 1933). Thomas L. Connelly launched a much more aggressive attack on Lee's role in the war in his 1977 book *The Marble Man: Robert E. Lee and His Image in American History* (New York: Alfred A. Knopf, 1977). Connelly's book attacked what the author called Lee's image as a "Marble Man" and brought forth spirited defenses of Lee from such writers as Albert Castel and Richard Roland. For these contributions as well as an excellent group of essays by other authors in this debate, see Gary W. Gallagher, ed., *Lee the Soldier* (Lincoln: University of Nebraska Press, 1996). We shall take a closer look at Lee and the debates over Confederate strategy later in this chapter.

4. This was a point that was not lost on early advocates of the Lost Cause. Jubal Early noted that the "fall of Richmond, and the surrender of the Army of Northern Virginia, were the consequences of events in the West and Southwest, and not directly of the operations in Virginia (Early, "Campaigns of Robert E. Lee," 67). He quickly added, however, that those armies also had "the disadvantage of overwhelming numbers and the other agencies that I mentioned, to contend against, and a truthful history of their deeds will confer upon them imperishable renown" (p. 67).

5. Shelby Foote, "Men at War: An Interview with Shelby Foote," *The Civil War: An Illustrated History*, ed. Geoffrey Ward (New York: Alfred A. Knopf, 1990): 272.

6. Willam C. Davis, *The Cause Lost: Myths and Realities of the Confederacy* (Lawrence: University of Kansas Press, 1996): 139.

7. Ibid.: 137.

8. For excellent account of the Battle of Second Manassas, see John J. Hennessy, *Return to Bull Run: The Campaign and Battle of Second Manassas* (New York: Simon & Schuster, 1993).

9. Quoted in Herman Hattaway and Archer Jones, *How the North Won: A Military History of the Civil War* (Champaign-Urbana: University of Illinois Press, 1983): 307.

10. A good collection of essays dealing with both the Battle of Chancellorsville and its aftermath is in Gary Gallagher, ed., *Chancellorsville: The Battle and Its Aftermath* (Chapel Hill: University of North Carolina Press, 1996).

11. The story of the Battle of Antietam has been told countless times, most recently by James M. McPherson, *Crossroads of Freedom: Antietam* (New York: Oxford University Press, 2002). In addition to this work, the description that follows has drawn particularly on two other works dealing with the battle: James V. Murfin, *The Gleam of Bayonets: The Battle of Antietam and the Maryland Campaign of 1862*, paperback ed. (Baton Rouge: Louisiana State University Press, 1965) and Stephen W. Sears, *Landscape Turned Red: The Battle of Antietam* (New York: Ticknor and Fields, 1983).

12. The orders were written to Confederate General D. H. Hill. Legend has it that they were found by a Union soldier named Barton Mitchell, who noticed a bulky envelope lying in the grass. He found the orders wrapped around three cigars inside the envelope. As James McPherson points out, whether or not this is the true story of how the orders fell into Union hands, the discovery of Lee's orders by the Union high command is "a remarkable example of the contingencies that change the course of history." McPherson, *Antietam*: 108.

13. Cited in Murfin, *The Gleam of Bayonets*: 133.

14. As in all Civil War battles, the number of casualties is at best an estimate. McPherson argues that a "fair estimate" of the Confederates killed outright

would be 2,000 men; for the Union the figure would be 2,300. In addition, there were 17,300 wounded men, of whom at least 2,000 died of their wounds. McPherson, *Antietam*: 177, n. 56. McWhiney and Jamieson place the total casualties at 11,724 for the Confederates and 11,657 for the Union, for a combined total of 23,381. Grady McWhiney and Perry D. Jamieson, *Attack and Die: Civil War Military Tactics and the Southern Heritage* (Tuscaloosa: University of Alabama Press, 1982): 8, Table 1.

15. Quoted in Murfin, *The Gleam of Bayonets*: 315.

16. Quoted in McPherson, *Antietam*: 141.

17. Quoted in Allan Nevins, *The War for the Union: War Becomes Revolution, 1862–1863*, vol. 6, *Ordeal of the Union* (New York: Charles Scribner's Sons, 1960): 231.

18. James Longstreet, "Lee's Invasion of Pennsylvania," *Battles and Leaders of the Civil War*, ed. Robert U. Johnson and Clarence C. Buel, vol. 3 (New York: Century Company, 1884): 247.

19. For an excellent description of the movement of the two armies leading up to the battle itself, see Noah Andre Trudeau, *Gettysburg: A Testing of Courage* (New York: HarperCollins, 2002), chs. 6 to 11.

20. Stuart's "raid" created a great deal of consternation among the Union commanders and succeeded in capturing a large cache of supplies as he moved north. However, by detaching himself from the main body of Lee's army, he deprived Lee of a valuable function of cavalry when the army was on the move: information on the whereabouts of the enemy. There is considerable debate over the extent to which Stuart's raid was a contributing factor to Lee's problems at Gettysburg.

21. Quoted in Trudeau, *Gettysburg*: 123.

22. Ibid.: 125.

23. Ibid.: 205.

24. James M. McPherson, *Ordeal by Fire: The Civil War and Reconstruction*, 3rd ed., vol. 2 (New York: McGraw-Hill, 2001): 352.

25. Trudeau, *Gettysburg*: 267–68.

26. "It is unhistoric to conclude that Ewell was necessarily wrong in his judgment," claimed Nolan. "His decision was reasonable in the circumstances." Alan T. Nolan, "R. E. Lee and July 1 at Gettysburg," *The First Day at Gettysburg*, ed. Gary Gallagher (Kent, Ohio: Kent State University Press, 1992): 28. Gary Gallagher points out that both A. P. Hill and Ewell had only recently been elevated to their commands following the death of Stonewall Jackson at Chancellorsville. Gallagher, ed., *The First Day at Gettysburg*. For a spirited defense of Lee and an equally sharp indictment of Ewell carried on in the best tradition of the Lost Cause, see Scott Bowden and Bill Ward, *Last Chance for Victory: Robert E. Lee and the Gettysburg Campaign* (Cambridge, Mass.: DaCapo, 2001): 176–209.

A more balanced interpretation of the first day's events is the summary given by Trudeau, *Gettysburg*: 267–72.

27. Bowden and Ward, *Last Chance for Victory*: 393.

28. Gary Gallagher, " 'If the Enemy Is There, We Must Attack Him': R. E. Lee and the Second Day at Gettysburg," *The Second Day at Gettysburg*, ed. Gary Gallagher (Kent, Ohio: Kent State University Press, 1993): 32. Gallagher's essay is one of the best summaries of the debates over the wisdom of Lee's decision to attack the left flank of the Union army rather than disengage after the first day. There is a large literature dealing with the reasons for the Confederate failure. In the years immediately following the war, Longstreet received much of the blame because of his failure to get his troops into position earlier in the day. Critics alleged that he deliberately obstructed movements of his troops because he believed Lee's plans to be fatally flawed. Historians have largely exonerated "Old Pete" of this charge, focusing instead on the problems of coordinating command among the Confederate generals, on the one hand, and the ability of Meade to move troops to the right place soon enough to stop any breakthrough, on the other. "Meade," writes Russell F. Weigley in his summary of the battle, "thoroughly outgeneraled Lee by putting "the right subordinate in the right place with the right understanding of his mission throughout the battle with almost uncanny consistency." Weigley, *A Great Civil War: A Military and Political History, 1861–1865* (Bloomington: Indiana University Press, 2000): 254.

29. Noah Trudeau, one of the most recent historians of the battle, sums up Lee's role as well as anyone: "If July 1 was the battle of accidental encounters and July 2 the fight for dominant position, then the combat on July 3 was driven solely by Robert E. Lee's desire for a decisive victory. . . . There were indications, for those who wanted to see it that way, that the Union army was tottering; but there were signs, too again, for those who wished to think so that it remained resilient and strong. Lee chose to join the former group." Trudeau, *Gettysburg*: 526.

30. Foote, "An Interview with Shelby Foote": 268.

31. Quoted in Willam L. Shea and Terrence J. Winschel, *Vicksburg Is the Key: The Struggle for the Mississippi River* (Lincoln: University of Nebraska Press, 2003): 178.

32. Russell Weigley notes that throughout the Vicksburg campaign, Grant "marched rapidly, shifted direction deftly, hit hard when fighting became necessary, but achieved its objectives less through battles with its casualties than by deceptive maneuver." Weigley, *A Great Civil War*: 269–70. William Sherman later credited the success of Grant's army maneuvering without supply lines south and east of Vicksburg as the basis for his own decision to march through Georgia and live off the land in late 1864.

33. In capturing Jackson and tearing up the rail lines, Sherman showed the thoroughness that was to make him famous throughout Georgia a year and a half later. For an account of his raid on Jackson, see Shea and Winschel, *Vicksburg Is the Key*: ch. 15.

34. Hattaway and Jones, *How the North Won*. The authors cite a comment by James Longstreet that the West was already largely cut off from the rest of the Confederacy, and "as to the Yankees using the river for trade, it cannot be done as long as we have the banks" (p. 175).

35. Kentucky had been invited to be part of the Confederacy. This action by the two CSA generals was in accordance with the recognition of Kentucky as a state in the Confederacy. Bragg hoped to utilize the authority of his secessionist government to gain troops through conscription. We shall return to the pivotal position occupied by Kentucky in the future of the Confederacy in chapter 4.

36. For more on the Battle of Stones River, or Murfreesboro, see James Lee McDonough, *Stones River: Bloody Winter in Tennessee* (Knoxville: University of Tennessee Press, 1980).

37. Cited in James Lee McDonough, *Chattanooga: A Death Grip on the Confederacy* (Knoxville: University of Tennessee Press, 1984): 28. McDonough's book provides one of the best accounts of what he terms the war between the generals on the Confederate staff and the battle for Chattanooga that followed. For more on the problems Bragg had with his staff see Grady McWhiney, *Braxton Bragg and Confederate Defeat: Field Command* (New York: Columbia University Press, 1969).

38. Reinforcements to Grant's army brought the number of Union troops in Chattanooga to about seventy thousand. The departure of Longstreet and Wheeler reduced the Confederate army to about forty thousand men.

39. Sherman's march to the sea has been documented many times. Among the best accounts of the campaign are the books by Joseph T. Glatthaar, *The March to the Sea and Beyond: Sherman's Troops in the Savannah and Carolinas Campaigns* (New York: New York University Press, 1985); John F. Marszalek, *Sherman: A Soldier's Passion for Order* (New York: Free Press, 1993); and Theodore P. Savas and David A. Woodbury, eds., *The Campaign for Atlanta and Sherman's March to the Sea: Essays on the American Civil War in Georgia*, 2 vols. (Athens, Ga.: Savas Woodbury Publishers, 1994). For an interesting take on the "new" form of warfare instituted by Sherman, see Charles Royster, *The Destructive War: William Tecumseh Sherman, Stonewall Jackson, and the Americans* (New York: Alfred A. Knopf, 1991).

40. The term "Fabian strategy" dates from the strategy employed by the Roman General Quintus Fabius in defeating the invasion of Italy by the Carthaginian general Hannibal during the Second Punic War. Though the Romans suffered

numerous defeats at the hands of Hannibal, they were able to maintain an army in the field. Eventually the Carthaginian army was worn down to where Hannibal, unable to resupply his army in Italy, was forced to give up the invasion and return home. Rome was subsequently able to force Carthage into signing an unfavorable peace treaty to end the war. Two of the most celebrated examples of this strategy being successfully employed in modern times were the Russian response to invasions in 1812–13 by Napoleon and by the Nazi *Blitzkrieg* in 1942–45. In each case the Russian armies retreated far into the interior of their country and exposed the invaders to serious problems of supply as the result of distance and the Russian winter. Eventually the Russians were able to counterattack and drive the foe from their country.

41. The figures are from McWhiney and Jamieson, *Attack and Die*: Table 1, p. 8. The data cover men killed or wounded in the following battles: Shiloh, Fair Oaks, Seven Days, Second Manassas, Antietam, Perryville, Murfreesboro, Chancellorsville, Vicksburg, Gettysburg, and Chickamauga. The estimates are those presented in Thomas L. Livermore, *Numbers and Losses in the Civil War in America 1861–1865* (Boston and New York: 1901). As we note below, there are many ambiguities in these numbers. Appendix 1 examines Livermore's estimates in greater detail. Detailed estimates of the casualty data for Confederate losses in specific battles in the Virginia campaigns of 1864–65 are very incomplete, and it is therefore difficult to assess the merits of the argument relating to relative losses beyond the campaigns of 1862–63.

42. McWhiney and Jamieson, *Attack and Die*: 7.

43. McWhiney, *Braxton Bragg*: Table 4, p. 19. McWhiney and Jamieson are not alone in their criticism that Lee wasted his men by taking offensive actions that produced excessive casualties. Others who have presented lengthy arguments supporting the claim that the South paid too high a price for Lee's actions in northern Virginia include: Connelly, *The Marble Man*; Allan T. Nolan, *Lee Reconsidered: Robert E. Lee and Civil War History* (Chapel Hill: University of North Carolina Press, 1991); and Robert D. McKenzie, *Uncertain Glory: Lee's Generalship Re-Examined* (New York: Hippocrene Books, 1997).

44. Quoted in Hattaway and Jones, *How the North Won*: 307. Actually, Johnston got his chance to repulse such a charge on a somewhat smaller scale when, in 1864, Sherman launched a bloody attack on Confederate troops dug in on Kennesaw Mountain, Georgia. Sherman's force suffered more than two thousand casualties; Johnston's losses were about one-tenth of that total.

45. Thus, for example, Gary W. Gallagher insists that "many critics fail to give Lee credit for what he accomplished through aggressive generalship." He points out that Lee's victories managed to "push the eastern military frontier back to the Potomac and confronted Lincoln with a major crisis at home and abroad." Gallagher, "Another Look at the Generalship of R. E. Lee," *Lee the Soldier*, ed.

Gary W. Gallagher (Lincoln: University of Nebraska Press, 1996): 283. Gallagher expands on the same point, *The Confederate War: How Popular Will, Nationalism, and Military Strategy Could Not Stave Off Defeat* (Boston: Harvard University Press, 1997). Others have also argued that the value of Lee's victories more than offset their cost in terms of casualties. See, for example, Joseph L. Harsh, *Confederate Tide Rising: Robert E. Lee and the Making of Strategy, 1861–1862* (Kent, Ohio: Kent State University Press, 1998) and James M. McPherson, "Failed Southern Strategies," *With My Face to the Enemy*, ed. Robert Cowley (New York: Berkley Books, 2001).

46. Perhaps the most complete statement of these claims is in the volume of essays edited by Richard E. Beringer, Herman Hattaway, et al., *Why the South Lost the War* (Athens: University of Georgia Press, 1986): 16.

47. This section draws very heavily on arguments presented in Gallagher, *The Confederate War: How Popular Will, Nationalism, and Military Strategy Could Not Stave Off Defeat* and Robert G. Tanner, *Confederate Strategy Reconsidered* (Wilmington, Del.: Scholarly Resources, 2001).

48. Barbara Fields, "Who Freed the Slaves?," *The Civil War: An Illustrated History*, ed. Geoffrey Ward (New York: Alfred A. Knopf, 1990): 181

49. Writing in 1985, Herman Hattaway and Archer Jones observed that "under Davis' leadership the Confederacy skillfully reconciled the defense of exposed territory against raids with powerful resistance on the main lines of operations." Hattaway and Jones, *How the North Won*: 696. The authors went on to cite particularly the success of the Confederates in using their rail system to coordinate defenses. Interestingly, Archer Jones was initially a severe critic of Davis. See his remarks in the preface to the 1991 edition of Archer Jones, *Confederate Strategy from Shiloh to Vicksburg* (Baton Rouge: Louisiana State University Press, 1991), first published in 1961.

50. See in particular Harsh, *Confederate Tide Rising: Robert E. Lee and the Making of Strategy, 1861–1862* and Gary Gallagher, "When Lee Was Mortal," *With My Face to the Enemy*, ed. Robert Cowley (New York: Berkley Books, 2001). Steven E. Woodworth argues that Davis and Lee often offset each other, with Davis urging a more conservative policy and Lee a more offensive posture. Though the two did not always agree on the best strategy, Woodworth concedes that the combination of views often produced an effective strategy. Woodworth, *Davis and Lee at War* (Lawrence: University Press of Kansas, 1995).

51. There is an extensive literature on this issue. A sampling of works supporting the argument that the Southern strategy was in fact a reasonable response to the situation at hand would include: Gallagher, *The Confederate War: How Popular Will, Nationalism, and Military Strategy Could Not Stave Off Defeat*: ch. 3; Tanner, *Retreat to Victory?* ; and McPherson, "Failed Southern Strategies."

Chapter 3. Against All Odds:
The Anatomy of a Southern Victory

1. Forrest actually did escape with about a thousand of his men. On the prospect that he might have done more given the opportunity, see Kendall D. Gott, *Where the South Lost the War: An Analysis of the Fort Henry—Fort Donelson Campaign, February 1862* (Mechanicsburg, Pa.: Stackpole Books, 2003): 238–41.

2. In the actual battle, Sherman was instrumental in rallying his troops. In the process of doing so, he had his horse shot out from under him on three occasions. He sustained a wound in his hand: A bullet that glanced off a buckle would have disabled him had it been inches to either side. Victor Hanson provides an excellent account of Sherman's role at Shiloh: *Ripples of Battle: How Wars of the Past Still Determine How We Fight, How We Live, and How We Think* (New York: Doubleday, 2003): ch. 2.

3. The demotion of Grant in the event of defeat at Shiloh would be a foregone conclusion. As historian James Lee McDonough comments in his assessment of the actual battle, if things had gone any worse for the Union at Shiloh, Grant "would have been discredited, especially so when news spread of how the army was surprised while its commander was residing in a mansion nine miles down the river": McDonough, *Shiloh—in Hell before Night* (Knoxville: University of Tennessee Press, 1977): 222.

4. There were actually several battles that occurred around Corinth and Iuka in the Civil War. Our version of the October battle, with Grant as the attacker and the Confederates defending the towns, has the roles reversed. In the actual fighting it was the Confederate army under Van Dorn attacking the Union forces that had occupied Corinth and Iuka since shortly after Shiloh.

5. This hypothetical account of the Vicksburg campaign follows the actual course of events rather closely with two important changes. The first change is that the campaign takes place roughly four months later than the campaign described in chapter 2. Vicksburg actually fell after a forty-eight-day siege on July 4, 1863; in our counterfactual account it capitulated without a fight on November 2, 1863. The second change is that in our counterfactual the bulk of the forces stationed in Vicksburg under Pemberton left Vicksburg when Grant's army successfully crossed the Mississippi south of the city. In fact, General Pemberton remained in the city with his entire command and eventually surrendered twenty-nine thousand Confederate troops to the Union force. One of the points frequently made by commentators is the effect that these troops, together with those that surrendered at Fort Donelson, would have on the

availability of troops to defend the Mississippi area. In our counterfactual example, Johnston and Pemberton have roughly thirty thousand more troops than were actually available.

6. Up to this point, the counterfactual account follows the same path as the narrative for the Tennessee and Kentucky theater we presented in chapter 2.

7. We discussed the problems with Bragg and his generals in chapter 2. As we noted there, virtually every historian agrees that Davis's failure to replace Bragg after Chickamauga (or better yet, after Murfreesboro) was a serious error. The most significant difference between the actual situation and the one posed in our counterfactual is that Albert Sidney Johnston, for whom Davis had a very high regard, was alive to corroborate the need for a change in command.

8. Quoted in Willam L. Shea and Terrence J. Winschel, *Vicksburg Is the Key: The Struggle for the Mississippi River* (Lincoln: University of Nebraska Press, 2003): 177.

9. The accounts of these battles were summarized in chapter 2. Our counterfactual scenario assumes that the events of these battles (with one notable exception) were essentially unchanged. The exception, as we note below, was that in our counterfactual world Stonewall Jackson did not die of his wound at Chancellorsville. We are assuming that Jackson recovered and rejoined Lee's army in the fall of 1863.

10. The Battle of Antietam is a popular choice to be the turning point at which a Southern victory might allow the Confederacy to win a counterfactual civil war. One of the most ingenious scenarios is that of James McPherson, who outlines a counterfactual campaign in which Lee's invasion of Maryland in the fall of 1862 culminates in a titanic battle at Gettysburg. Dug in on the south edge of town, the Confederates wait for McClellan to attack. The Union attacks fail, and in the ensuing counterattacks by the Confederates, McClellan is killed. The Army of the Potomac disintegrates, and with no Union army to oppose him, Lee has a free hand to roam through the Northeast. Meanwhile, Bragg and Kirby Smith, encouraged by the victory at Gettysburg, resume their campaign in Kentucky, putting further pressure on Lincoln and his government to seek a speedy solution to the war. With Confederate armies poised to go on the offensive in Kentucky and the east, the Union president accedes to the pressures of Congress and accepts an armistice to end the fighting. See James M. McPherson, "If the Order Hadn't Been Lost," *What If ?*, ed. Robert Cowley (New York: G. P. Putnam's Sons, 1999). Michael Hathaway presents one of the most detailed counterfactual analyses of the consequences of a Confederate victory over McClellan's army in the fall of 1862. Hathaway places the battle on the eastern side of South Mountain, near Frederick, Maryland. Following his victory at the Battle of Frederick, Lee is able to wage a successful campaign in the North that eventually allows the Army of Northern Virginia to occupy the city

of York, Pennsylvania. Impressed by the string of Confederate victories, the British and French offer to mediate the conflict. With Union morale rapidly falling in the North, there is a massive financial crisis in New York at the end of October. The inability of the government to stem the continuing financial crisis, together with the failure of the Union military to contain Lee, leads to an overwhelming defeat of the Republicans in the November 1862 elections. A treaty between the United States and the Confederacy ending the war is finally signed in August 1863. See Michael Hathaway, "When the Bottom Fell Out: The Crisis of 1862," *Dixie Victorious*, ed. Peter G. Tsouras (Mechanicsburg, Pa.: Stackpole Books, 2004): 89–131. Both McPherson's and Hathaway's counterfactual accounts of Lee's invasion are quite plausible, and Hathaway's account of the disruption that a Confederate victory might cause in the North is particularly interesting. He is one of the few writers to explore carefully the details of negotiations that would be necessary to end the war at that time. My problem with both these essays is that I do not believe that morale in North was so fragile in the fall of 1862 that a single victory by the Army of Northern Virginia would cause the government in Washington, D.C., to capitulate.

11. The details of both these battles are covered in chapter 2. Stonewall Jackson was wounded in his arm as he returned on a scouting mission late in the afternoon. The wound was not thought to be serious at first; however, it became infected, and he died several days later. In our counterfactual scenario we assume that Jackson did not die of the wound, though it did keep him out of the Gettysburg campaign.

12. The Army of Northern Virginia was organized then into three corps, commanded by James Longstreet, Richard Ewell, and A. P. Hill (filling in for the injured Jackson).

13. The failure of the Confederates to take Culp's Hill on the first day of battle was one of the most serious errors of the entire battle. Isaac Trimble really did plead with Ewell to occupy the hill, claiming that a brigade of men could walk over and occupy the high ground. We have only slightly altered history by having Trimble convince the North Carolinians to do his bidding.

14. The decision by Daniel Sickles to place III Corps far in front of the rest of the Federal line did in fact take place. However, unlike the actual battle, where Sickles's move very nearly created a Union disaster by opening a gap in the Union line, in the counterfactual scenario Sickles's daring is rewarded when his troops seriously disrupt the Confederate plan to flank the Union left wing.

15. The struggle for control of Little Round Top is one of the great legends of the Gettysburg battle. Colonel Joshua Chamberlain and the 20th Maine held their position on the hill until they ran out of ammunition, whereupon Chamberlain ordered the men to form up and led a bayonet charge down the hill that successfully stopped the last Confederate effort to take the hill. Whether such

heroics were necessary in our counterfactual battle is left to the imagination of the reader.

16. There are of course a multitude of scenarios that could produce a Confederate victory. The simplest and most common way is to have Pickett's charge on the third day succeed in breaking through the Union line and delivering Lee the victory. However, unless something in the earlier fighting had favored the Confederates, it is highly unlikely that Pickett's charge could have succeeded. The counterfactual Battle of Gettysburg outlined in the text is based on my discussion of the actual battle presented in chapter 2. The pivotal change was the decision by Trimble to send troops on to Culp's Hill. Most writers agree that the failure of Richard Ewell to take Cemetery Hill and Culp's Hill was a critical mistake. If the Confederates had taken the hill, as they do in our counterfactual scenario, the famous fishhook that had been formed by the Union army on the first day of battle would not have been possible. My decision to have Lee attack the Federals on Cemetery Hill in force early on the second day follows from everything we know about Lee's propensity to seize the tactical offensive when the opportunity arose. My counterfactual scenario also addresses Lee's rejection of Longstreet's argument that the Confederates should not attack the Union position on the second day and the argument that this accounts for Longstreet's sluggish performance in moving into position to attack the left wing of the Union line. In my counterfactual battle, I assume that Longstreet did not object to an attack on the exposed right wing of the Union Army. He would also be more comfortable with Lee's suggestion that he march around the Union left flank. The rest of the counterfactual battle rests largely on my imagination.

The account of a Southern victory at Gettysburg that comes closest to agreeing with mine is that presented by Newt Gingrich and William R. Forstchen, *Gettysburg: A Novel of the Civil War* (New York: St. Martin's Press, 2003). In their scenario, the first day of fighting follows the action as it actually occurred. That evening Lee concedes that Longstreet is probably correct in his assessment that the Union position is too strong to be stormed. The two men then agree on a daring plan not unlike the one that Lee and Stonewall Jackson devised for Chancellorsville a few months earlier. Longstreet will take his division and march completely around the Union left flank, going all the way to Taneytown while part of Ewell's corps and Stuart's cavalry create enough of a diversion that Meade will believe the main Confederate attack will come from the north. The plan works. Longstreet occupies Taneytown and quickly moves on to capture the Union supply base in Westminster and in so doing places his forces between the Union army and Washington, D.C. Meade is forced to attack the Confederates with disastrous results, and Lee is able to achieve his great victory on July 4, 1863. This is a wholly creditable scenario, though one that requires far higher risks on the part of the Confederates than what I have described in this chapter. But as we noted earlier in our story, war is a gamble, and counterfactual history is not about what was *likely* but about what might have been *possible*. Like the account described above, Gingrich and Forstchen base their story on a firm grasp of reality combined with a heavy dose of imagination.

17. The raid described in the text is loosely based on a real event. In July 1864 Lee sent Jubal Early with a force of about fourteen thousand on a route similar to the one described above taken by Jackson. Early actually did get all the way to the northern outskirts of Washington at Fort Stevens. Though most of the Union troops had been removed from the Washington garrison, Early's force was too small to accomplish much more than burn a few houses in the suburbs. When Grant finally reacted to the raid by detaching Wright's corps to defend the capital, Early retreated back into northern Virginia. His army was eventually destroyed at the Battle of Winchester in late 1864. For more on Early's raid, see Benjamin Franklin Cooling, *Jubal Early's Raid on Washington, 1864* (Knoxville: University of Tennessee Press, 1989). Kevin Kiley presents a counterfactual account of Early's raid in which he also has Cleburne's forces reinforce Early. The Confederate troops reach Fort Stevens just outside Washington, D.C., where an excessively curious Abraham Lincoln is shot and killed while looking over one of the fort's parapets at the Confederate forces. Lincoln's death, together with the victory gained by Early and Cleburne over Philip Sheridan's army at Winchester, turns the tide against the Union forces. See Kevin Kiley, "Terrible as an Army with Banners: Jubal Early in the Shenandoah Valley," *Dixie Victorious*: 252–72.

18. There is no reliable way to estimate the outcome of the 1864 election, given the changed conditions from the actual situation. Harry Turtledove has constructed a very plausible scenario involving a four-candidate race among Lincoln, George McClellan, John Frémont, and Horatio Seymour. Seymour and the Democratic Party emerge as the eventual winners. Turtledove, *The Guns of the South* (New York: Ballantine Books, 1992): "Historical Notes," pp. 559–63. I have elected to omit McClellan's candidacy from the picture because I believe that in our scenario McClellan would have remained in the Democratic Party. George Hunt Pendleton was the actual vice presidential candidate of the Democratic Party in 1864 along with George McClellan.

Chapter 4. The King Is Dead, Long Live the King: The Future of the Slave South

1. Quoted in James M. McPherson, *Crossroads of Freedom: Antietam* (New York: Oxford University Press, 2002): 142.

2. The other country that bought significant amounts of cotton from the United States was France. However, as David Pinkney argues, the textile industry in France was not important enough to cause disruption throughout the entire economy, and by 1863 the French industrialists had successfully replaced American cotton with imports from India and Egypt. David H. Pinkney, "France and the Civil War," *Heard round the World*, ed. Harold Hyman (New York: Alfred A. Knopf, 1969): 128–30.

3. For more on the argument that the British military were not interested in getting involved with the war, see Russell F. Weigley, *A Great Civil War: A Military and Political History, 1861–1865* (Bloomington: Indiana University Press, 2000): 81.

4. Cited in David P. Crook, *The North, the South, and the Powers, 1861–1865* (New York: John Wiley, 1974): 64.

5. The prospect of foreign involvement in the American war was further diminished because the reasons for intervention varied widely among the European states. France, in particular, was concerned over the prospect that a British victory over the United States would substantially increase the relative power of a country the French still regarded with considerable suspicion. As one official in Douai noted in a report to the government in Paris, "At no price would one want to make common cause with England to destroy a navy that could someday be her rival, for us an auxiliary." Quoted in Pinkney, "France and the Civil War," 101.

6. November 12, 1862; cited in Crook, *The North, the South, and the Powers*: 252.

7. Cited ibid.: 219.

8. In a comparable situation following the armistice declared in November 1918 that ended the fighting in the First World War, the British refused to relax their blockade of the Central Powers until a peace treaty had been signed. By keeping the economic pressure on their enemies, the Allies effectively pressured Germany into accepting a peace treaty that imposed harsh terms that could not be refused six months after the armistice.

9. Much has been made in American accounts of the Civil War about how the battle of the *Merrimack* and the *Monitor* off the coast of Virginia in 1862 made wooden ships obsolete. In fact, neither the *Monitor* nor the *Merrimack* was a warship that could operate on the open seas. The Union monitors, while effective as a weapon to prevent the Southern navy from breaking the blockade of Southern ports, were in reality little more than floating batteries and would have been no match for the faster and more maneuverable British ships, both of which seriously outgunned their American counterparts.

10. Delaware, which had only 1,798 slaves in 1860 out of a total population of 112,221, saw relatively little pressure for secession. For an interesting analysis

of slavery in Delaware, see Patience Essah, *A House Divided: Slavery and Emancipation in Delaware, 1638–1865* (Charlottesville: University of Virginia Press, 1996).

11. The Union would be in a strong position to enforce any such arrangements, since many areas of the Confederacy depended on the Ohio and Tennessee river systems as their primary transportation routes to the outside world via the Mississippi. Union naval forces could close the Ohio River and the northern sections of the Mississippi, a situation that would seriously damage Confederate commerce to New Orleans.

12. It required all of Lincoln's political skill to get the Thirteenth Amendment passed by a lame-duck Congress in December 1864. The amendment was not formally proclaimed as being in effect until December 18, 1865, after it had been ratified by three-fourths of the states. In our counterfactual world it is likely that the amendment would not even have been passed by Congress following the 1864 elections. It is also likely that efforts to emancipate slaves in the Border States would be stalled.

13. A point that is often overlooked in the efforts to enact emancipation in Northern states before the war is that as the threat of emancipation neared, slaveowners could either migrate South or sell their slaves to buyers in the slave states to avoid any economic loss.

14. An example of such a pessimist would be Paul Escott, who argues that "the Confederacy was collapsing from within long before Federal Armies managed to apply irresistible pressure from without." Escott, *After Secession: Jefferson Davis and the Failure of Confederate Nationalism* (Baton Rouge: Louisiana State University Press, 1978): 272.

15. Noting that recent scholarship has "highlighted social tensions and fissures to create a portrait of Confederate Society crumbling from within," Gary Gallagher insists that Confederate nationalism was far stronger than the pessimistic arguments suggest. "Historians," he notes, "have worked backward from Appomattox to explain that failure." Gallagher, *The Confederate War: How Popular Will, Nationalism, and Military Strategy Could Not Stave Off Defeat* (Boston: Harvard University Press, 1997): 3. George C. Rable echoes this theme when he argues: "What remains remarkable about the Confederacy is not its internal weaknesses—political, social or economic—but its staying power and especially the ability of so many men and women to endure and make sacrifices." Rable, *The Confederate Republic: A Revolution against Politics* (Chapel Hill: University of North Carolina Press, 1994): 300.

16. More than 200,000 men served in the Continental army out of a population of about 2.5 million. There were about 10,000 casualties, a figure that is tiny compared with those of the Civil War. However, the damage from the fighting, which lasted for seven years and covered virtually the entire coast

from Boston to Charleston, was probably greater in relative terms for the country as a whole than was the case of the Civil War. Whereas every major city in the colonies was occupied by British troops at least once, the interior of the Confederacy was largely untouched at the time of the cease-fire in 1865.

17. On the economic prospects of the new nation and the impact of the Napoleonic Wars during the 1790s, see Douglass C. North, *The Economic Growth of the United States, 1790–1860* (Englewood Cliffs, N.J.: Prentice Hall, 1961).

18. A copy of the Confederate Constitution is reprinted in Appendix 3.

19. The areas of greatest damage were northern Virginia, Kentucky, and Tennessee, where the bulk of the fighting took place. In our counterfactual world Sherman would not have marched through Georgia and South Carolina, and the Union raids into Alabama and Mississippi in 1864–65 would not have taken place. On the speed with which the defeated South actually did recover from the physical destruction of the war, see Roger L. Ransom and Richard Sutch, "The Impact of the Civil War and of Emancipation on Southern Agriculture," *Explorations in Economic History* 12 (January 1975).

20. The figures on actual Confederate expenditures are from Richard C. K. Burdekin and Farrokh K. Langdana, "War Finance in the Southern Confederacy," *Explorations in Economic History* 30 (July 1993): 354–55. They are estimated from the reports of the Confederate Treasury and cover the period from February 1861 through September 1864. Burdekin and Langdana estimate the total expenditure of the government over this period to be $2.1 billion. These estimates correspond well to those of Claudia Goldin and Frank Lewis, "The Economic Costs of the American Civil War: Estimates and Implications," *Journal of Economic History* 35 (June 1975).

21. The Confederate government actually did enact a major reform of the currency in April 1864, effectively reducing the money supply by one-third. Figure 4.1 shows that in the period when Grant and Sherman were held at bay, the reform had the desired effect on prices. However, when Atlanta fell and Lincoln was reelected, expectations sank to new lows, and prices resumed their rise to new heights. We assume that in our counterfactual world, where the Confederates were winning the war in 1864, the reform of the currency would have had the desired effect of reducing prices sharply in the second quarter of 1864 and that the rate of inflation thereafter would have roughly followed the expansion of the money supply. On the currency reform undertaken by the Confederate government in the spring of 1864, see Richard C. Todd, *Confederate Finance* (Athens: University of Georgia Press, 1954): 111–15; Burdekin and Langdana, "War Finance"; and George K. Davis and Gary M. Pequet, "Interest Rates in the Civil War South," *Journal of Economic History* 50 (March 1990).

22. The securities backed by cotton rather than gold were called Erlanger Bonds after the French firm that underwrote the issues. They were first issued

in Amsterdam in 1863, and despite the obvious failures of the Confederate military effort in 1864, they were still trading at a price of thirty-three dollars (or about one-third their par value) the week that Lee surrendered. See Marc Weidenmier, "The Market for Confederate Bonds," *Explorations in Economic History* 37 (January 2000) and Roger L. Ransom, "The Historical Statistics of the Confederacy," *The Historical Statistics of the United States, Millennial Edition*, ed. Susan Carter and Richard Sutch (New York: Cambridge University Press, 2005).

23. The price of cotton quoted in pence at Liverpool rose from six to twenty-seven. The Liverpool price of a pound of cotton in 1860 was eleven cents. Because of inflation in the United States, cotton prices peaked at over one dollar in late 1864, a rise of ten times. The blockade prevented cotton from leaving the South, so the price of cotton in the Confederacy remained almost constant through 1863 in spite of the inflation noted in Figure 4.1. See Ransom, "The Historical Statistics of the Confederacy."

24. In constructing the counterfactual scenario for the Confederacy, we shall frequently have reason to draw on the actual experience of the defeated American South in the years after the Civil War. To simplify the discussion, when describing developments in our counterfactual world in which the South won the Civil War, we shall refer to the South as the Confederacy or the CSA; when we refer to actual events that happened in the Southern states that lost the Civil War, we shall refer to the postbellum American South.

25. See North, *Economic Growth*: chs. 1–3 on the economic changes after 1790. Douglass C. North, *Growth and Welfare in the American Past: A New Economic History* (Englewood Cliffs, N.J.: Prentice Hall, 1966) discusses the "economics" of the Constitutional Convention and its eventual success.

26. This estimate is based on data from Thomas Ellison, *The Cotton Trade of Great Britain* (London: Frank Cass & Company, 1886); also see the discussion in Ransom, "The Historical Statistics of the Confederacy," ch. 6.

27. Robert W. Fogel, *Without Consent or Contract: The Rise and Fall of American Slavery* (New York: W. W. Norton, 1989): 14. Fogel bases his projection of the Confederacy's economic future on a counterfactual scenario in which the South manages to leave the Union without a war. He argues that his conjectures represent "a very creditable sketch" of what might have happened if the South had been allowed to go free. Since the argument rests primarily on the South's control of cotton, the results would not be greatly different in our counterfactual scenario of a long and costly war. Cotton, as we noted above, would still be the staple crop of Southern agriculture.

28. Ibid.: 14

29. On the importance of the cotton boom and its importance to antebellum growth, see Gavin Wright, "Slavery and the Cotton Boom," *Explorations in Eco-*

nomic History 12 (October 1975); North, *Economic Growth* ; and Roger L. Ransom, *Conflict and Compromise: The Political Economy of Slavery, Emancipation, and the American Civil War* (New York: Cambridge University Press, 1989): ch. 3.

30. We focus on the period after 1840 because that is the first year for which we can make meaningful estimates of national income. The regional per capita national income data for the United States were developed by Richard A. Easterlin, "Regional Income Trends, 1840–1950," *American Economic History*, ed. Seymour E. Harris (New York: McGraw-Hill, 1961), "Interregional Differences in Per Capita Income, Population, and Total Income: 1840–1950," *Trends in the American Economy in the Nineteenth Century*, vol. 24, Studies in Income and Wealth (Princeton: Princeton University Press, 1960). Regional estimates of per capita income for 1860 were developed by Stanley L. Engerman, who is responsible for developing the argument that the South maintained a level of antebellum growth equal to that of the rest of the country. Engerman, "The Economic Impact of the Civil War," *Explorations in Entrepreneurial History* 2nd Series 3 (Spring 1966).

31. The most notable proponent of this view was Charles W. Ramsdell, "The Natural Limits of Slavery Expansion," *Mississippi Valley Historical Review* 16 (September 1929). For more on the importance of Western settlement and the "territorial imperative" of the slave economy, see Ransom, *Conflict and Compromise*: ch. 5.

32. In 1899 Southern states spent an average of just over fifty cents per tilled acre on fertilizer, compared with a national average of about thirteen cents. See Roger L. Ransom and Richard Sutch, *One Kind of Freedom: The Economic Consequences of Emancipation*, 2nd ed. (New York: Cambridge University Press, 2001): 187–89 and Tables 9.9 and 9.10.

33. For a further discussion of this pessimistic outlook of the international cotton market and its impact on the South, see Ransom and Sutch, *One Kind of Freedom*: 188–93. Gavin Wright presents data on the role of other countries that were suppliers of cotton in the international market both before and after the war. Wright, "Cotton Competition and the Post-Bellum Recovery of the American South," *Journal of Economic History* 34 (September 1974): 621–22.

34. For an excellent exposition of the economic situation of yeoman farms in the antebellum South, see Gavin Wright, *The Political Economy of the Cotton South: Households, Markets, and Wealth in the Nineteenth Century* (New York: W. W. Norton, 1978).

35. For an analysis of the relative risks of cotton and corn facing the operators of small farms in the South, see Gavin Wright and Howard Kunreuther, "Cotton, Corn and Risk in the Nineteenth Century," *Journal of Economic History* 35 (September 1975).

36. Viken Tchakerian insists that "the evidence suggests that southern manufacturing enterprises may not have been any different from those in the Midwest with respect to their degree of flexibility and dynamism. . . . Perhaps the thesis of 'southern backwardness' needs to be revised": Tchakerian, "Productivity, Extent of Markets, and Manufacturing in the Late Antebellum South and Midwest," *Journal of Economic History* 54 (September 1994): 520. He concedes, however, that small markets probably hindered the expansion of industry. On the same point, see Fogel, *Without Consent or Contract*: 102–11.

37. Raimondo Luraghi, "The American Civil War and the Modernization of American Society: Social Structure and Industrial Revolution in the Old South before and during the War," *Civil War History* 18 (September 1972).

38. Historian Richard B. Latner argues that "the crisis laid bare southern anxieties about maintaining slavery and evidenced a determination to devise barriers against encroachments on southern rights": "The Nullification Crisis and Southern Subversion," *Journal of Southern History* 43 (1977). The definitive work on the Nullification Crisis is William Freehling, *Prelude to Civil War: The Nullification Crisis in South Carolina: 1816–1836* (New York: Harper & Row, 1965).

39. The Constitution also prohibited any "bounties" from being disbursed by the treasury. See Appendix 3, Article 1, Section 8.1.

40. See Appendix 3, Article 1, Section 9.6.

41. See Appendix 3, Article 2, Section 1.1.

42. See the discussion of urbanization in chapter 1 above and in Roger L. Ransom and Richard Sutch, "Conflicting Visions: The American Civil War as a Revolutionary Conflict," *Research in Economic History* 20 (2001). Two of the best statements of the relationship between slave plantations and the lack of urban markets are by Douglas Dowd, "A Comparative Analysis of Economic Development in the American West and South," *Journal of American History* 16 (December 1956) and Eugene Genovese, *The Political Economy of Slavery: Studies in the Economy and Society of the Slave South* (New York: Vintage Books, 1965).

43. Economists call the phenomenon described in the text a "crowding out" of investment funds as the result of the presence of slave assets. In our example, the value of slave assets in the planter's portfolio reduces the need to accumulate other financial or "real" assets, thus lowering the rate of investment. This is similar to the effect that large amounts of government debt can have in reducing capital available for investment needs in the contemporary capital markets of the United States. The crowding out theory proposed here is not the same as a popular argument at the time of the Civil War that the need to spend money on the purchase of slaves "absorbed" funds that would otherwise have been invested in real capital formation. That argument confuses physical capi-

tal with financial capital. The purchase of a slave does not destroy the money spent by the person buying the slave; it simply transfers the funds to some other investor who can still invest the money. The crowding out approach actually reduces the savings rate in the economy by reducing the amount people wish to save. See Roger L. Ransom and Richard Sutch, "Capitalists without Capital: The Burden of Slavery and the Impact of Emancipation," *Agricultural History* (Fall 1988): 138–41.

44. After the Civil War Longstreet became engaged in a long and bitter battle over his role in the Battle of Gettysburg. Jubal Early and other adherents to the Lost Cause claimed that Longstreet, who disagreed with Lee's strategy of attacking the Federal position after the first day of fighting, was responsible for the Confederate defeat. Longstreet further alienated many voters by supporting the Republican Party in the South. One can assume his political future would follow a somewhat different course as a politician in an independent Confederacy.

45. Jackson's situation might be compared to that of William Tecumseh Sherman following the North's victory in the war. Sherman, who was immensely popular, replied to an offer of presidential candidacy that "if nominated I will not run; if elected I will not serve." Like Sherman, Jackson would likely wind up as commander in chief of his country's armed forces.

46. For an excellent biography of Breckinridge, see William C. Davis, *Look Away!: A History of the Confederate States of America* (New York: Free Press, 2002): 63.

47. Our earlier discussion concluded that prices would have risen in the Confederacy by a factor of at least ten. We have not speculated on the course of inflation after 1865. The statement in the text should be interpreted to mean that slave prices would have returned to their prewar level in terms of the prices of 1860. See Appendix 2 for an elaboration of this point.

48. One should note that given the ability of slaves in the American system of agriculture *always* to produce enough food to support themselves and provide at least a small surplus, the value of slaves would never sink to zero. However, the decline in value compared with 1860 could be enormous, and the slaveholder who formerly made ends "meet" by selling slaves would find there was no market for his chattel labor. Slaves could feed themselves, but they would no longer be the key to prosperity and wealth.

49. The provisions for amendment of the Confederate Constitution required that two-thirds of the states approve the amendment. See Article V in Appendix 3.

50. If these costs seem large relative to the values of slaves discussed in chapter 1, it is because our calculations assume that despite the efforts to control inflation during and just after the war, prices in the 1880s would probably be

roughly ten times what had have been twenty years earlier. See the discussion in Appendix 2 for a more detailed explanation of the calculations.

51. The one development that might mute the economic boost from the bonds would be a situation in which a significant amount of the debt was transferred into foreign hands and the interest payments became a problem in the balance of payments. Yet even were this to happen, the transfer of capital represented by the initial sale of bonds to foreigners could have a positive effect on domestic capital formation in the Confederacy.

52. For more on the impact of emancipation and the problems of the postbellum American South, see Ransom and Sutch, *One Kind of Freedom*, which includes an extensive bibliography of work appearing after the publication of the first edition in 1977.

53. A point that is often overlooked in the discussion of emancipation—both in America and elsewhere—is that the process of emancipation dramatically changes the options of freed slaves with regard to how much they are willing to work. Plantations were organized around a gang system that was extremely regimented and in many instances forced slaves to endure a level of brutality that no free person would willingly endure. One reason many planters resisted emancipation is that they feared they would lose their labor. And if the experience of the American South during Reconstruction is any guide, these fears were justified. Blacks in the postbellum American South chose to work substantially fewer hours as free workers than their masters had made them work as slaves. This was not, as their former masters supposed, a reflection of the alleged laziness or inferiority of black workers; it was simply a case of free people choosing not to work "like slaves." In other words, the freed slaves were no longer willing to give their former masters that extra portion of labor that was extracted through the compulsion of slavery. See Stanley Engerman, "The Economic Response to Emancipation and Some Economic Aspects of the Meaning of Freedom," *The Meaning of Freedom*, ed. Frank McGlynn and Seymour Drescher (Pittsburgh: University of Pittsburgh Press, 1992) and Ransom and Sutch, *One Kind of Freedom*: ch. 3.

54. Notable examples of this view of the antebellum South include: Louis Hacker, *The Triumph of American Capitalism: The Development of Forces in American History to the End of the Nineteenth Century* (New York: Columbia University Press, 1940); Genovese, *The Political Economy of Slavery: Studies in the Economy and Society of the Slave South* and Eugene D. Genovese, *Roll, Jordan, Roll: The World the Slaves Made* (New York: Pantheon, 1974); Dowd, "Comparative Analysis"; and Raimondo Luraghi, *The Rise and Fall of the Plantation South* (New York: New Viewpoints Press, 1978). With regard to the postbellum failure to grow and diversify, see Jay R. Mandle, *The Roots of Black Poverty: The Southern Plantation Economy after the Civil War* (Durham, N.C.: Duke Univer-

sity Press, 1978); Harold D. Woodman, *King Cotton and His Retainers: Financing and Marketing the Cotton Crop of the South, 1800–1925* (Lexington: University of Kentucky Press, 1968); Jonathan Wiener, "Social Origins of the New South: Alabama, 1865–1885," *Journal of Interdisciplinary History* 7 (1978). Cliometric historians have challenged that view, arguing that the South's failure to develop industry was a result of small markets, not an anticapitalist attitude on the part of planters. They have a point, but it does not change the essential point of the text, which is that an independent Confederacy would have problems industrializing, whichever view was correct. One might note that Adam Smith's dictum that specialization is limited by the extent of the market suggests that these two views of Southern economic performance reinforce each other. If investment opportunities are limited by the extent of the market, that will surely restrain entrepreneurial activity, which in turn would add to the persistence of small markets.

55. Gavin Wright notes that an obstacle to growth in the postbellum American South was the extent to which ownership of manufacturing capital by groups outside the South created a situation in which decisions regarding management, the development of new technology, and the type of machinery used were made by groups outside the South. Wright, *Old South, New South: Revolutions in the Southern Economy since the Civil War* (New York: Basic Books, 1986).

Chapter 5. What Might Have Been: The Civil War and the "Whole Family of Man"

1. For an excellent statement on how the "Second American Revolution" had a profound effect in reinvigorating liberal movements throughout the world, see James McPherson, " 'The Whole Family of Man': Lincoln and the Last Hope Abroad," *Drawn with the Sword: Reflections on the American Civil War*, ed. James McPherson (New York: Oxford University Press, 1996). Two other excellent works that deal with the war in an international context are David P. Crook, *The North, the South, and the Powers, 1861–1865* (New York: John Wiley, 1974): ch. 1, and Harold Hyman, ed., *Heard round the World: The Impact Abroad of the Civil War* (New York: Alfred A. Knopf, 1969); particularly the selection by H. C. Allen.

2. Reprinted in Edward McPherson, *The Political History of the United States of America during the Great Rebellion* (Washington, D.C.: Philp and Solomons, 1864): 334.

3. O. P. Morton, "Oration of Governor O. P. Morton at the Dedication of Soldiers Monument, Gettysburg National Soldiers' Cemetery, 4 July 1869," *The*

Soldiers. National Cemetery at Gettysburg, ed. John Russel Bartlett (Providence, RI: Providence Press, 1874): 100–01.

4. Historian Richard F. Bensel argues that "the state that early American nationalists had previously attempted to establish at the Constitutional Convention in 1787 had become a mere shell . . . a government with only a token administrative presence in most of the nation and whose sovereignty was interpreted by the central administration as contingent upon the consent of the individual states": *Yankee Leviathan: The Origins of Central State Authority in America, 1859–1877* (New York: Cambridge University Press, 1990): ix. Richard D. Brown makes a similar point: *Modernization: The Transformation of American Life, 1600–1865* (New York: Hill and Wang, 1976): ch. 7.

5. Quoted in Bensel, *Yankee Leviathan*: 62.

6. In December 1814 representatives of the Federalist Party in New England gathered in Hartford, Connecticut, to protest the failure of the Monroe administration to find a way to end the war against England, a war that was having a ruinous effect on the New England economy. As it turned out, the Treaty of Ghent ended the war in February 1815, and the convention quietly disbanded without ever revealing the details of its deliberations. However, one of the key items that had been discussed by the delegates was a proposal that the New England states should leave the Federal Union if the government was unable to negotiate an immediate peace with Britain.

7. In chapter 1 we discussed the specific legislative actions relating to this Republican agenda and noted that all the principal measures were passed by the Thirty-seventh Congress in 1862. Since this would have occurred before the fortunes of war turned strongly against the Union, we assume that the legislation would have passed in our counterfactual world as well.

8. This assessment of postwar strength is based on the pattern of Republican voting in Map 1.7.

9. An estimated 1.85 million men who served in the Union army survived as veterans. The numbers for our counterfactual world would be the same order of magnitude.

10. On the situation of American labor in the last part of the nineteenth century, see Melvyn Dubofsky, *Industrialism and the American Worker, 1865–1920* (New York: Cromwell, 1975); Nell Irvin Painter, *Standing at Armageddon: The United States, 1877-1919* (New York: W. W. Norton, 1987); and David Montgomery, *The Fall of the House of Labor: The Workplace, the State, and American Labor Activism, 1865–1925* (New York: Cambridge University Press, 1987). On the demise of tradesmen and the rise of managerial capitalism, see Alfred D. Chandler, "The Emergence of Managerial Capitalism," *Business History Review* 58 (Winter 1984) and *The Visible Hand: The Managerial Revolution in American*

Business (Cambridge, Mass.: Harvard University Press, 1977). We assume that the forces driving industrial growth before the war would still be powerful in our counterfactual world.

11. The expansion of markets for American grains began in the late 1840s and lasted through the 1880s. For an excellent analysis of this phenomenon, see Morton Rothstein, "America in the International Rivalry for the British Wheat Market, 1860–1914," *Mississippi Valley Historical Review* 47 (December 1960) and "The International Market for Agricultural Commodities, 1850–1873," *Economic Change in the Civil War Era*, ed. David T. Gilchrist and David Lewis, vol. 62–72 (Greenville, Del.: Eleutherian Mills-Hagley Foundation, 1965). Though this growth might have been tempered somewhat by the diminished size of the U.S. market and the possibility of strained relations between Britain and the United States, the expansion of the world market for grains was something that did not depend on the outcome of the American Civil War.

12. This discussion of the politics of a counterfactual United States is patterned after the actual rise of the Populist Party in the United States after the North's victory in the Civil War. At its peak in the 1892 presidential election, the Populist candidate received almost 10 percent of the popular vote. In our counterfactual world, we assume that the Populists gained considerably more support, perhaps as much as 25 percent of the popular vote.

13. Fixing the rate at which the pound sterling would be exchanged for gold greatly reduced the need to actually transport gold from one country to another. Since pounds were "as good as gold" so long as the British were willing to convert them at any time into a fixed amount of gold, the need to actually convert the currency was limited to settling the excess demand or supply of pounds over time.

14. Countries adopting some variant of a gold standard between 1875 and 1880 included Germany, France, Belgium, Holland, Switzerland, and the Scandinavian nations. The United States established convertibility of dollars into either gold or silver with the Resumption Act of 1879.

15. Greenbacks were paper money that were issued by the U.S. Treasury during the war but that were not backed by gold. Though the United States resumed payment of gold in 1879, the country did not officially go on the gold standard. For twenty years the Treasury bought silver and issued silver certificates, backed by silver rather than gold. While this violated the unwritten rules of the gold standard, the amount of silver added to the money supply was not enough to disrupt seriously the gold value of the dollar. Most writers consider the United States on a de facto gold standard after 1879. For the standard source on the economics of this policy, see Milton Friedman and Anna J. Schwartz, *A Monetary History of the United States* (Princeton: Princeton University Press, 1963); for a more recent view of the politics, see Richard Bensel,

The Political Economy of American Industrialization, 1877–1900 (New York: Cambridge University Press, 2000): ch. 6.

16. This policy would not be without its problems. The United States at this time was not in a position to control the international currency markets. Thus, even after the Treasury adjusted the price of gold immediately after the war, the United States would face the prospect of continued deflation as the level of world prices continued to decline throughout the last third of the nineteenth century. In a world of multinational trade, countries were in the grips of the gold standard whether or not they wanted to peg their currencies to gold. If they didn't do it, someone else would.

17. As legal scholar Bernard Schwartz notes, "When the ultimate protection of person and property was transferred from the states to the nation, the judicial trend in favor of the corporation also became a national one. The role of the corporate person made use of the amendment to safeguard such persons a natural development." Schwartz, *From Confederation to Nation: The American Constitution, 1835–1877* (Baltimore: Johns Hopkins Press, 1973): 203.

18. There is an enormous literature on this issue. We have already mentioned the Beard-Hacker thesis; the best exposition of this point is Louis Hacker, *The Triumph of American Capitalism: The Development of Forces in American History to the End of the Nineteenth Century* (New York: Columbia University Press, 1940). Perhaps the finest exposition of corporate growth in the United States is Chandler, *The Visible Hand*.

19. Chandler, *The Visible Hand*, explores this point; also see the essays in Lance E. Davis et al., *American Economic Growth: An Economist's History of the United States* (New York: Harper & Row, 1972). Economic historians who have paid particular attention to the integration of capital markets as a stimulus to development include: Lance E. Davis, "The Investment Market, 1870–1914: The Evolution of a National Market," *Journal of Economic History* 25 (September 1965); John A. James, *Money and Capital Markets in Postbellum America* (Princeton: Princeton University Press, 1978); Kerry A. Odell, "The Integration of Regional and Interregional Capital Markets: Evidence from the Pacific Coast," *Journal of Economic History* 49 (June 1989); and Richard E. Sylla, "Federal Policy, Banking Market Structure, and Capital Mobilization in the United States, 1863–1913," *Journal of Economic History* 29 (December 1969).

20. The most obvious examples would be the more extreme variants of mercantilism that flourished in the seventeenth and eighteenth centuries and the "beggar thy neighbor" policies adopted by many countries in the midst of the Great Depression of the 1930s.

21. The population of the United States at the time of the Civil War was 31.5 million, with slightly more than a third of that total living in the Confederacy. By 1900 the census reported a population of 76 million living in the United

States. Of that total, just over 21 million—or just over a quarter of the total—lived in the twelve states that make up our counterfactual Confederacy. We do not have population figures for our counterfactual world; however, we argue in the text that the Confederacy would probably have fared as well as or better than the postwar defeated South, while the United States would probably *not* grow as fast because of the limitations of political uncertainty and smaller markets. This means that the actual figures represent an upper limit to the disparities in income and population between the two countries in our counterfactual world.

22. Even though it lacked the military capability to enforce the doctrine, the United States did manage to curtail European involvement in the Western Hemisphere before 1860. In 1833 Britain occupied the Falkland Islands; however, with the aid of the British Navy the United States kept France from intervening in South America.

23. The United States had steadfastly continued to recognize Juárez and his supporters as the legitimate government of Mexico; however, with the preoccupation of the Civil War, it could offer little more than moral support. Immediately after the Confederate surrender, President Andrew Johnson sent General Philip Sheridan and a sizable force of U.S. troops to the Mexican border in a show of force to back up the American government's support for Juárez. The Juárez forces, led by General Porfirio Díaz, eventually reoccupied Mexico City, and Maximilian surrendered to rebel forces at Querétaro in 1867. The deposed "emperor" was executed by a firing squad shortly after his surrender. Juárez was once again elected president of Mexico in December 1867. However, his triumph was short-lived; he died in 1872.

24. The counterfactual events described here roughly parallel the outcome of the Spanish-American War, which ended with the Treaty of Paris in 1898. Under the terms of that treaty all the territories mentioned were ceded to the United States, with Spain receiving an indemnity of twenty million dollars from the United States.

25. The U.S. Congress did appropriate money several times for a canal project in Central America in the 1890s, and in 1901 the United States and Britain signed the Hays-Pauncefote Treaty allowing the United States to build the canal. The country of Panama was created in 1903 with American backing, and the new nation agreed to allow the Americans to have a perpetual lease on a section of central Panama sixteen kilometers (ten miles) wide, where the canal could be built. Our counterfactual version of the construction of the Panama Canal roughly follows the actual course of events, though we have sped up the historical clock by a few years. What is missing from our counterfactual account, of course, is the Spanish-American War, which many people believe

was important in arousing American interest in the canal project. In our counterfactual world, that interest would be spurred on by the earlier development of the West Coast of the United States and the rivalry of the three countries in the Caribbean.

26. Bismarck was not successful in mitigating the animosity between Austria-Hungary and Russia, so he drew Italy into the Triple Alliance in 1882 and continued to pursue the objective of bilateral nonaggression agreements with Russia. One of the best descriptions of the treaty system is Joachim Remak, *The Origins of World War I*, 2nd ed. (New York: Harcourt Brace, 1995). We are assuming that in our counterfactual world the diplomatic manipulations undertaken by Bismarck followed the course of events actually charted in the years up to 1890.

27. To this point our counterfactual world coincides with what actually happened. The Schlieffen plan is one of the most famous plans in military history. It called for the German Army in the west to invade neutral Belgium and move in a wide arc that would eventually carry it west of Paris, a maneuver that would catch the French Army in a scissors and result in the capture of Paris. Meanwhile, a skeleton force was expected to hold off any activity in the East that might be caused by the Russian Army. It almost worked. For an excellent account of the early months of war, see Barbara Tuchman, *The Guns of August* (New York: Macmillan, 1962). Also see John Keegan, *The First World War* (New York: Alfred A. Knopf, 1998) and Martin Gilbert, *The First World War: A Complete History* (New York: Henry Holt, 1994)

28. For an excellent account of the arms race in Europe, see David G. Herrmann, *The Arming of Europe and the Making of the First World War* (Princeton: Princeton University Press, 1996). In our counterfactual world, we assume that the armaments race would involve the United States and the Confederacy as well as the major powers of Europe.

Appendix 1. Measuring Casualties in the Civil War

1. Thomas L. Livermore, *Numbers and Losses in the Civil War in America 1861–1865* (Boston and New York: 1901).

2. Among general works that rely on Livermore's figures for estimates of battle losses are: Craig L. Symonds, *A Battlefield Atlas of the Civil War*, 2nd ed. (Baltimore: The Nautical and Aviation Publishing Company of America, 1983); Herman Hattaway and Archer Jones, *How the North Won: A Military History of the Civil War* (Champaign-Urbana: University of Illinois Press, 1983); Grady McWhiney and Perry D. Jamieson, *Attack and Die: Civil War Military Tactics and*

the Southern Heritage (Tuscaloosa: University of Alabama Press, 1982); and Russell F. Weigley, *A Great Civil War: A Military and Political History, 1861–1865* (Bloomington: Indiana University Press, 2000).

3. Examples of researchers who have constructed careful estimates of each unit engaged in a battle on both sides are those for Perryville: Kenneth Noe, *Perryville: This Grand Havoc of Battle* (Lexington: University of Kentucky Press, 2001); for Chancellorsville: Stephen W. Sears, *Chancellorsville* (New York: Houghton Mifflin, 1996); and Gettysburg: Noah Andre Trudeau, *Gettysburg: A Testing of Courage* (New York: HarperCollins, 2002) and Scott Bowden and Bill Ward, *Last Chance for Victory: Robert E. Lee and the Gettysburg Campaign* (Cambridge, Mass.: DaCapo, 2001).

4. The most important instances of this problem relate to several of the major engagements in Virginia during the 1864–65 campaign, for which the Confederates gave no figures for losses.

5. Livermore, *Numbers and Losses*: 66.

6. To account for these problems, see the discussion ibid.: 66–70.

7. As we noted in the discussion of Confederate strategy in chapter 2, whether or not these figures are included in the data has a noticeable effect on the overall rate of casualties for Confederate armies. There were other actions on both sides where sizable bodies of troops surrendered; however, in most of these cases it is difficult to ascertain exactly how many troops surrendered. There do not appear to be other instances where such a large number of prisoners were taken and then paroled on the spot.

8. Stephen W. Sears, *To the Gates of Richmond: The Peninsula Campaign* (New York: Ticknor and Fields, 1992): 355.

Appendix 2. The Costs of Emancipation in 1880

1. A number of economic historians have dealt with the economic feasibility of emancipation schemes in the United States before the Civil War. The most complete study is Claudia Dale Goldin, "The Economics of Emancipation," *Journal of Economic History* 33 (March 1973); also see Roger L. Ransom and Richard Sutch, "Who Pays for Slavery?," *Race, Restitution, and Redistribution: The Present Value and Distribution of the Benefits of Slavery and Discrimination*, ed. Richard F. America (London: Greenwood Press, 1990), "Capitalists without Capital: The Burden of Slavery and the Impact of Emancipation," *Agricultural History* (Fall 1988); and Jeremy Atack and Peter Passell, *A New View of American History from Colonial Times to 1940*, 2nd ed. (New York: W. W. Norton, 1994): 358–59.

2. The age at which the child would be freed from apprenticeship in the emancipation scheme introduced in the Northern states varied. See the discussion in Goldin, "Economics of Emancipation": 66–72.

3. We do not know the exact population of our counterfactual Confederacy. If we assume that there was not a great deal of migration into the region in the years immediately after the war, then the population would probably approximate that of the U.S. South in 1880, which was 15.2 million people.

BIBLIOGRAPHY

Atack, Jeremy, and Peter Passell. *A New View of American History from Colonial Times to 1940*, 2nd ed. New York: W. W. Norton, 1994.

Beard, Charles, and Mary Beard. *The Rise of American Civilization*. 2 vols. Vol. 1. New York: Macmillan, 1927.

Bensel, Richard. *The Political Economy of American Industrialization, 1877–1900*. New York: Cambridge University Press, 2000.

Bensel, Richard F. *Yankee Leviathan: The Origins of Central State Authority in America, 1859–1877*. New York: Cambridge University Press, 1990.

Beringer, Richard E., Herman Hattaway. et al. *Why the South Lost the War*. Athens: University of Georgia Press, 1986.

Bowden, Scott, and Bill Ward. *Last Chance for Victory: Robert E. Lee and the Gettysburg Campaign*. Cambridge, Mass.: DaCapo, 2001.

Brown, Richard D. *Modernization: The Transformation of American Life, 1600–1865*. New York: Hill and Wang, 1976.

Burdekin, Richard C. K., and Farrokh K. Langdana. "War Finance in the Southern Confederacy." *Explorations in Economic History* 30 (July 1993): 352–77.

Carr, Edward Hallett. *What Is History? The George Macaulay Trevelyan Lectures*. New York: Alfred A. Knopf, 1961.

Carter, Susan; Roger Ransom; and Richard Sutch. "The Decline in Fertility and the Life Cycle Transition in the Antebellum United States." In *History Matters: Economic Growth, Technology, and Population*, ed. Timothy W. Guinnane, William A. Sundstrom, and Warren Whatley. Palo Alto, Calif.: Stanford University Press, 2002.

Chandler, Alfred D. *The Visible Hand: The Managerial Revolution in American Business.* Cambridge, Mass.: Harvard University Press, 1977.

———. "The Emergence of Managerial Capitalism." *Business History Review* 58 (Winter 1984): 473–503.

Clausewitz, Carl von. *On War,* trans. Michael Howard and Peter Paret. Princeton: Princeton University Press, 1976.

Cochran, Thomas C. "Did the Civil War Retard Industrialization?" *Mississippi Valley Historical Review* 48 (September 1961): 197–210.

Connelly, Thomas L. *The Marble Man: Robert E. Lee and His Image in American History.* New York: Alfred A. Knopf, 1977.

Conrad, Alfred H., and John R. Meyer. "The Economics of Slavery in the Ante Bellum South." *Journal of Political Economy* 66 (April 1958): 93–130.

Cooling, Benjamin Franklin. *Jubal Early's Raid on Washington, 1864.* Knoxville: University of Tennessee Press, 1989.

Cooper, William J., Jr., and Thomas E. Terrill. *The American South: A History,* 2nd ed. New York: McGraw-Hill, 1996.

Cowley, Robert, ed. *What If ?: The World's Foremost Military Historians Imagine What Might Have Been.* New York: G. P. Putnam's Sons, 1998.

Cronon, William. *Nature's Metropolis: Chicago and the Great West.* New York: W. W. Norton, 1991.

Crook, David P. *The North, The South, and the Powers, 1861–1865.* New York: John Wiley, 1974.

Davis, George K., and Gary M. Pequet. "Interest Rates in the Civil War South." *Journal of Economic History* 50 (March 1990): 33–147.

Davis, Lance E. "The Investment Market, 1870–1914: The Evolution of a National Market." *Journal of Economic History* 25 (September 1965).

———, et al. *American Economic Growth: An Economist's History of the United States.* New York: Harper & Row, 1972.

Davis, Willam C. *The Cause Lost: Myths and Realities of the Confederacy.* Lawrence: University of Kansas Press, 1996.

———. *Look Away!: A History of the Confederate States of America*. New York: Free Press, 2002.

Dowd, Douglas. "A Comparative Analysis of Economic Development in the American West and South." *Journal of American History* 16 (December 1956): 558–74.

Downing, David. *The Moscow Option: An Alternative Second World War*. London: Greenhill Books, 2001.

Dubofsky, Melvyn. *Industrialism and the American Worker, 1865–1920*. New York: Cromwell, 1975.

Dudley, Wade G. "Be Careful What You Wish For: The Plan Orange Disaster." In *Rising Sun Victorious*, ed. Peter Tsouras. London: Greenhill Books, 2001: 39–61.

Early, Jubal A. "The Campaigns of Robert E. Lee." In *Lee the Soldier*, ed. Gary W. Gallagher. Lincoln: University of Nebraska Press, 1996: 37–73.

Easterlin, Richard A. "Interregional Differences in Per Capita Income, Population, and Total Income; 1840–1950." In *Trends in the American Economy in the Nineteenth Century*. Vol. 24. Studies in Income and Wealth. Princeton: Princeton University Press, 1960: 73–140.

———. "Regional Income Trends, 1840–1950." In *American Economic History*, ed. Seymour E. Harris. New York: McGraw-Hill, 1961: 525–47.

Ellison, Thomas. *The Cotton Trade of Great Britain*. London: Frank Cass & Company, 1886.

Engerman, Stanley. "The Economic Response to Emancipation and Some Economic Aspects of the Meaning of Freedom." In *The Meaning of Freedom*, ed. Frank McGlynn and Seymour Drescher. Pittsburgh: University of Pittsburgh Press, 1992: 49–68.

Engerman, Stanley L. "The Economic Impact of the Civil War." *Explorations in Entrepreneurial History* 2nd Series 3 (Spring 1966): 176–99.

Escott, Paul D. *After Secession: Jefferson Davis and the Failure of Confederate Nationalism*. Baton Rouge: Louisiana State University Press, 1978.

Essah, Patience. *A House Divided: Slavery and Emancipation in Delaware, 1638–1865*. Charlottesville: University of Virginia Press, 1996.

Ferguson, Niall. "Virtual History: Towards a 'Chaotic' Theory of the Past." In *Virtual History: Alternatives and Counterfactuals*. London: Macmillan, 1997: 1–90.

Fields, Barbara. "Who Freed the Slaves?" In *The Civil War: An Illustrated History*, ed. Geoffrey Ward. New York: Alfred A. Knopf, 1990: 178–81.

Fogel, Robert, and Stanley Engerman. "The Economics of Slavery." In *The Reinterpretation of American Economic History*. Ed. Robert Fogel and Stanley Engerman. New York: Harper & Row, 1971: 311–41.

Fogel, Robert W. *Without Consent or Contract: The Rise and Fall of American Slavery*. New York: W. W. Norton, 1989.

———, and Stanley L. Engerman. *Time on the Cross: The Economics of American Negro Slavery*. 2 vols. New York: Little, Brown, 1974.

———. *Time on the Cross: The Economics of American Negro Slavery*, new ed. New York: W. W. Norton, 1989.

Foner, Eric. *Free Soil, Free Men and Free Labor: The Ideology of the Republican Party before the Civil War*. New York: Oxford University Press, 1970.

———. "Politics, Ideology and the Origins of the American Civil War." In *A Nation Divided*, ed. George Fredrickson. New York: Oxford University Press, 1975.

———. *Politics and Ideology in the Age of the Civil War*. New York: Oxford University Press, 1980.

Foote, Shelby. "Men at War: An Interview with Shelby Foote." In *The Civil War: An Illustrated History*, ed. Geoffrey Ward. New York: Alfred A. Knopf, 1990: 264–73.

Freehling, William. *Prelude to Civil War: The Nullification Crisis in South Carolina: 1816–1836*. New York: Harper & Row, 1965.

Friedman, Milton, and Anna J. Schwartz. *A Monetary History of the United States*. Princeton: Princeton University Press, 1963.

Fuller, J. F. C. *Grant and Lee: A Study in Personality and Generalship*. London: Eyre and Spotswood, 1933.

Gallagher, Gary, ed. *The First Day at Gettysburg: Essays on Confederate and Union Leadership*. Kent, Ohio: Kent State University Press, 1992.

———. "'If The Enemy Is There, We Must Attack Him': R. E. Lee and the Second Day at Gettysburg." In *The Second Day at Gettysburg*, ed. Gary Gallagher. Kent, Ohio: Kent State University Press, 1993: 1–32.

———, ed. *Chancellorsville: The Battle and Its Aftermath*. Chapel Hill: University of North Carolina Press, 1996.

———. *The Confederate War: How Popular Will, Nationalism, and Military Strategy Could Not Stave Off Defeat*. Cambridge, Mass.: Harvard University Press, 1997.

———. "When Lee Was Mortal." In *With My Face to the Enemy*. Ed. Robert Cowley. New York: Berkley Books, 2001: 245–60.

Gallagher, Gary W. "Another Look at the Generalship of R. E. Lee." In *Lee the Soldier*, ed. Gary W. Gallagher. Lincoln: University of Nebraska Press, 1996: 275–90.

———, ed. *Lee the Soldier*. Lincoln: University of Nebraska Press, 1996.

Genovese, Eugene. *The Political Economy of Slavery: Studies in the Economy and Society of the Slave South*. New York: Vintage Books, 1965.

Genovese, Eugene D. *Roll, Jordan, Roll: The World the Slaves Made*. New York: Pantheon, 1974.

Gienapp, William, ed. *Essays on American Antebellum Politics, 1840–1860*. Arlington: Texas A & M University Press, 1982.

Gienapp, William E. *The Origins of the Republican Party, 1852–1856*. New York: Oxford University Press, 1987.

Gilbert, Martin. *The First World War: A Complete History*. New York: Henry Holt, 1994.

Gingrich, Newt, and William R. Forstchen. *Gettysburg: A Novel of the Civil War*. New York: St. Martin's Press, 2003.

Glatthaar, Joseph T. *The March to the Sea and Beyond: Sherman's Troops in the Savannah and Carolinas Campaigns*. New York: New York University Press, 1985.

Goldin, Claudia Dale. "The Economics of Emancipation." *Journal of Economic History* 33 (March 1973): 66–85.

Goldin, Claudia, and Frank Lewis. "The Economic Costs of the American Civil War: Estimates and Implications." *Journal of Economic History* 35 (June 1975): 299–326.

Gott, Kendall D. *Where the South Lost the War: An Analysis of the Fort Henry-Fort Donelson Campaign, February 1862*. Mechanicsburg, Pa.: Stackpole Books, 2003.

Gunderson, Gerald. "The Origin of the American Civil War." *Journal of Economic History* 34 (December 1974): 915–50.

Hacker, Louis. *The Triumph of American Capitalism: The Development of Forces in American History to the End of the Nineteenth Century.* New York: Columbia University Press, 1940.

Hamilton, Holman. *Prologue to Conflict: The Crisis and Compromise of 1850.* New York: W. W. Norton, 1964.

Hanson, Victor Davis. *Ripples of Battle: How Wars of the Past Still Determine How We Fight, How We Live, and How We Think.* New York: Doubleday, 2003.

Harsh, Joseph L. *Confederate Tide Rising: Robert E. Lee and the Making of Strategy, 1861–1862.* Kent, Ohio: Kent State University Press, 1998.

Hattaway, Herman, and Archer Jones. *How the North Won: A Military History of the Civil War.* Champaign-Urbana: University of Illinois Press, 1983.

Hawthorn, Geoffrey. *Plausible Worlds: Possibility and Understanding in History and the Social Sciences.* New York: Cambridge University Press, 1991.

Hennessy, John J. *Return to Bull Run: The Campaign and Battle of Second Manassas.* New York: Simon & Schuster, 1993.

Herrmann, David G. *The Arming of Europe and the Making of the First World War.* Princeton: Princeton University Press, 1996.

Holt, Michael. *The Political Crisis of the 1850's.* New York: W. W. Norton, 1978.

———. *The Rise and Fall of the American Whig Party: Jacksonian Politics and the Onset of the Civil War.* New York: Oxford University Press, 1999.

Huston, James L. "Property Rights in Slavery and the Coming of the Civil War." *Journal of Southern History* 65 ((May 1999): 249–86.

———, *Calculating the Value of the Union: Slavery, Property Rights, and the Economic Origins of the Civil War.* (Chapel Hill: University of North Carolina Press, 2004).

Hyman, Harold, ed. *Heard round the World: The Impact Abroad of the Civil War.* New York: Alfred A. Knopf, 1969.

James, John A. *Money and Capital Markets in Postbellum America.* Princeton: Princeton University Press, 1978.

Jones, Archer. *Confederate Strategy from Shiloh to Vicksburg.* Baton Rouge: Louisiana State University Press, 1991.

Jordan, Winthrop. *White over Black: American Attitudes toward the Negro: 1550–1812*. Chapel Hill: University of North Carolina Press, 1968.

Kantor, MacKinlay. *If the South Had Won the Civil War*. New York: Bantam Books, 1961.

Keegan, John. *The First World War*. New York: Alfred A. Knopf, 1998.

Latner, Richard B. "The Nullification Crisis and Southern Subversion." *Journal of Southern History* 43 (1977): 19–33.

Livermore, Thomas L. *Numbers and Losses in the Civil War in America 1861–1865*. Boston and New York: 1901.

Longstreet, James. "Lee's Invasion of Pennsylvania." In *Battles and Leaders of the Civil War*, ed. Robert U. Johnson and Clarence C. Buel. Vol. 3. New York: Century Company, 1884: 244–51.

Luraghi, Raimondo. *The Rise and Fall of the Plantation South*. New York: New Viewpoints Press, 1978.

———. "The American Civil War and the Modernization of American Society: Social Structure and Industrial Revolution in the Old South before and during the War." *Civil War History* 18 (September 1972): 230–50.

Mandle, Jay R. *The Roots of Black Poverty: The Southern Plantation Economy after the Civil War*. Durham, N.C.: Duke University Press, 1978.

Marszalek, John F. *Sherman: A Soldier's Passion for Order*. New York: Free Press, 1993.

McDonough, James Lee. *Shiloh: In Hell before Night*. Knoxville: University of Tennessee Press, 1977.

———. *Stones River: Bloody Winter in Tennessee*. Knoxville: University of Tennessee Press, 1980.

———. *Chattanooga: A Death Grip on the Confederacy*. Knoxville: University of Tennessee Press, 1984.

McKenzie, Robert D. *Uncertain Glory: Lee's Generalship Re-Examined*. New York: Hippocrene Books, 1997.

McPherson, Edward. *The Political History of the United States of America during the Great Rebellion*. Washington, D.C.: Philp and Solomons, 1864.

McPherson, James M. "Antebellum Southern Exceptionalism: A New Look at an Old Question." *Civil War History* 29 (September 1983): 230–44.

————. "'The Whole Family of Man': Lincoln and the Last Hope Abroad." In *Drawn with the Sword: Reflections on the American Civil War*, ed. James McPherson. New York: Oxford University Press, 1996: 208–30.

————. "If the Order Hadn't Been Lost." In *What If ?*, ed. Robert Cowley. New York: G. P. Putnam's Sons, 1999: 223–40.

————. "Failed Southern Strategies." In *With My Face to the Enemy*, ed. Robert Cowley. New York: Berkley Books, 2001: 72–86.

————. *Ordeal by Fire: The Civil War and Reconstruction*. 3rd ed. Vol. 2. New York: McGraw-Hill, 2001.

————. *Crossroads of Freedom: Antietam*. New York: Oxford University Press, 2002.

McWhiney, Grady. *Braxton Bragg and Confederate Defeat: Field Command*. New York: Columbia University Press, 1969.

————, and Perry D. Jamieson. *Attack and Die: Civil War Military Tactics and the Southern Heritage*. Tuscaloosa: University of Alabama Press, 1982.

Montgomery, David. *The Fall of the House of Labor: The Workplace, the State, and American Labor Activism, 1865–1925*. New York: Cambridge University Press, 1987.

Moore, Ward. "Bring the Jubilee." In *The Fantastic Civil War*, ed. Frank McSherry, Charles G. Waugh, and Martin Harry Greenberg. New York: Bren Books, 1952: 17–136.

————. *Bring the Jubilee Again*. New York: Farrar, Straus and Young, 1952.

Morton, O. P. "Oration of Governor O. P. Morton at the Dedication of Soldiers Monument, Gettysburg National Soldiers' Cemetery, 4 July 1869." In *The Soldiers. National Cemetery at Gettysburg*, ed. John Russel Bartlett. Providence, R.I.: Providence Press, 1874: 100–01.

Murfin, James V. *The Gleam of Bayonets: The Battle of Antietam and the Maryland Campaign of 1862*, paperback ed. Baton Rouge: Louisiana State University Press, 1965.

Nevins, Allan. *The Fruits of Manifest Destiny, 1847–1852*. Vol. 1. *Ordeal of the Union*. New York: Charles Scribner's Sons, 1947.

————. *The Emergence of Lincoln: Douglas, Buchanan, and Party Chaos, 1857–1859*. Vol. 3. *Ordeal of the Union*. New York: Charles Scribner's Sons, 1950.

———. *The Emergence of Lincoln: Prologue to Civil War, 1859–1861*. Vol. 4. *Ordeal of the Union*. New York: Charles Scribner's Sons, 1950.

———. *The War for the Union: War Becomes Revolution, 1862–1863*. Vol. 6. *Ordeal of the Union*. New York: Charles Scribner's Sons, 1960.

Noe, Kenneth. *Perryville: This Grand Havoc of Battle*. Lexington: University of Kentucky Press, 2001.

Nolan, Alan T. "R. E. Lee and July 1 at Gettysburg." In *The First Day at Gettysburg*, ed. Gary Gallagher. Kent, Ohio: Kent State University Press, 1992: 1–29.

———. *Lee Reconsidered: Robert E. Lee and Civil War History*. Chapel Hill: University of North Carolina Press, 1991.

North, Douglass C. "Location Theory and Regional Economic Growth." *Journal of Political Economy* 63 (June 1955): 243–58.

———. *The Economic Growth of the United States, 1790–1860*. Englewood Cliffs, N.J.: Prentice Hall, 1961.

———. *Growth and Welfare in the American Past: A New Economic History*. Englewood Cliffs, N.J.: Prentice Hall, 1966.

North, Jonathon, ed. *The Napoleon Options: Alternate Decisions of the Napoleonic Wars*. London: Greenhill Books, 2000.

Odell, Kerry A. "The Integration of Regional and Interregional Capital Markets: Evidence from the Pacific Coast." *Journal of Economic History* 49 (June 1989): 297–310.

Painter, Nell Irvin. *Standing at Armageddon: The United States, 1877–1919*. New York: W. W. Norton, 1987.

Parker, Geoffrey. "The Repulse of the English Fire Ships." In *What If ?*, ed. Robert Cowley. New York: G. P. Putnam's Sons, 1999: 141–54.

Pinkney, David H. "France and the Civil War." In *Heard round the World*, ed. Harold Hyman. New York: Alfred A. Knopf, 1969: 97–144.

Potter, David. *The Impending Crisis: 1848–1861*. New York: Harper Torchbooks, 1976.

Potter, David M. "Why the Republicans Rejected Compromise and Secession." In *The Crisis of the Union*, ed. George H. Knoles. Baton Rouge: Louisiana State University Press, 1965: 90–106.

Rable, George C. *The Confederate Republic: A Revolution against Politics.* Chapel Hill: University of North Carolina Press, 1994.

Ramsdell, Charles W. "The Natural Limits of Slavery Expansion." *Mississippi Valley Historical Review* 16 (September 1929): 151–71.

Ransom, Roger L. *Conflict and Compromise: The Political Economy of Slavery, Emancipation, and the American Civil War.* New York: Cambridge University Press, 1989.

———. "Fact and Counterfact: The 'Second American Revolution' Revisited." *Civil War History* 45 (March 1999): 28–60.

———. "The Historical Statistics of the Confederacy." In *The Historical Statistics of the United States, Millennial Edition,* ed. Susan Carter and Richard Sutch. New York: Cambridge University Press, 2005.

———, and Richard Sutch. "The Impact of the Civil War and of Emancipation on Southern Agriculture." *Explorations in Economic History* 12 (January 1975): 1–28.

———. "Growth and Welfare in the American South in the Nineteenth Century." *Explorations in Economic History* 16 (April 1979): 207–35.

———. "Capitalists without Capital: The Burden of Slavery and the Impact of Emancipation." *Agricultural History* (Fall 1988): 119–47.

———. "Who Pays for Slavery?" In *Race, Restitution, and Redistribution: The Present Value and Distribution of the Benefits of Slavery and Discrimination,* ed. Richard F. America. London: Greenwood Press, 1990: 31–54.

———. "Conflicting Visions: The American Civil War as a Revolutionary Conflict." *Research in Economic History* 20 (2001): 249–301.

———. *One Kind of Freedom: The Economic Consequences of Emancipation,* 2nd ed. New York: Cambridge University Press, 2001.

Rawley, James A. *Race and Politics: "Bleeding" Kansas and the Coming of Civil War.* Philadelphia: J. B. Lippincott Company, 1969.

Remak, Joachim. *The Origins of World War I.* 2nd ed. New York: Harcourt Brace, 1995.

Rothstein, Morton. "America in the International Rivalry for the British Wheat Market, 1860–1914." *Mississippi Valley Historical Review* 47 (December 1960): 401–18.

————. "The International Market for Agricultural Commodities, 1850–1873." In *Economic Change in the Civil War Era*, ed. David T. Gilchrist and David Lewis. Vols. 62–72: Eleutherian Mills-Hagley Foundation, 1965.

Royster, Charles. *The Destructive War: William Tecumseh Sherman, Stonewall Jackson, and the Americans*. New York: Alfred A. Knopf, 1991.

Savas, Theodore P., and David A. Woodbury, eds. *The Campaign for Atlanta and Sherman's March to the Sea: Essays on the American Civil War in Georgia*. 2 vols. Athens, Ga.: Savas Woodbury Publishers, 1994.

Schwartz, Bernard. *From Confederation to Nation: The American Constitution, 1835–1877*. Baltimore: Johns Hopkins Press, 1973.

Sears, Stephen W. *Landscape Turned Red: The Battle of Antietam*. New Haven: Ticknor and Fields, 1983.

————. *To the Gates of Richmond: The Peninsula Campaign*. New York: Ticknor and Fields, 1992.

————. *Chancellorsville*. New York: Houghton Mifflin, 1996.

Sellers, Charles. *The Market Revolution: Jacksonian America, 1815–1846*. New York: Oxford University Press, 1991.

Shea, Willam L., and Terrence J. Winschel. *Vicksburg Is the Key: The Struggle for the Mississippi River*. Lincoln: University of Nebraska Press, 2003.

Silbey, Joel, ed. *The Transformation of American Politics, 1840–1860*. Englewood Cliffs, N.J.: Prentice Hall, 1967.

Stampp, Kenneth M. *The Imperiled Union: Essays on the Background of the Civil War*. New York: Oxford University Press, 1980.

Sylla, Richard E. "Federal Policy, Banking Market Structure, and Capital Mobilization in the United States, 1863–1913." *Journal of Economic History* 29 (December 1969): 657–86.

Symonds, Craig L. *A Battlefield Atlas of the Civil War*, 2nd ed. Baltimore: Nautical and Aviation Publishing Company of America, 1983.

Tanner, Robert G. *Confederate Strategy Reconsidered*. Wilmington, Del.: Scholarly Resources, 2001.

Tchakerian, Viken. "Productivity, Extent of Markets, and Manufacturing in the Late Antebellum South and Midwest." *Journal of Economic History* 54 (September 1994): 497–525.

Todd, Richard C. *Confederate Finance.* Athens: University of Georgia Press, 1954.

Trevor-Roper, Hugh. "History and Imagination." In *History and Imagination: Essays in Honour of H. R. Trevor-Roper,* ed. Hugh Lloyd-Jones, Valerie Pearl, and Blair Worden. London: Gerald Duckworth, 1981: 356–69.

Trudeau, Noah Andre. *Gettysburg: A Testing of Courage.* New York: Harper-Collins, 2002.

Tsouras, Peter. *Gettysburg: An Alternate History.* London: Greenhill Books, 1997.

———, ed. *Dixie Victorious: An Alternative History of the Civil War.* Mechanicsburg, Pa.: Stackpole Books, 2004.

Tuchman, Barbara. *The Guns of August.* New York: Macmillan, 1962.

Turtledove, Harry. *The Guns of the South.* New York: Ballantine Books, 1992.

———. *How Few Remain: A Novel of the Second War between the States.* New York: Ballantine Books, 1997.

———. *The Great War: American Front.* New York: Ballantine Books, 1998.

———. *The Great War: Breakthrough.* New York: Ballantine Books, 2000.

———. *The Great War: Walk in Hell.* New York: Ballantine Books, 1999.

United States Bureau of the Census. *Historical Statistics of the United States, Colonial Times to 1970.* 2 vols. Washington, D.C.: U.S. Government Printing Office, 1975.

Weidenmier, Marc. "The Market for Confederate Bonds." *Explorations in Economic History* 37 (January 2000): 76–97.

Weigley, Russell F. *A Great Civil War: A Military and Political History, 1861–1865.* Bloomington: Indiana University Press, 2000.

Wiener, Jonathon. "Social Origins of the New South: Alabama, 1865–1885." Baton Rouge: Louisiana State University Press, 1978.

Woodman, Harold D. *King Cotton and His Retainers: Financing and Marketing the Cotton Crop of the South, 1800–1925.* Lexington: University of Kentucky Press, 1968.

Woodworth, Steven E. *Davis and Lee at War.* Lawrence: University Press of Kansas, 1995.

Wright, Gavin. "New and Old Views on the Economics of Slavery." *Journal of Economic History* 33 (June 1973): 452–66.

―――. "Cotton Competition and the Post-Bellum Recovery of the American South." *Journal of Economic History* 34 (September 1974): 610–35.

―――. "Slavery and the Cotton Boom." *Explorations in Economic History* 12 (October 1975): 439–52.

―――. *The Political Economy of the Cotton South: Households, Markets, and Wealth in the Nineteenth Century.* New York: W. W. Norton, 1978.

―――. *Old South, New South: Revolutions in the Southern Economy since the Civil War.* New York: Basic Books, 1986.

―――, and Howard Kunreuther. "Cotton, Corn and Risk in the Nineteenth Century." *Journal of Economic History* 35 (September 1975): 526–51.

INDEX

Page numbers in *italics* refer to maps and illustrations.